The State in the Forest

THE STATE IN THE FOREST.
CONTESTED COMMONS IN THE
NINETEENTH CENTURY VENETIAN ALPS

Giacomo Bonan

British Library Cataloguing in Publication Data
A catalogue record for this book is available from the British Library

ISBN 978-1-912186-08-2 (HB)
ISBN 978-1-912186-11-2 (ebook)
ISBN 978-1-912186-67-9 (PB)

Cover image 'Giacomo Della Lucia called Bozze miraculously saved with three raftmen,
7 May 1883, ex voto'. Source: Church of Beata Vergine dei Caduti (Belluno).

TABLE OF CONTENTS

Giacomo Bonan

When the axe comes into the forest, the trees say: Look! The handle is one of us!

John Berger, *Once in Europa*

ACKNOWLEDGEMENTS

This book is the result of a research path that began with an M.A. thesis at the Ca' Foscari University of Venice and continued with a Ph.D. at the University of Bologna. Before starting on this path, if someone had asked me to sum up the characteristic activity of historical research, I would probably have conjured up the image of a solitary person poring over a book, an archival folder or a computer screen. Days of this character have certainly not been lacking in recent years but, with hindsight, the most rewarding aspect of this work has been the opportunity to meet, discuss and collaborate with many people, to whom my gratitude extends for the friendship and help they have generously given me.

First of all, Ilaria Porciani has supported me along this path with dedication, always willing to share her knowledge and experience, but also her enthusiasm and curiosity for things yet to be discovered. Much of what I know about the rural Veneto in the nineteenth century I have learned from Piero Brunello, sometimes on walks not far from the places that will feature in the following pages. Two periods at the Division of History of Science, Technology and Environment at the Royal Institute of Technology in Stockholm – the first at the beginning of the Ph.D., the second as a post-doctoral fellow – allowed me to reflect on my work from a different perspective, in particular thanks to conversations with Marco Armiero and Arne Kaijser.

I was able to discuss the initial results of my research in various locations; I would like to recall a workshop organised by José-Miguel Lana and Tine De Moor at the University of Pamplona; two sessions on the theme of common forests at the European Rural History Conferences in Girona and Leuven coordinated by Anna Stagno and Vittorio Tigrino; and the seminars on the History of the Alps organised by Luigi Lorenzetti and Roberto Leggero. The Department of History and Cultures at the University of Bologna, the Laboratory of the History of the Alps at the University of Italian Switzerland and the C.M. Lerici Foundation in Stockholm have generously supported my research.

Anyone who has tried to venture among the files of the *camerale* section of the Austrian government, in the Venice State Archive, will understand the debt of gratitude I owe to Antonio Lazzarini for making his notes available to me. Federico Budel, Orietta Ceiner, Gabriele Contri, Alberto Fiocco, Alice Gazzi, Antonio Genova, Matteo Guerriero, Davide Marchet, Silvia Miscellaneo, Elena Nart, Noemi Nicolai, Luisa Oliveti, Natascia Pecorari, David Rosini and Eurigio Tonetti all facilitated my wanderings amongst archives and libraries. Marco Armiero, Loredana Corrà, Angela De Benedictis, Laura Di Fiore, Claudio Lorenzini, Marco Meriggi, Michele Nani and Ilaria Porciani have read and commented on various versions of the text. Simon Stott's help has been instrumental in the preparation of the English version of the manuscript. Sarah Johnson at The White Horse Press has travelled the editorial path with passion and cordiality.

I have lost count of debts accumulated with Claudio Lorenzini in recent years. With Paolo Maoret the debts have been accumulating since childhood. Elisa has had the patience to stand by me and to support me along this path; and the journey would not have been possible without my parents, Donatella and Valter, to whom I dedicate this work.

LIST OF ABBREVIATIONS

ACA: Archivio Comunale di Auronzo

ACCS: Archivio Comunale di Comelico Superiore

AMC: Archivio Museo Correr

AMCF: Archivio Magnifica Comunità di Fiemme

ASBl: Archivio di Stato di Belluno

ASCB: Archivio Storico Comune di Belluno

ASMi: Archivio di Stato di Milano

ASVe: Archivio di Stato di Venezia

ASVeG: Archivio di Stato di Venezia, Giudecca

BCF: Biblioteca Comunale di Feltre

BCU: Biblioteca Comunale di Udine

BSC: Biblioteca Storica Cadorina di Vigo di Cadore

b. bb.: folder/folders

cf.: *confer*

f. ff.: file/files

ms.: manuscript

p. pp: page/pages

INTRODUCTION

In recent years, the theme of the commons (both as common land and as common rights over land) has been the focus of much attention. This interest, I believe, stems from the growing concern for environmental issues in academia and, more widely, in the public sphere. This is because the commons is a field of study where the links between environmental, social and political problems (and conflicts) are more evident.[1] It is in this context that the historical approach assumes particular relevance, since it allows us to reflect on the dynamic and conflictual construction of territorial structures and on the active role played by local actors in these processes.[2]

The most recent studies on this theme have been mainly concerned with the organisational aspect of the commons, focusing particularly on the *ancien régime*, a period in which specific local institutions were often associated with these lands. Less attention has been paid to the following period, when these bodies were no longer formalised and legitimised at the institutional level, leading to the criminalisation of the traditional use of their associated resources, rather than the disappearance of these practices.[3] In much of Europe, this process should be placed within the context of the comprehensive socio-economic change that transformed the continent between the eighteenth and nineteenth centuries and one of whose features was the drive towards agrarian individualism.[4]

The development of agrarian individualism, at the expense of more open and hybrid forms of land tenure, took place as a result of two interrelated processes, which followed autonomous and sometimes divergent paths. The first has been a much-debated subject of research in the past and concerns the privatisation of common land during the

---

1. Bonan 2015, pp. 108–13; see also Wall 2014.
2. Ingold 2008; Tigrino 2015.
3. For two thematic reviews, cf. Cristoferi 2016; Bonan 2018.
4. The milestone on this is Bloch 1930a-b.

Giacomo Bonan

spread of capitalism in the countryside.[5] The second one has also been a long-standing historiographical theme, but its implications in the dynamics of the use of common resources have been investigated to a lesser extent: this is the process of state centralisation.[6]

This book explores the relationship between administrative modernisation and the criteria for using natural resources. In particular, I have sought to examine how, and to what extent, certain institutional changes introduced during the nineteenth century, and linked to the dynamics of state centralisation, influenced the systems and practices traditionally associated with the common use of the woodlands.

The research has been carried out in a geographically circumscribed area – some valleys in the eastern Alps that make up the territory of Cadore, in the higher reaches of the Piave river – and within a relatively limited time period – the six decades between the introduction of the Napoleonic administrative model at the start of the nineteenth century and the period immediately following the annexation of these territories to the Kingdom of Italy.

The choice of woodlands as the focus of analysis was motivated by their importance for all the social and institutional players involved in their management. In the areas covered by this study, the woodland and the different uses made of it represented the main resource for the population and were of vital importance, in order to cope with the chronic problems of food supply that characterised the Alpine regions. At the same time, the control of forest resources, both to ensure the flow of timber to the urban areas and to limit hydrogeological instability, was considered a strategic issue by the government, and its importance grew during the process of centralisation of state power in the course of the nineteenth century.

From the methodological point of view, I have tried to combine the well-established strengths of political-institutional history with the recent propositions of environmental history. In the former field, recent decades have been characterised by a growing interest in the 'spatial dimension' of the process of construction of the modern state;

5.   Cf. Démelas, Vivier 2003; Congost, Lana 2007.
6.   Caffiero 1990, p. 74; Serrano 2014; Ingold 2018.

this has allowed both the problematisation of the relationship between institutional structures and related territorial configurations, and a more in-depth examination of the role played by local actors in these dynamics.[7] At the same time, environmental historians have started to examine the relationship of mutual redefinition between environmental and institutional contexts, identifying in forest history a significant field of study in this respect.[8]

The small-scale local analysis undertaken in this study is different from the usual approach to these issues, which has tended to favour research on broader territorial areas, either national or regional.[9] This more local approach has allowed me to focus the analysis not only on the forestry policies adopted at governmental level, together with the administrative apparatus set up to implement them and the guiding role played by the nascent science of silviculture,[10] but also on their concrete reception and application – and also negotiation – at the local level. This has been especially the case in those areas where there was an established 'environmental vocation' linked to the exploitation of forest resources.[11]

While most of the research carried out on macro-areas, partly as a result of the scale of observation adopted, has only examined forestry policies, the micro-analytical approach has allowed me to relate these aspects to other factors, both institutional and socio-economic, that influenced in equal (or greater) measure the management of forest resources. As well as these advantages, the adoption of a local scale of analysis also has some disadvantages. In summary, one can question to what extent the local events studied in this work are useful to understand better and in more depth certain global (historiographical) issues.

I have tried to respond to this question in two complementary

---

7.   Cf. Bordone et al. 2007; Blockmans et al. 2009; Torre 2011; Meriggi 2016.

8.   To pick a few, cf. Sivaramakrishnan 1999; Armiero 1999; Sansa 2003; Appuhn 2009; Wing 2015.

9.   Cf. the previous note; there are exceptions: see Warde 2006a; Bertogliati 2014.

10.   Aspects which have already been studied in some depth: see Lazzarini 2009.

11.   On the concept of environmental vocation, see Gambi 1972.

ways. The first is based on the conviction that from a particular perspective it is possible to reconsider certain general assertions or to propose new lines of interrogation that are also valid for other, and perhaps wider, contexts. The second concerns the model according to which this work has been articulated, in that there is a continuous juxtaposition of local and wider events, of conjunctural and long-term elements, in an attempt to explore the interconnections between them as much as possible.

My hope is that this will not disorientate the reader, but rather open up perspectives that, from the starting point of the Cadore woodlands, will allow us to reflect on different themes: the role of local actors in the dynamics of state building; the European debates on the deforestation of the eighteenth and nineteenth centuries; the process of privatisation of common land; the changing relationship between populations and resources in the Alpine regions during the nineteenth century.

As for chronology, I have chosen as my starting point the introduction of the Napoleonic reforms in the area covered by the present study. It almost goes without saying that there were prodromes to the Napoleonic administrative system, and that there were various developments of the system in the European states after the Restoration. Furthermore, much remains to be written on the actual impact of Napoleonic legislation at the local level. However, it is difficult to deny that this period was one of considerable discontinuity with respect to the models of organisation of power that had been experienced up until then across most of Europe.

The change initiated in those years can be observed and analysed from different points of view: the criteria used to operate and recruit to the bureaucratic machine, the methods used to identify and control people, the relationship between executive and legislative power, or that between the army and society, just to give a few examples. Here it is worth remembering that a new way of describing the territory, and therefore of relating to it, was also imposed during that period.[12] For the region that concerns us, this watershed can be ex-

---

12. Sereno 1991; Barca 2010. On forest management, see Grewe 2010, pp. 47, 53–54.

emplified by the start of work, later completed during the Restoration, on drawing up the new cadastre, and by the administrative reorganisation that led to the creation of a homogeneous and rigidly hierarchical institutional space.

I shall say more about the end point of the research in the final chapter. For now, it is enough to suggest that the chosen timespan of six decades is more than sufficient for my purposes since, in order to evaluate the ever-changing relationship between institutions and individuals, I consider it appropriate to adopt the lifespan of an individual.

The most important sources for my research have been those preserved in the municipal and local archives of the Cadore area. Initial investigations had enabled me to identify a series of archives in which the documentation seemed sufficiently extensive for the period I was proposing to study. This documentation was then combined with that produced by the different levels of governments and forest administrations that succeeded each other from the setting up of the Piave department during the Napoleonic period up to the annexation of these territories by the Kingdom of Italy. These documents are kept in the State Archives of Belluno, Milan and Venice.[13]

There is a phrase of Franz Kafka that could also sum up several of his stories: 'the chains of tortured humanity are forged out of *Kanzleipapier*', the paper of officialdom or red tape.[14] This came often to mind while I was reading the accounts that made up this research and leafing through those papers: the reports and memos written across half a page on a white form or the minute notes on blue sheets. I read them whilst trying to understand the costs at local level of the process of state modernisation; and I was reading from the very sheets that, according to Kafka, are one of the most oppressive symbols of that process.

On that account, the choice of aspects to be explored was driven

---

13. In some instances, especially in the case of papers kept in the municipal archives, the documents are organised into folders but not files. In such cases, after the folder number, I have added the date of drafting of the document as an alternative reference.

14. Löwy 2007, p. 11. I owe this quote – and the meaning it can assume for those who spend time amongst archival papers – to conversations with Piero Brunello, see https://storiamestre.it/2008/02/notes-nodi/ (accessed 31 Jan. 2019).

first of all by my interests, which include a certain attraction to those incidents that broke, at least a little, the 'chains' of the bureaucratic treadmill. At the same time, I hope that the events I have analysed, as they unfold, will also allow us to understand better what could, on the surface, seem rather ordinary.[15] The results of my research are presented chronologically, but I have aimed to organise the chapters around key themes.

In the first chapter, I set out the premises of the research and establish the starting point. Although this book focuses on the period when the *ancien régime* was overturned, I have spent some time defining some of the features of the area covered by the study (the Cadore) and the governmental structure in which it was inserted in the early modern period (the Republic of Venice). I have brought together here the information that is necessary to understand the nineteenth century developments analysed in the remaining chapters, rather than weighing down the text with long digressions. In this respect, the number of studies produced recently on these issues for the Venetian period has facilitated my work. In the concluding part of this first chapter, I have illustrated some of the features of that institutional rupture represented by the period of French rule in north-eastern Italy. Regarding forest law, I have focused also on the ideological presuppositions that directed legislation on the subject. In fact, although concerns about the disappearance of woodlands and the increase in the price of timber were themes that cyclically re-emerged in early modern Europe, in the eighteenth century these preoccupations assumed unheard-of proportions, in terms of both their wide diffusion and the severity of the language in which they were couched. From these preoccupations emerged the forestry policies introduced across most of Europe in the eighteenth and nineteenth centuries.

In the second chapter, I have described the region where the effects of the changes presented in a general sense in the previous

---

15. This particular archival path may perhaps be understood with reference to the famous oxymoron of the 'exceptional normal' proposed in Grendi 1977. On the multiple interpretations of this term, see Revel 2006, pp. 36–38.

chapter are evaluated. The local context and its transformation during the nineteenth century are delineated according to three criteria: institutions, population and resources. These aspects are closely intertwined, especially the last two, and their evolution during the course of the century is only comprehensible within the context of their mutual interaction.

In the third chapter, I give an account of the first attempts to apply the new legislation, in particular forest legislation, in the Cadore area; the resistance that these attempts provoked; and the negotiations and/or conflicts that ensued.

The fourth chapter discusses the issue of common resources which, in many ways, coincides with that of the forests. Throughout the early modern period, the majority of the woodlands of the Eastern Italian Alps – and the same can be said for the pasture lands – was managed in common, according to various rights, by village communities. The administrative reforms of the early nineteenth century led to a redefinition of the legal status of these lands and of the constraints to which their use was subjected. Moreover, during the course of the century, there were more concerted attempts by landowners and by the government to privatise these resources, as was the case in much of the continent. By analysing the conflicts that these phenomena caused, I shall re-discuss certain assumptions about the role of common resources in the process of social and economic change that swept through Europe in these decades.

In the fifth and final chapter, I have placed the issues discussed within the context of wider events: the relationship between the rural population and the Risorgimento movement, with particular reference to the revolutions of 1848; the process of criminalisation of customary practices, upon which the treatment of forestry violations throws a clear spotlight; some disputes arising from the management of forest resources after the annexation of these territories to the Kingdom of Italy. Finally, I have tried to justify why the last third of the nineteenth century can be considered the end point of the events analysed in the course of this book and, at the same time, the starting point for new dynamics that resulted in a reconfiguration of the relationships between institutions, population and resources.

Giacomo Bonan

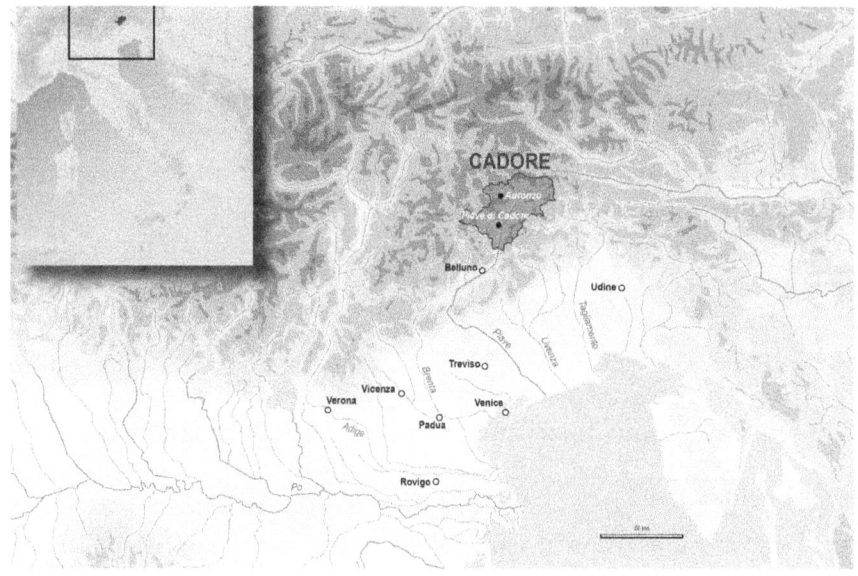

Map 1.

Location of Cadore in the North-East of Italy. Cartography by Nieves López Izquierdo.

1.

PROLOGUE. COMMON LAND AND FOREST RESOURCES: FROM THE ANCIEN RÉGIME TO THE NEW ORDER

The source of all wealth, the cause of all discord

If we climb from the bottom of the plain up into the mountains, we find a very different social order ... In some mountain areas private owner-ship is still an exception; the community possesses the pasture land and forest, also the water sources and the mines. Nor is it always sufficient to be born of parents born in the village; rather one must belong to one of the patrician families of the community, appertaining to the original inhabitants.[1]

With these evocative words, Carlo Cattaneo introduced the reader to the alpine zone of Lombardy, having taken him first through the plains and the hills. And Cattaneo famously describes how in this Alpine area there existed, in a widespread and established form, what he called 'another way of owning' – that is, ownership in common.[2]

This picture drawn by Cattaneo was not limited to Lombardy. It is well documented that the common management of resources was one of the essential assets of the Alpine communities and the corner-stone on which the life of the community, and the institutions ema-nating from it, was founded.[3] These institutions might have different names, and could differ in size, internal organisation, complexity and level of formalisation of their statutory rules, but they all shared one thing: it was the common land, and particularly the woods and pas-ture land, that defined their very identity; and the right to use these lands marked the dividing line between those who were members of

1. Cattaneo 1844, pp. cv–cvi.
2. Cattaneo 1956, pp. 187–88. Cf. Grossi 1977.
3. Cf. Furter, Head-König, Lorenzetti 2014.

the community and those who were excluded from it.[4]

In the more distinctly Alpine areas, the central importance of common land, given also the constraints that environmental characteristics placed on the expansion of cultivated land, enabled the consolidation of institutions with a high degree of autonomy. This consolidation was also associated with the weaker pressure exerted by feudalism and urban landowners compared to the lowlands. In the mountains of the Veneto region, these institutions were called *vicinie* or *regole*. Among the main *regole* of that area, both in terms of the historical traditions and in terms of the scope of the common patrimony, were those present in the Cadore Community.

The Cadore Community was a federative organisation of pyramidal structure, whose summit was represented by the general council and at whose base were the domestic aggregates that formed the various village communities.[5] In the centuries between the drafting of the first statutes of the Cadore Community during the lordship of da Camino (1245), through their reconfirmation during the dominion of the patriarchs of Aquileia (1338) and then in the period following the dedication to Venice (1420) up until the fall of the Serenissima (1797), the relationships between and within the various levels of this pyramidal organisation were constantly changing. It is not possible here to present a detailed analysis of the organisation of the Cadore Community and its evolution during the late Middle Ages and then the period of the Venetian domination. I shall confine myself to presenting some aspects of these events that will elucidate what happened during the nineteenth century, when the whole institutional system appertaining to the Cadore Community was abolished in the course of a comprehensive phase of territorial reorganisation; and I shall refer to the cited bibliography from time to time for those desiring further information.

A fundamental element of the life of all the Cadore communities was the assembly, in which a representative from each household

---

4.   Corona 2010.

5.   On this institutional structure, see Bonazza 2009. Hereafter, when I use Community I refer to the federative organisation, whereas when I use community(ies) I refer to the village community(ies).

(*fuoco* or hearth) could participate – the head of the family or a person delegated by him. Such assemblies were called *regole* (or sometimes *fabule*). During the earliest phase, these terms referred not only to the institutional assembly, but also to the territory it controlled, showing the link between institutions and territory from an etymological point of view.[6] These institutions had the task of establishing the norms regulating the internal life of the community (*laudi*) and of electing the officers appointed to enforce these statutes.[7]

The different *regole* of Cadore were grouped by geographical area into ten *centenari* that constituted a second level of this pyramidal structure. The *centenari* were responsible for the organisation of defence and for taxation, divided between the different villages according to the number of hearths and the extent of the woodlands. Furthermore, it was on the basis of the *centenari* that political representation was established within the general council.[8]

The general council constituted the top tier of the internal management of the territory. The council was responsible for the appointment of the main administrative, accounting and judicial (civil, penal and ecclesiastical) officers. It was the responsibility of the council to decide on economic, tax and administrative organisation, as well as on licences to practise particular professions (notarial and some commercial activities).[9]

The inclusion of these territories in the Venetian territorial state, in the dedication of 1420, did not substantially modify this administrative structure.[10] On this occasion, in line with the policies of the Serenissima, which was careful to keep the consent of the peripheral areas, especially those located on strategic boundaries, the Cadorini obtained the reconfirmation of their pre-existing internal institu-

6.   Felice, Battisti 1949.
7.   Several *laudi* have been published and analysed: see the bibliography in Zanderigo Rosolo 2013.
8.   Pozzan 2013, pp. 56, 69.
9.   Pozzan 2013, pp. 34–37.
10.   Cadore became part of *Patria del Friuli*; the two local representatives of Venetian administration were the *capitano* and *vicario*: see Sacco 2007.

tional structure, as well as fiscal, military and patrimonial privileges.[11]

The annexation of these areas to the Republic of Venice formalised the ties that, from an economic and commercial point of view, had been developing for some time. The driver that had encouraged the penetration of Venetian capital into Cadore was the timber trade, which is well documented from the thirteenth century.[12] The growing demand for timber, from the Veneto plain and in particular the urban centres, prompted many Venetian merchant houses to become increasingly integrated into Cadore society: they formed a stable presence, and they consolidated their political and commercial ties with the local notables. As a result, Venetian influence strengthened in this area, with important implications from the symbolic, social and cultural points of view too.[13]

At the local level, the economic and social changes triggered by this massive exploitation of forest resources and by the growing influx of Venetian financial capital, provoked a progressive escalation of the conflict linked to the two different approaches to the common patrimony, especially wooded resources. Indeed, this continued to play a fundamental role in supporting the weaker sections of the population, who could obtain free firewood or work timber from these areas, as well as important supplementary income thanks to their participation in forestry work. From this point of view, the common lands not only had an economic function but also a symbolic and cultural one, reinforcing the solidarity bonds within the village communities. These traditional bonds were strengthened above all in response to external factors, such as boundary conflicts concerning the common land between two neighbouring villages; claims made by outsiders to benefit from the customary rights appertaining to the original inhabitants; or the interference of some Venetian magistrate aiming to regulate or prevent the exploitation of certain lands.[14]

Alongside – and in many ways opposed to – this customary,

---

11. Colle 2007; Pozzan 2013, pp. 21–32.
12. Fabbiani 1959; Braunstein 1988; Vendramini 1988, pp. 7–8.
13. Concina 1982a-b.
14. Similarly to what happened in the neighbouring region of Carnia: cf. Bianco 2000a; Bianco 2005; Lorenzini 2006.

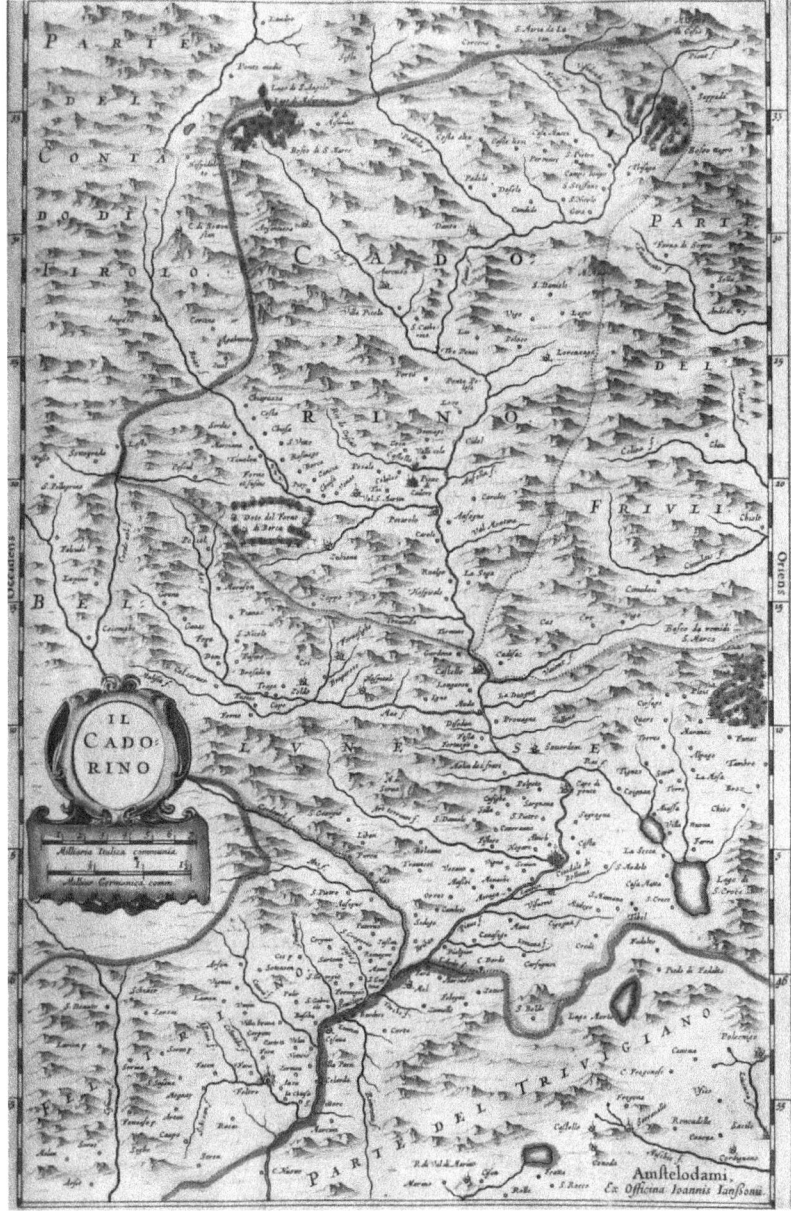

Figure 1.

Cadore in a sixteenth century map. Source: Giovanni Antonio Magini, *Il Cadorino* (Bologna: Sebastiano Bonomi, 1620).

collective approach to the common assets, there was another trend, represented by the growing importance of the timber market and the speculative practices connected to it. This led to the growth of social differentiation and to the consolidation of family factions that contended for control of the main elected offices.[15] Some families managed to accumulate large fortunes by exploiting their positions in local institutions (especially in the general council) to take advantage of the lucrative timber trade, initially as intermediaries or partners of the Venetian merchants and then taking over when, during the seventeenth century, the ruling classes of the Serenissima gradually moved their capital from commercial activity to land ownership.[16]

There were two particularly controversial and closely related issues, which caused various clashes of competencies to emerge between the different levels of the Cadore Community, in particular between the general council and the *regole*. These concerned the definition of the *regolieri* and the ownership of common resources. In both cases the main cause of conflict was economic in character; but the solution had important political, juridical and symbolic implications.

Regarding the first aspect, as mentioned earlier, the right to participate in the village assembly, as well as that to use the common assets, were not assigned individually but to the family group, identified by the household (*fuoco*). In this sense, the allocation of rights to use the common assets on a family basis represented a factor that was both conservative and equalising.[17] It was conservative because, unlike other management systems of common resources regulated just by residency, it placed greater restraints on the use of these resources, thus limiting the risks of over-exploitation. It was equalising because the method for awarding community rights was established according to relatively fair criteria, unlike other systems where they were allocated on the basis of property holdings (e.g. the number of

---

15. Bianco 2000b; Sacco 2007. For a comparison with other European regions, cf. Lana 2008; De Moor 2010.

16. Zannini 2011.

17. On the homeostatic function of these rules on the relation between population and resources, see Lorenzetti, Merzario 2005, pp. 31–54.

agricultural lands or animals owned by the respective households).[18]

In addition to the benefits deriving from membership of the assembly, each household was subject to equally distributed obligations (the construction or maintenance of buildings or communal infrastructures; the obligation to attend the assembly and to carry out the tasks that were assigned by it annually etc.). Rights and duties were acquired by patrilineal descent, with a few exceptions that allowed for female succession.[19]

These rules, the origin of which was traced back to the links of consanguinity between the families that had colonised the territory, served to reinforce the bonds of identity between members of the community, the original inhabitants (*originari*). At the same time, they served to set up barriers to all that was external, in accordance with the well-known model of the closed corporate community that was widespread in many pre-industrial societies.[20]

Those who were not part of the original families were defined as foreigners – not only the non-Cadorini, but also those Cadorini who came under another *regola*.[21] The rules that limited the rights of foreigners residing in the territories of the *regola* were all the more detailed, whilst the vaguest provisions were those that aimed at establishing the ways in which a foreigner could become part of the community of original inhabitants. This situation led to continuous disputes between the village assemblies and the general council on the criteria for admission to the community organisations.[22]

Another issue concerned the ownership of the common patrimony, on the legal position of which there are still differing opinions, partly because it involves outstanding issues between the *regole,* as reconstituted post-World War II, and the municipal administrations. The most controversial issue, due to its high economic value, concerned – and concerns – the ownership of woodlands. The interpretative

18. For an overview of systems regulating access to common land in various regions of North-West Europe, cf. De Moor, Shaw-Taylor, Warde 2002.

19. Zanderigo Rosolo 1982, pp. 99–134.

20. Wolf 1957.

21. Zanderigo Rosolo 2013, pp. 70–72.

22. Pozzan 2013, pp. 79–83.

line that I adopt here is that identified by Giandomenico Zanderigo Rosolo and recently revived by Annamaria Pozzan: it argues that, from an initial freer use of the common lands by all members of the Cadore Community, there developed a progressive division between the respective *regole* relating to the pasture land and the woods.[23] In this sense, the statutory provision that stated 'all the woods located in Cadore are, and should be, common to the men of Cadore, and not to any foreigners' had a predominantly symbolic value, in order to legitimise the Cadore prerogatives with respect to the Republic of Venice and its attitude towards the common property and forest resources of the Venetian mainland.[24]

The Lion, the communities, the forests

With its conquest of the mainland, accomplished in stages between the fourteenth and fifteenth centuries, Venice came into possession of a vast and varied region stretching from the Adriatic coast to the peaks of the Alps, from the coasts of Istria to the provinces of eastern Lombardy.

The Venetian ruling class immediately realised the problems related to the management and exploitation of wooded areas in the new territories. The Venetian patricians had been interested and involved in the timber market from at least the thirteenth century; however, it was in the second half of the fifteenth century that the Serenissima developed systematic forestry legislation.[25] From then on, the attitude of the Republic of Venice always oscillated between two poles: the need to valorise and the desire to protect forest resources – that is, the urge to exploit the resources, arising from the growing need for wood due to the increase in population and consumption; and the conservative desire to guarantee long-term supplies (in particular for certain productive sectors), as well as to preserve important territorial balances.

23. Pozzan 2013, pp. 95–97; Zanderigo Rosolo 1982, pp. 57–81.

24. *Statuti della Communità di Cadore (Venezia MDCXCIII)* 1987, p. 63. (original edition 1338).

25. Vergani 2006, p. 401.

Prologue: Common land and forest resources

As regards territorial protection, the forestry policy of the Republic was driven primarily by the wider defence needs of the Venetian lagoon.[26] In fact, even if in this period there was a lack of in-depth scientific knowledge of the relationship between deforestation, hydro-geological instability, river flooding and the burying of the lagoon environment, the Venetian ruling class realised by the first half of the fifteenth century that these factors were interconnected. In the following century, the links are explicitly referred to in legislation adopted by the Senate and the Council of Ten.[27]

However, these measures to protect the territory were always subordinate to the economic-productive needs of the Republic.[28] Moreover, it could not have been otherwise in a period characterised by the omnipresence of wood in every aspect of daily life, so much so that Fernand Braudel has suggested that pre-industrial Europe should be defined as the 'civilisation of wood'.[29] This definition could be applied to Europe as a whole before the use of fossil fuels, but it takes on a particular significance in the case of Venice. This is first of all due to the peculiar environmental characteristics of the city: 'no one should be surprised to see the deforestation of the Alps of Venice and Istria if they think of the trees buried in our lagoon', wrote Agostino Sagredo in the middle of the nineteenth century, referring to the piles on which the foundations of most of the buildings were built; to which must be added the trunks used to mark out the lagoon and for the sea defences.[30]

To the importance of wood used for public and private buildings in the city must be added its use in shipbuilding, on which the fortunes of the Serenissima had been founded for centuries. In this area, the best known and most studied example, although certainly not the only one, is the military shipyards of the Arsenal which, by virtue of their

---

26. Caniato 1997.
27. Appuhn 2000, p. 869; Vergani 2010, p. 188.
28. Lazzarini 2009, p. 18.
29. Braudel 1981, p. 362.
30. Quoted in Lazzarini 2009, p. 14–15.

strategic importance, always obtained a privileged supply of timber.[31]

In addition to being a crucial raw material for construction, ship-building and craft work, wood (in its natural state or as charcoal) was also the main source of energy for heating and cooking in a city which, despite its relative decline, was still one of the most populous of early modern Europe.[32] As well as these domestic uses, fuel was also needed for the bakeries and various manufactories, among which the furnaces of the Murano glassworks stood out for their importance and high consumption.[33]

In terms of population and industrial activities, Venice presented the highest demand for timber within the Republic, but there were also the needs of the other cities of the Veneto plain, which was one of the most densely populated areas of early modern Europe and, at the same time, devoid of adequate forest resources. This was due to the lowland woods having been in retreat since the fifteenth century and, in any case, never having been large enough to satisfy the demands of the urban centres.[34]

This high demand was met for the most part by the Alpine and Perialpine territories closest to the Veneto plain. For this region to serve as the main supply area for the needs of Venice and the cities of the mainland, not only was it important that it possessed large quantities of the most sought-after arboreal species (fir and larch for construction, beech as an energy source); equally crucial were its relative proximity to the urban centres (the main areas involved were just over 100 kilometres from Venice) and, above all, the morphology of the territory. Indeed, the value of a resource depends more on the possibility of commercialising it than on its nature.

In the period before rail transport, a necessary precondition for the development of a wood supply chain was the presence of waterways capable of transporting timber from the cutting areas to the points of sale.

---

31. This is a popular topic among historians: cf. the bibliography quoted in Lazzarini 2014.
32. Beloch 1994.
33. Trivellato 2000; Lazzarini 2006a.
34. On the population of this area, Beltrami 1954; on the woods, Barbacetto 2008, p. 18.

Prologue: Common land and forest resources

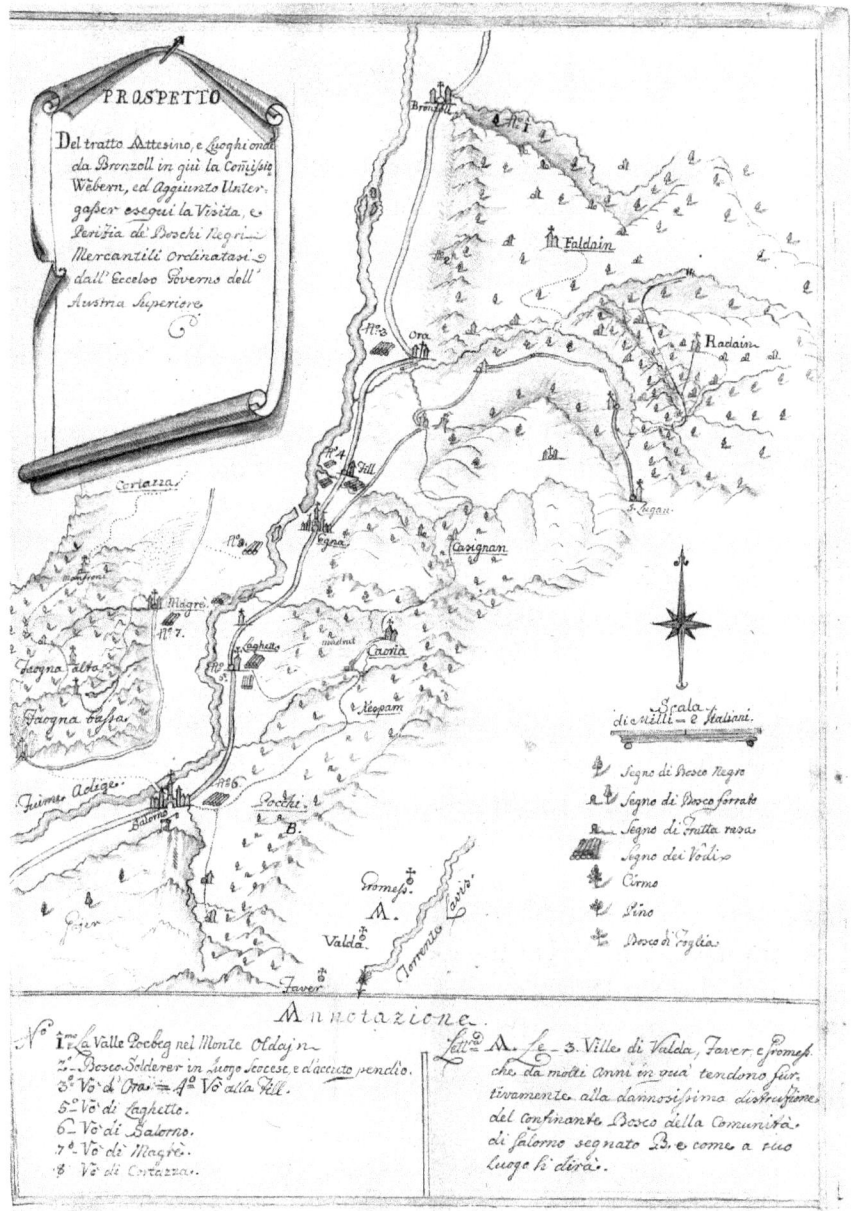

Figure 2.

One of the 'timber roads' to Venice: the Adige river. Source: AMCF, b. 68, f. 369.

The transport of timber to the Venetian plain, and particularly to the Venetian market, developed along the main fluvial arteries that descend from the Alpine chain to the Adriatic coast, according to a model that was already in place at the time of the Republic's expansion onto the mainland, and that lasted until the second half of the nineteenth century.[35] The main traffic routes consisted of the most important rivers of the area – the Piave, Adige, Brenta and Tagliamento – to which goods coming from the various tributaries were channelled. It was a huge trade, and not limited only to the territories under the control of the Serenissima, as large quantities of timber also flowed towards Venice from Trentino, Tyrol and Carinthia.[36]

It is difficult to quantify this traffic in monetary terms, due to the widespread smuggling, the fragmented nature of the documents and the wide range of products and arboreal species sold.[37] The available data nevertheless suggest the importance of this commercial sector. For example, it has been estimated that at the start of the seventeenth century, the only river port of Fonzaso (on the Cismon torrent) handled timber of a value equal to the annual revenue of the Republic of Venice in the same period.[38] In those years, it is possible to estimate that the timber trade had a total value far greater than that in woollen fabrics (the most important manufactured product of the Republic between the fifteenth and seventeenth centuries) and was comparable only to the market for cereals in terms of the capital involved.[39] However, during the Venetian period, the market for timber over and above cereals steadily improved, making it one of the most profitable activities of the time.[40]

Within this market there were very different, and often opposed, interests: public interests that favoured the protection of the tree species

35. Lazzarini 2009, pp. 195–208. For a European overview see Hollister-Short 1994. On the Milan timber supply system, see a Marca 2001.

36. Occhi 2015; Lorenzini 2012.

37. Corazzol 1997, p. 222.

38. Occhi 2006, p. 59.

39. Zannini 2011, p. 475.

40. Corazzol 1997, p. 223.

required in shipbuilding and other privileged sectors; those of the timber merchants who very often belonged to the Venetian ruling class and influenced its policy, despite obvious conflicts of interest; the urban interests (domestic and artisan) of Venice and the cities of the mainland; and finally those of the mountain communities, which boasted of rights of various kinds over the woodlands, and which obtained products for the local economy from these resources, as well as essential assets to compensate for their chronic deficit in the grain balance.[41]

Venetian forest policy, in the decades following the conquest of the mainland, was mainly directed to ensuring supplies for public uses, especially those that were considered strategic, such as shipbuilding, in line with the priorities set out in the legislation of the fourteenth century.[42]

There were two main ways in which the Republic tried to guarantee supplies for the Arsenal. A first provision, issued in 1479, reserved all existing oaks in the territories east of Lake Garda. The law set out the obligation to conserve obligation to conserve all the oak trees (*Quercus sp.*), fundamentally important species in the shipbuilding industry because they were the most suitable for the construction of the frames and hulls of ships.[43] However, it seems that the Venetian legislation in this area was ineffective: given that the obligation to conserve and enhance supplies of oak fell on the owners of the land, the most common practice amongst private individuals and communities was to fell seedlings not yet registered by the Venetian magistrates.[44]

A second device used was to issue a proclamation assigning exclusive use of a wood to the needs of the Arsenal. Following a model already tried for the forest of Montona in Istria – which was set aside at the end of the fourteenth century because it was rich in oaks that were curved and particularly suited to the making of hulls

---

41. On the different actors involved, cf. Lorenzini, Bernardin 2013; Zannini 2010.
42. On the Venetian forest legislation, see Lazzarini 2014; Lazzarini 2018; cf. a different evaluation in Appuhn 2009.
43. Agnoletti 2004.
44. Vergani 1991.

– between the fifteenth and sixteenth centuries around 65 woods had bans placed on their use. These also were chosen because they contained species necessary for shipbuilding. Many of these forests – for example those located in Carnia – were hardly used at all for logistical reasons, while the exploitation of timber was mainly from three woods (in addition to the aforementioned Montona): Cansiglio, Montello and Somadida. This last, the smallest of the four, was located in Cadore, near Auronzo. It was only 400 hectares in size, but had a high concentration of precious firs for masts.[45]

Unlike what happened with the legislation on oak, it is agreed in the literature on the subject that the public protection of these areas, which remained state property (*demanio*) even after the fall of the Republic, had positive results from the environmental point of view. However, it is still necessary to investigate the social costs that the restrictions imposed by Venice inflicted on the populations living near these woods, who found themselves excluded.[46]

However, these woodlands, over which the Venetian authorities did exercise effective control, represented a minimal portion of the Veneto forest area – about six per cent, of which more than two thirds were concentrated in the Cansiglio area.[47] There were also woods owned by private individuals or ecclesiastical bodies, but the majority of forest areas – and in the mountain areas almost all – were the assets of the local communities and were collectively used by the local populations, as was the rest of the uncultivated land.[48]

In the second half of the fifteenth century, a period of much activity with regard to forestry legislation, Venice intervened to regulate the management of the common forests too, with a series of measures issued at the beginning of 1476.[49] The regulations

---

45. Vergani 2006.

46. Cf. Zannini 2012c; Appuhn 2000; Vergani 2006; Lazzarini 2006b.

47. Before Italian unification, the Veneto area also included the provinces of Udine and Pordenone (nowadays in Friuli Venezia-Giulia). The area of state forests is estimated from nineteenth century data: Lazzarini 2009, pp. 60–61.

48. Bianco 2001.

49. Appuhn 2009, pp. 111–24.

prescribed a ten-year cycle for felling in the woodlands, as well as limiting access by herds and the lighting of fires in wooded areas. In their practical implementation, these rules had a very limited impact, since they were not backed up by adequate means of enforcement and the local populations continued freely to use their own woodlands.[50] However, it was at this point that a distinction was introduced that was to become usual in subsequent legislation, and whose effects were to extend well beyond the period of Venetian domination over these territories: the distinction between *beni comuni* and *beni comunali*.[51] This distinction affected not just forest lands but also all the uncultivated land managed collectively by the communities of the Venetian mainland, from the marshes and fishing valleys of the low plains to the pastures and woodlands of the mountainous areas.[52]

The lands that the populations used according to ancient custom, but which lacked property titles and the possession of which often depended upon the formula *ab immemorabili*, became state property of the Serenissima. The Republic then granted them in usufruct to the same communities through renewable grants, with a constraint of inalienability and restrictions of use. These lands were classed as *beni comunali*. On the other hand, other communities were able to demonstrate legitimate ownership of the lands they were profiting from 'thanks to documented purchases or special privileges, such as those recognised in Cadore at the time of its dedication to Venice'; these lands were called *beni comuni*.[53] While *beni comunali* were state property, and therefore exempt from taxation, *beni comuni* were registered on the tax estimates as allodial assets.

It should, however, be kept in mind that common land, regardless of its legal definition, was the subject of long-running disputes between various parties (the Venetian magistrates, bordering commu-

---

50. Zannini 2012b, p. 104.
51. Barbacetto 2008, p. 21.
52. For a bibliography on the Venetian legislation on common land, see Bragaggia 2012, p. 50 n. 42.
53. Pitteri 2006, p. 58.

nities, private individuals), who asserted their various rights to these assets in a constant jostling to redefine power relations.[54]

The distinction between *beni comuni* and *beni comunali* was reconfirmed in subsequent Venetian legislation on the subject, particularly in the first half of the seventeenth century when, to stem the continuous erosion of *beni comunali* through undue appropriations by private individuals – the so-called encroachers – the Venetian authorities undertook the huge task of officially registering the property granted in usufruct to the populations of the Venetian mainland. *Beni comuni* considered as belonging to the respective communities were exempted from this procedure, as in the case of Cadore.[55] In the same way, they were exempted some years later, when the official registration work undertaken by Venice to restrict or prevent attempts to privatise *beni comunali* proved useful for this purpose. In fact, in order to meet the debts contracted to finance the wars of Candia and Morea against the Turks, Venice decided for the first time systematically to sell the *beni comunali* in the territories east of the river Mincio.[56]

It must be said that the impact of these sales, which took place over more than eighty years (1646–1727), was concentrated mainly in the Veneto-Friuli plain, which was radically transformed during this period (total sales amounted to almost 90,000 ha), while the Republic tried to reconcile its financial needs with the desire to safeguard the territory through a series of measures that reaffirmed the inalienability of the *beni comunali* if they were wooded, or situated in the mountain areas or along the Piave river.[57]

Symptoms and remedies

The huge amount of legislation produced by Venice on forestry matters, independently of any evaluation of its effects, is the best evi-

54. Bragaggia 2012.
55. Zanderigo Rosolo 2013, pp. 87–91.
56. Barbacetto 2000, pp. 84–85.
57. For a quantitative analysis of the sales, see Beltrami 1961. For the exceptions, see Barbacetto 2008, p. 174.

dence for the attention given to these issues by the Venetian ruling classes. However, from the mid-eighteenth century, issues related to the management of woodlands took on a new importance. Two interconnected factors were influential in this respect: on the one hand, the development of a scientific approach to forestry problems inspired by the ideas of the Enlightenment; on the other, a widespread alarm among contemporary elites concerning the 'disappearance of the woodlands' and the problems associated with this. Neither factor was confined to the territories under the control of the Republic of Venice; they were shared, albeit with differing nuances and characteristics, by a large part of the European continent.[58]

Firstly, the breadth of the debate changed – it no longer involved only the government apparatus, but also the wider cultural world – and so did the ways in which these issues were dealt with. Within the context of the more general reform movement that developed in Italy in the second half of the eighteenth century, great importance was given to agronomic issues. The main centres of this debate, especially with regard to the Republic of Venice, were the agricultural academies, whose publications also concerned themselves with forestry issues, which might be analysed independently or in relation to other topics.[59]

A common feature of these writings was the search for the most scientific approach possible. The profile of the authors was varied, but they were usually either agronomists, Enlightenment reformers or hydraulic scientists.[60] The problems discussed were the same as those that had inspired the legislative measures of previous centuries, namely the need to ensure timber supplies for urban centres and the relationship between deforestation and hydrogeological instability. This last issue was felt more keenly in the Veneto area than elsewhere, given the absence of lakes to slow down the impetus of the waters and the presence of many torrential rivers.[61] One of those who concerned himself with this issue, at the University of Padua,

---

58. Cf. Harrison 1992, pp. 114–24; Warde 2006b.
59. Simonetto 2009a-b; Berengo 1962.
60. Vecchio 1974; see also Vecchio 2010.
61. Lazzarini 2002a.

was Pietro Arduinio, who held the first chair in agriculture set up in Europe (1765).[62]

Even though forestry issues were studied in relation to different themes, since the profiles of the authors varied, one thing distinguishes all these writings: the tone used to describe the condition of the forests. The state of the woodlands is described with alarm; often the subject of description is not the forests, but their disappearance. Antonio Carrera, archpriest of Castion, a town near the city of Belluno, south of the Cadore region, writes in 1774: 'The territory of Belluno a century ago was almost all forested', but 'as time has passed, things have completely changed. The mountain is all bare and open; now one seeks in vain any vestige or sign of the ancient forest, which used to stand there everywhere in all its fullness'. Already at the start of the piece, the author is aware that he is not confronting a problem limited to the territory of Belluno:

> It is now felt over almost all of Europe that wood has become a thing of great scarcity; and we see, unfortunately, that compared to times past, prices have climbed to such an extent that the poor of the city in the raw winter, struggle more to keep the fire lit than to have enough food to eat.[63]

Deforestation is attributed to different causes, the incidence of which varies mainly according to the geographical context. Where the morphology of the territory allows it, the desire to expand agricultural areas causes the ploughing up of the woods; in some other cases, the main cause is excessive commercial pressure linked to the timber trade; in others it is caused by grazing in the wooded areas – or other practices deplored in contemporary writings – leading to a slow deterioration. Deforestation was often not provoked by specific human activities but, more generally, by the system of ownership of the woodlands: 'common land, when it becomes the object of a special discourse, becomes so almost always because its state, usually not flourishing, is recognised as being the result of its system of ownership'.[64]

62. Gloria 1855, pp. 724–56.

63. *Giornale d'Italia* **10** (1774): 389–90. On Carrera see Preto 1978.

64. Vecchio 1974, p. 49. See also Warde 2015, p. 157.

This last aspect was especially debated in the Veneto-Friuli mountains where, as has been seen, most of the wooded areas were used collectively by the local populations in different ways.

> The daily need for firewood, as well as the urge to profit from the sale of bundles of wood for various uses, led the mountain people to the woodlands, where the sovereign munificence had granted them the right to use the woods in common. And since they were interested in satisfying their own needs and interests with the least possible expenditure of time and effort, they pounced on the nearest wood. This woodland could be profited from by every community, and it benefited each equally, so any affection or attachment on the part of the beneficiaries was effectively extinguished.[65]

This was the opinion of Giuseppe Antonini, a member of the agricultural academy of Udine, on the use made by the populations of the Carnic Alps of their woodlands.

Even in the district of Feltre, in the southern part of the current province of Belluno, the obstacles to agricultural development were well known to Bartolomeo Dal Covolo, a member of the local academy: 'The first thing is the daily tilling of the common lands by the villagers'.[66]

The reason for this attitude is illustrated by the Dean of Belluno, the noble Lucio Doglioni: 'No one takes great care of that which belongs to everyone. People only love their own property. Therefore, the public pastures are barren; the mountains are mostly bare of woodlands that can be used for firewood.'[67] The topos according to which what belonged to everyone was used – or, rather, overused – as if it belonged to no one, was so widespread among reformers of the time that when it came to intervening with legislation, it was always re-stated as a natural assumption, instead of a subjective evaluation linked to specific territorial areas. Yet the same Doglioni, after having affirmed it, notes that 'woodlands are preserved, however, in the more distant parts, and especially in the mountains; and these woodlands supply commercial timber, which by means of the Piave is transported to the Treviso area

---

65. Antonini 1789, p. 122. On Antonini see Bianco 2008a.

66. *Giornale d'Italia* **5** (1769): 402.

67. Doglioni 1816, p. 10.

and up to Venice'.[68] But the woods that were envied by Doglioni – who was certainly referring to the Cadore area – were almost entirely the common property of the Cadore populations. This is confirmed by another member of the Belluno aristocracy of that time, Count Francesco Piloni, who describes in similar tones the flourishing trade in timber extracted from the Cadore woods.[69]

There were certainly exceptions. One of these of particular interest is found in the writings of Giovanni Gervasis, if only because it raises the issue in terms of social relations, evoking the theme of the means of production well before the well-known nineteenth-century developments.[70] Gervasis agrees that the condition of most of the common land of Belluno was poor. However, he notes that conditions had been different in previous centuries and that they were still different in some areas of the district. In the Agordino, Longaronese and Zoldano districts, the common woodlands and pastures were kept in good condition and brought considerable income to the respective communities. On the other hand, in the other parishes, the common property was in a state of advanced decay. According to Gervasis, this discrepancy was due to the fact that private land and common land held complementary functions. In those areas where direct management of farmland dominated, the population also looked after the maintenance of the common land. On the other hand, the deterioration of the common land was more marked in those zones where there had been an expansion of city land ownership in the rural areas, with the consequent expropriation and impoverishment of the rural population.[71]

Just as the reasons for deforestation were more complex than those identified in many writings of the time, so the actual extent of the phenomenon is also far from clear. In fact, in recent decades, a renewed historical interest in these issues has allowed us to relativise contemporary descriptions of forest degradation. According to this

68. Doglioni 1816, pp. 10–11.

69. Quoted in Vecchio 1974, p. 68 n. 42.

70. Simonetto 2001, p. 120.

71. Gervasis 1790.

revision, what at the time was seen as a general forest crisis, with a serious risk of the woodlands disappearing, was in reality a forest resource crisis.[72] There was a distribution crisis, due to various factors including the increase in population and industrial activities, and a real – albeit limited – retreat of forest cover, particularly in those areas closest to urban centres. The combined effect of the growth in demand and the increase in transport costs caused a significant increase in the price of timber – especially that used as an energy source – and made it impossible sometimes to meet market needs.[73] This dynamic was also detected in the Veneto area by Antonio Lazzarini.[74] However, even if the degradation of woodland heritage was more perceived than real, it was from such convictions that the nascent forest science developed, and also subsequent nineteenth-century legislation inspired by it.

Although works had already been published in previous centuries dedicated specifically to trees and woodlands, it is from the eighteenth century that treatises with a scientific vocation first appear.[75] The watershed is usually seen to be the publication of *Traité complet des bois et des forêts* by Henri-Louis Duhamel du Monceau, the importance of which was also immediately clear to contemporaries. As can be seen from the titles of the various volumes that make up the work,[76] Duhamel covers every possible topic related to the management and exploitation of forest areas, from the preparation of land and the choice of seeds to the organisation of transport and the sale of timber.[77] The importance of this work lies not only in its huge size or in the attention given to every single aspect. There are two approaches that distinguish Duhamel's writing from most previous

---

72. Grewe 2000.
73. Cf. Corvol 2000a; Sansa 2003; Radkau 2012.
74. Lazzarini 2008b.
75. Armiero 1999, pp. 213–14.
76. *Traité des arbres et arbustes* (1755); *La physique des arbres* (1758), *Des semis et plantations des arbres* (1760); *De l'exploitation des bois* (1764); *Du transport, de la conservation et de la force des bois* (1767).
77. Matteson 2015, p. 65. Cf. Corvol 2000b.

Figure 3.

Works in a coppice woodland. Source: H. Duhamel du Monceau, *De l'exploitation des bois* (Paris: H.L. Guerin & L.F. Delatour, 1764) Vol. I, p. 250.

works: an analysis devoid of aesthetic considerations and careful only to scientifically evaluate the function and utility of the objects being discussed; and an intention to consider the woodland as a cultivated field, an area in which the processes of sowing, growing and 'harvesting' ought to be directed by human action.[78]

However, if the *Traité complet des bois et des forêts* was probably the most read and debated work of the period, it was the silvicultural approach developed in the German-speaking countries between the end of the eighteenth and beginning of the nineteenth centuries that became the reference model for the main European forest administrations.[79]

To respond to the increasing difficulties of timber procurement, German silviculture developed a method based on the concept of sustainable yield (*Nachhaltigkeit*). Thanks to the contribution of other disciplines that were developing in this period, such as cartography, geometry, mathematics and statistics, German foresters developed a system of management of wooded areas aimed at ensuring the largest possible production of wood mass without compromising the continuity of extraction over the long term. At the root of this system was the attempt to quantify and lay out parameters such as the real dimensions of a wood, the volume of wood mass contained in it and, consequently, the monetary value of the product obtainable from it.[80] Once these parameters had been defined, as well as the time needed to allow the reproduction of the wood itself, the area was divided into subsections that were cut in annual rotation so that the end of the cutting cycle coincided with the period established to best guarantee the reproduction of the forest (regular section cut). To facilitate the homogenisation of the different sections that made up the wood and thus make the calculations that were the basis of this system easier, the most suitable cutting method was clear-cutting.[81]

It is useful to look at two consequences of this geometric approach to

---

78. Sansa 1997, pp. 98–100.

79. On the influence of German silviculture in other European countries, cf. Guha, Gadgil 1989; Sansa 1997; Whited 2000.

80. Lowood 1991.

81. Ravi Rajan 2006, pp. 35–44.

forest resources, one social and the other environmental. From the social point of view, any human activity capable of altering the parameters on which the cutting criteria were based had to be limited and, where possible, prevented. In other words, and in accordance with a predominant trend in every agronomic consideration, the customary activities practised by local populations in forest areas were not compatible with the new principles of forest management. From an environmental point of view, the cutting systems adopted by German silviculture, based on the hypothesis of being able to calculate the exact wood mass contained in each wooded area, favoured the spread of 'pure' woods – that is, woods characterised by the prevalence of a single tree species.[82]

The debates arising from the development of silvicultural science also aroused interest in the Veneto region. Attention was paid above all to the treatises in French (not yet those in German), and an Italian translation of the first two parts of *Traité complet des bois et des forêts* by Henry-Louis Duhamel du Monceau was published in Venice, as a result of a state initiative.[83]

It is clear, therefore, that there was widespread interest in this region in the new and innovative theories emerging from the field of silviculture; however, what was lacking in the leaders of the Venetian republic was the ability to translate these reflections and debates into a comprehensive reform project.[84]

From a formal point of view, the forestry sector was a notable exception to the general pattern of legislative inconclusiveness that characterised most of the reform projects launched by the Venetian establishment at the end of the eighteenth century, since in 1792 a new forest law was enacted. However, although this new legislation was innovative in various ways – particularly in the criteria laid out for selecting forest personnel and the organisational structure – there were difficulties in implementing it, as highlighted by Antonio Lazzarini: conflicts of competency between different magistrates, a lack

82. Scott 1998, pp. 11–22; Grewe, Hölzl 2018, pp. 22–28.

83. Duhamel du Monceau 1772; Duhamel du Monceau 1774. On this initiative, see Lorenzini 2018, pp. 127–29.

84. Simonetto 2001.

of financial support and poor cooperation between the government and the scientific community.[85]

Moreover, as with previous legislation in this sector, the forest law of 1792 lacked an overview of the forest question and of its role in an overall policy of land management. In fact, its action was limited to the state forests and to those containing oaks. Therefore, most of the forest area in the Alpine districts was excluded from the legislation; in these areas, the exploitation criteria continued to be determined on the basis of the needs of local communities and the interests of merchants operating in the timber trade.[86]

The growing crisis of the Serenissima, and then its sudden collapse on 12 May 1797 with the arrival of the French troops, prevented further modifications to the system described so far. Even the first Austrian domination, which replaced the brief democratic interregnum following the Treaty of Campoformio (17 October 1797) maintained, in all essentials, the territorial governmental system inherited from the Venetians, as regarded both forestry legislation and the distinction between *beni comuni* and *beni comunali*.[87] However, quite another attitude was adopted after the Peace of Pressburg (26 December 1805), when the Venetian territories became part of the Kingdom of Italy controlled by the French.

From community to municipality

In the territories belonging to the Republic of Venice, as in most of Europe, the few years of Napoleonic administration coincided with a phase of profound modernisation, especially as concerned legislative models and administrative structures.[88]

During that period, for the first time a centralised form of territorial government was imposed, which was maintained during the following decades. Indeed, as will be seen, some of the principal laws promulgated

---

85. Lazzarini 2009, pp. 13–38.
86. Lazzarini 2009, pp. 25, 27.
87. Massarotto 1998.
88. For a general overview of this period, see Donato et al. 2015.

by the French stayed in force well beyond the half century of Austrian domination and remained points of reference after Italian unification. Moreover, even where there was a formal discontinuity between the French and the Lombardo-Venetian regulations, the Austrian administration was constantly stimulated by comparisons with the Napoleonic experience, of whose effectiveness the new state was fully aware. In this sense there is no doubt that, at least from the institutional point of view, the period of reforms initiated during the French occupation and continued after the Restoration can be seen as a turning point, the long-term significance of which must be properly assessed.[89]

However, if it is possible to attribute to this institutional break an explanatory and not merely an events-based significance, this must be done in the knowledge that the issuing of new legal provisions or principles does not necessarily mean that they were effectively enforced, especially in such a 'peripheral' area as this.

'From the day when the Napoleonic Code is put into operation, the Roman law, the ordinances, general and local customs, statutes and regulations will cease to have the force of general or particular law in the matters that are the subject of the provisions contained in Napoleonic Code'.[90] This preamble to the Italian edition of the *Code Civil* of 1804, which well represents the intentions of the French legislature, has often been read as if it had a performative efficacy, as if the simple statement of it created a *tabula rasa* of a whole world of custom, social relations and territorial particularism.[91]

I propose here to examine briefly some aspects of this legislation, being mindful that its reception and reprocessing at the local level must then be analysed, in order to understand how these regulations were constantly being mediated, resisted or invoked – more or less instrumentally – by the host of actors involved.

The aspects on which I shall focus are those to which I have already referred regarding previous periods – that is, the legislation on forests and use of common land. However, as part of the more com-

---

89. Laven, Riall 2000; Meriggi 2011.

90. *Codice di Napoleone il Grande pel Regno d'Italia* 1806, p. 3.

91. Viggiano 2009, p. 179.

prehensive reform plan implemented in these years, and limiting the analysis only to institutional changes, these aspects are closely linked to at least two other themes: fiscal reform and administrative reform. Fiscal reform, in terms of the predial tax, initiated the operations that led to the setting up of the new cadastre. Administrative reform led to the creation of departments and municipalities as modern administrative bodies. I shall return to the former in the next chapter; here the latter will be briefly considered.

After the Peace of Pressburg, the laws in force in the Kingdom of Italy were extended to the so-called ex-Venetian territories. As had already happened in Lombardy, the administrative structure was reorganised according to territorial departments. Each department was in turn subdivided into districts, cantons and municipalities. The territory of the upper basin of the Piave, which for centuries had been fragmented into the three areas of Feltrino, Bellunese and Cadore, was merged to form the department of the Piave, thus creating an administrative unit that lasted over the following centuries, despite some territorial changes.[92]

The new area, formed as a result of territorial contiguity, did not take into account historical traditions and well-established economic interests. Cadore was traditionally linked to Friuli from an institutional point of view, while it had strong economic ties both with the Carnic Alps and the neighbouring German-speaking territories. As for Feltrino, its traditional interests were directed more towards the South and West (Primiero, Trevigiano and Vicentino) rather than the Belluno area located in the Northeast. The same city of Belluno, in terms of size, population and historical importance, certainly could not compete with the capitals of the other territorial departments of the Kingdom[93].

The artificiality of the aggregations was even more acute at the local level, where the administrative reform led to a drastic simplification of the institutional fabric. In rural areas, local institutions such as the *regole*, which had been the basic administrative unit of the territory for centuries, were suppressed and replaced by municipalities.

There were notable differences between the two bodies. The first

92.   Netto 1967.
93.   Cf. Mancuso, De Vecchi 1991.

was geographic: the new entity, even with different administrative pro-
cedures and practices, did not coincide with the territory previously
managed by the *regoliere* assembly. In most cases, the municipality
imposed by the French encompassed more conterminous communities. And the amalgamations were maintained even after the return of
the Austrians, who merged neighbouring communities that (precisely
because they were neighbouring) had often been in conflict. This territorial expansion was matched by an increase in the administrative
burden imposed on the municipalities. As a result, they faced a considerable increase in both ordinary and extraordinary expenses.[94]

It is not possible here to analyse in detail the administrative reforms
implemented by the French in Italy, but one can identify two guiding principles behind the legislation of those years: uniformity and
centralisation.[95] The best-known and most representative symbol of
centralisation was undoubtedly the prefect. Among his tasks was that
of supervising the municipal administration, either directly or through
the deputy prefects, who were assigned to the various cantons into
which a department was subdivided. This hierarchy remained valid,
despite nominal changes, during the Austrian domination.[96]

If the vertical structure reveals the centralist character of the new administrative system, the horizontal one is characterised by an attempt to
homogenise the space. The territory is no longer divided into different
realities, each one with its own internal arrangements, its own privileges
and, above all, specific criteria of citizenship. Rather, it is 'rationalised'
according to uniform parameters in which the functions of the local administration, the criteria of citizenship and the forms of representation
are the same and are predetermined according to a hierarchy that divides
the municipalities according to size into three classes of membership.[97]

This redefinition of the territory created the deepest fractures in

94. Zannini, Gazzi 2003, p. 56.

95. Cadore Community sent a petition to Napoleon in March 1806, asking for an exemp-
     tion from the new legislation on the basis that 'a new, general and uniform legislation
     cannot be applied in this territory without undermining its existence and patriarchal
     system', in ASMi, *Archivio Aldini*, b. 42, section 6, f. III/4.

96. Antonielli 1983.

97. On the evolution of the municipal legislation during this period, see Aimo 2005.

rural areas. Here the ancient territorial bodies were indistinguishable from the family groups that composed them. The main local institution, the assembly of family heads, was identified – etymologically and ideally – with the group of original inhabitants and the territory itself. As already mentioned, the principles of autonomy and equality on which these assembly institutions were founded were more formal than real. However, they were the basis of accepted values and identity that were deeply rooted in the rural world.

The new municipality undermined this identification. In the first place, because it often incorporated more than one rural community; secondly, because the criteria for participation in the municipal forum were no longer linked to patrilineal descent, but associated with land tenure and taxation; finally, because the municipality became an administrative organ within a complex institutional system of vertical structure. The difference is shown if the criteria used to select local representatives are considered: once the expression of the will of the heads of families gathered in the assembly, now the process was under the jurisdiction of a prefect nominated by the government.[98]

The suppression of the ancient rural institutions left open the problem of what to do with the property associated with them, those lands owned or used by the village communities. In the French legislation, specifically Article 542 of the Napoleonic Code, municipal property was defined as 'property or produce to which the inhabitants of one or more municipalities have an acquired right'.[99] This is a broad definition, which encompassed both types of asset provided for in the previous Venetian legislation: the *beni comunali* granted in usufruct to the communities and the *beni comuni* owned in freehold by the communities. Even if the question is not resolved in Article 542, interpretations of it agree in assessing that the original wording *communes* should be understood to refer not to the municipality as an administrative body (which in French was called *municipalité)*, but to the villages from which it was formed (*section*), thus maintaining the possibility of separate budgets in the event of the amalgamation of

98. Corbellini 1992, pp. 106–09. On this see also Mannori 2008, pp. 38–39.
99. *Codice di Napoleone il Grande pel Regno d'Italia* 1806, p. 112.

several village communities to form a single administrative entity.[100]

In the spring of 1806, all the municipalities of the Kingdom were requested to inform the government of the quantity and quality of the property in their possession. A few months later, the government planned and arranged to privatise all uncultivated common land that was in excess of the grazing needs of the residents' livestock. This was in the wake of a similar operation attempted in France in the previous decade, inspired by the theories of the physiocratic school, which considered full and absolute possession of property to be a necessary condition for agricultural development.[101]

The provision was ineffective for various reasons: an unstable political situation; the repeated failure of several municipalities to assess their assets or the portion to be kept in common pasture; the resistance of some administrators, who were fearful of provoking unrest and revolt in rural areas.[102] In addition, there was a particular reason in the area previously under the dominion of the Serenissima: the drawing up of the inventories of common property required by the government triggered the claims of those inhabitants who considered themselves the descendants of the original families, and therefore believed that they held particular rights over those lands.[103]

To resolve the disputes arising between the original inhabitants and foreigners, and to clarify the position of the citizens of the new municipalities who were not heirs of members of the ancient rural communities, the Napoleonic government issued a new decree; the importance of this becomes clear in later legislation on the subject, but it was destined to give rise to further problems. The decree of

---

100. Barbacetto 2008, pp. 274–78. Over the following decades, these lands were the object of constant dispute between different social and institutional actors. This dispute also related to the formal definition of these territories. Hereafter, when I talk about them in a general sense, I shall use the expression 'common land(s)'; even if, from an official point of view, they were considered municipal lands.

101. Decree 25 July 1806 n. 147, see *Bollettino delle leggi del Regno d'Italia*, II, 1806, p. 796. On physiocratic theories cf. Vardi 2012; Jones 2016. On the privatisation of common land in France, see Plack 2009.

102. Barbacetto 2008, p. 278; Bianco 2003, p. 41; Bianco 2000a, p. 87.

103. See the report in BCU, *Manoscritti, Fondo Principale*, n. 989.

25 November 1806 n. 225 transferred to the municipal administration all 'the property that at the end of the Venetian Republic had been under the administration of the so-called bodies of the *antichi originari* (the original inhabitants)', unless they were able to prove that they had purchased the said property with a money payment, an eventuality that was subject to further limiting constraints.[104]

The intent of the French legislature, to impose uniform and effective legislation on the whole Kingdom, is clear. It is equally clear that this decree was promulgated without due deliberation. In fact, it has already been seen that Article 542 of the Napoleonic Code referred both to the property over which the inhabitants had a right of ownership and to that over which they boasted a simple right of use. The subsequent French legislation, however, did not distinguish between *beni comunali* and *beni comuni*, a distinction that was typical under Venetian law. The new regulation, which the legislature intended to be general in character, referred only to property *in amministrazione* (under the administration) of the original inhabitants, leaving open therefore an interpretation limited to *beni comunali* as previously defined. This was all the more the case in that, in the preamble to the provision, two Venetian regulations were recalled that dealt with settling disputes between original inhabitants and foreigners with regard only to *beni comunali* (and limited to certain areas of the Republic of Venice).

Since subsequent legislation on the subject rested on this ambiguous formulation, as we shall see, any initiative taken by the legislature in the following decades to resolve these intricate issues became, in the rural areas, a pretext for reviving conflicts and latent claims.[105]

Although the main regulations regarding common resources were enacted in the months following the annexation of the former Venetian territories to the Kingdom of Italy, the replacement of the Venetian forestry legislation required more time.

To meet the costs of the war at sea with the British and to guarantee the necessary supplies for naval shipbuilding, the Napoleonic government adopted a series of measures between May and July 1808

---

104. *Bollettino delle leggi del Regno d'Italia*, III, 1806, pp. 1025–29 (quotation at p. 1026).
105. Pitteri 2005, p. 121.

to reform the forest administration.[106] Responsibility for this was as-signed to the general directorate of *Demanio* (state property) under the authority of the Ministry of Finance. The organisational struc-ture was reformed not only at its summit but also at the territorial level, with the establishment of a hierarchy made up of conservators of woodlands, inspectors, sub-inspectors and forest rangers. Different tasks and emoluments were assigned to each position. However, these early interventions were purely logistical, since there were no practical changes regarding the government of the woodlands beyond granting special prerogatives to the navy, thus following a tradition already in place during the Venetian period. On the contrary, it was expressly ordered that 'Until it is otherwise arranged, on the matter of the wood-lands the local laws and regulations will be observed'.[107]

Only three years later, on 27 May 1811, a complete forest reform was finally launched, organised into eight headings and 79 articles.[108] The first section laid out the criteria by which public woodlands of any kind were to be regulated, since the regime established for state-owned forests was also extended to municipal woodlands and to those belonging to other public bodies (§ 2). In order to correctly manage public forests, in accordance with the silvicultural precepts of the time, it was necessary to measure them precisely. Therefore, cadastres were to be prepared in which to map and describe all the public forests; the expenses of this operation were to be equally di-vided between the property owners and the usufructuaries (§ 3–5).

The second section dealt with the tasks and gratuities of the munici-pal foresters, based on the structure set up in the regulations of 1808, and to be further detailed over the following months.[109] It is worth re-membering that the salaries of these professional figures were deducted from the profits obtained from cutting in the municipal forests; where

---

106. Decrees 18 May 1808 n. 129 and 15 July 1808 n. 222 in *Bollettino delle leggi del Regno d'Italia*, I, 1808, pp. 322–24 and *Bollettino delle leggi del Regno d'Italia*, II, 1808, pp. 593–98.

107. *Bollettino delle leggi del Regno d'Italia*, II, 1808, pp. 598.

108. Decree 27 May 1811 n. 121 *Bollettino delle leggi del Regno d'Italia*, I, 1811, pp. 417–35.

109. Decrees 5 June 1811 n. 131 and 28 Sept. 1811 n. 236 n *Bollettino delle leggi del Regno d'Italia*, I, 1811, pp. 511–39 and n *Bollettino delle leggi del Regno d'Italia*, II, 1811, pp. 934–40.

these profits were insufficient, it was added as an additional expense to the municipal taxes (§ 10–12). In addition, the municipal foresters could be used as a gendarmerie with military or police duties (§ 15).[110]

Section III laid out the criteria for felling in the public forests. The importance of giving priority to the needs of the navy was reiterated, and naval agents were able to make prior visits to public forests in order to choose the trees to be reserved for shipbuilding (§ 16–21).

Section IV dealt with rights of access and use within the public forests. Within six months of the issuing of the decree, anyone holding rights or easements in the public forests had to present appropriate documents of proof at the offices of the local administration, and it was the task of the forest magistrates to decide – on the basis of the documents produced – which rights to confirm and which to abolish (§ 28–29). The most sensitive issue was that of grazing rights, which could be exercised only in those areas identified by the forest administration, with particular restrictions for small animals (§30–35).

Section V laid out the provisions applicable to private forests, over which the surveillance of the forest administration was extended. Section VI detailed the rules for planting trees along state and vicinal roads. Section VII laid out various prohibitions and their respective penalties. Even in the absence of specific contraventions, it was forbidden to enter a public forest with scythes, axes or suitable means to transport timber; the financial penalty imposed for these offences was doubled for repeat offenders or for those who committed them at night, while from the third offence the penalty became a custodial sentence (§ 63–65). It was forbidden to light fires within 500 metres of the forest areas and to build charcoal kilns or furnaces within two miles without a licence granted by the Ministry of Finance (§ 67–68). Section VIII laid out the procedure to be followed against offenders.

It is difficult to provide an unambiguous assessment of the forest law introduced by the French in 1811, even when limiting the analysis to the regulatory system, leaving the examination of its concrete application until later. This is because, as contemporaries themselves

---

110. See some examples of this military function in ASVe, *Ispettorato generale ai boschi, 1810–1815, atti riservati,* b. 668.

commented, the elements that were considered innovative were at the same time criticised as points of weakness in the legislation. Thus, the positive fact of having finally produced legislation that was valid throughout the national territory, was an achievement that in itself presented many drawbacks for the management of the woodlands. In fact, as noted by Domenico Aita, the director of state property in the Kingdom of Lombardy-Venetia – who had already been an official in the same department during the French period – the only cultivational distinction contained in the legislation, that between coppices and high stands, was insufficient considering the variety of altitudes and climatic and geomorphological conditions that existed in a kingdom that, at its largest, extended over a large part of central-northern Italy.[111] Likewise, the expansion of the forest administration's competency to also include private woodlands, as far as concerned naval needs, was held to be in violation of private law according to the opinion of Adolfo di Bérenger. However, it is necessary to remember that the latter was writing in a period – about half a century later – in which respect for liberal principles opposed any state intervention in the field of private property.[112] Moreover, both officials agreed in considering the 1811 decree to be merely a restating of the forestry legislation of the French Empire. It was therefore shaped by different needs from those of central and northern Italy at this time.[113]

Despite the criticisms, the modifications and several plans for complete overhauls after the return of the Austrians, for over half a century no one was able to make substantial improvements, and the 1811 decree remained in force in Veneto until 1877, when the first forestry legislation of united Italy was launched.[114]

In summary, this is the regulatory framework introduced by the French regarding forest resources and common land. It now remains to examine the reactions caused by the application of the regulations at the local level.

---

111. Quoted in Lazzarini 2009, pp. 120–21.
112. di Bérenger 1863, pp. 130–31. On this see Vecchio 1974, p. 240.
113. On the French legislation, see Centre national de la recherche scientifique 1987.
114. On the Austrian amendments see Guazzo 1853, II, pp. 484–541.

2.

THE SETTING. CADORE IN THE NINETEENTH CENTURY: INSTITUTIONS, POPULATIONS, RESOURCES

Territory and institutions

The territory on which I shall focus is made up of the northern part of the province (or delegation) of Belluno. After the return of the Austrians and the foundation of the Kingdom of Lombardy-Venetia, the province was established in the area previously belonging to the Department of the Piave, from which some of the municipal aggregates had been detached in 1810 (Ampezzo, Dobbiaco, Primiero).[1]

At the provincial level, the political administration was entrusted to the figure of the delegate, whose duties were similar to those previously borne by the prefect, while a superintendent of finance looked after the finances of the province. The territory was subdivided into districts organised according to the Napoleonic model of cantons. At the head of each district was a chancellor (from 1819, district commissioner). The chancellor carried out various fiscal, political and police duties within his district. It was also his job to oversee the activities of the municipal administrations and to ensure that their decisions were in conformity with the laws of the state. This made the chancellor, especially in rural areas, the one concrete reference to state power.[2]

The top central and local officials within the Austrian administration, namely the two governors established in Milan and Venice and the 200 and more commissioners distributed throughout the territory, had both political and financial remits. This was not the case within the intermediate levels of government. In both Veneto

---

1. For an overview on the institutional structure and the apparatus of the Kingdom of Lombardy-Venetia – to which I shall frequently refer in the following pages – cf. Meriggi 1987; Laven 2002. For a synthesis see Meriggi 2000.
2. Rossetto 2013.

and Lombardy, the government was divided into two sections, both presided over by the governor, headed respectively by the political senate – which was the reference point of the provincial delegates – and the finance senate (also known as the *camerale*). The general directorate of state property, to which the forest administration was delegated following the French reforms, also fell under this branch of government.

At the local level, the forest administration was subdivided into inspectorates whose responsibilities extended along territorial lines distinct from those of the delegates and organised according to the relative importance of the forest resources. There were eighteen inspectors subordinate to the finance senate of Venice, and one of these was in charge of the Cadore area.[3]

The progressive simplification of the territorial administration, to which I broadly referred in the previous chapter, also took effect in the Cadore area. Between 1797 and 1816, when the new Austrian legislation was applied, the 44 communities that composed the *centenari* of the Cadore Community were aggregated to form twenty municipalities (to which Sappada was added in 1852, while Danta was detached from San Nicolo in 1843), divided into two districts.[4]

The first district, in the southern part of the region and with its capital at Pieve, was made up of the municipalities of Pieve di Cadore, Borca, Calalzo, Cibiana, Domegge, Perarolo, Selva, Valle, San Vito, Ospitale, Vodo and Zoppè. The second district, situated in the north and with Auronzo as its capital, was composed of the municipalities of Auronzo, Comelico Superiore, Comelico Inferiore, Danta, Lorenzago, Lozzo, San Nicolò, San Pietro, Vigo and, from 1852, Sappada.

The territory within these administrative boundaries was located in the Alpine zone of the eastern Dolomites and corresponded almost

---

3. ASVe, *Ispettorato Generale ai Boschi*, Decreti di massima, 1806–1826, b. 117, f. 22. The department titles of the *camerale* administration changed over the years: in 1830 the finance senate became the *camerale* magistrature which, in turn, became the prefecture of finances after the 1848–1849 revolution: see Lazzarini 2006b, p. 143. For the establishment of the *camerale* magistrature in the province of Belluno, see ASVe, *Presidio di Governo*, 1815–1819, XII, b. 142, f. 6/1.

4. Migliardi O'Riordan, Testa Benzoni 2003, pp. 13–14.

entirely with the initial part of the catchment area of the river Piave, which has its source here on Mount Peralba. From a geographical point of view, Cadore is therefore an entirely Alpine region containing many common characteristics, as well as internal differences due to the constraints that the different altimetric, climatic, pedological and orographic conditions had imposed on anthropic action.

To summarise a picture that will be explored further in the following pages, the characteristics common to the whole area were: the chronic deficit in agricultural production, which conditioned any economic strategy; the productive centrality of those lands usually defined – using a formula that is more paradoxical here than elsewhere – as 'uncultivated'; the importance that certain natural forms of communication, using the Piave river and its tributaries, assumed for the economic activities of the area.

As for the differences within this territory, they can be illustrated by comparing the two administrative districts into which it was divided, even if this produces a slightly forced schematisation. The Pieve district was geographically less inaccessible, and here was concentrated the best part, both quantitatively and qualitatively, of the small amount of cultivable land. Furthermore, this district was closer to the foothills and the urban centres, and was crossed by one of the main communication routes of the time, the Alemagna road, which was completely remade between 1823 and 1832, becoming the fastest route of communication between the Adriatic Sea and the Tyrolean and German areas, at least until the opening of the Brenner railway line. Also as a result of this greater 'accessibility', various woodlands were described as depleted in the territory of the Pieve district, and pastoral farming was as important as forestry activities in order to produce a viable income. Conversely, in the Auronzo district the exploitation of the woodlands remained the pivot of the economic system.

In order to understand the territorial characteristics of Cadore more fully, it is important also to examine the link between population and resources. In the following sections, I shall analyse the different elements that contributed in defining this changing relationship and place them in their wider contexts – the province of Belluno, the Veneto-Friuli area, the Alpine chain – in order to understand the traits of the region that were distinctive and those that were shared with other contexts.

An exceptional demographic trend

In recent decades, there has been an important revision of the models used to represent the Alpine world.[5] A first phase of this revision took place during the 1980s, with some anthropological studies that were synthesised by Pier Paolo Viazzo in *Upland Communities*. The results of this research revised an excessively negative view of the Alpine area, which until then had been described as underdeveloped and overpopulated, with a constant imbalance between population and resources forcing continuous migration to the regions of the plains. From a demographic point of view, this new model was characterised by low pressure, marked by low birth and mortality rates and by the regulatory role played by marriage.[6]

However, as Jon Mathieu noted in a post-revisionist phase, the attention given to the 'homeostatic capacities' of the Alpine communities cannot be separated from an evaluation of the long-term demographic trend: the population of the Alpine chain almost tripled between 1500 and 1900.[7] In the wake of these important contributions, research has also been carried out on demographic trends in the Veneto mountain region, which was neglected in previous syntheses on the subject.[8] The research focused on the first half of the nineteenth century, 'one of the most interesting and potentially fruitful periods for the study of the transformation of mountain societies', since in this period the link between demographic transition and opportunities for the development of the mountain economies can be seen more clearly.[9]

5.   For a recent compendium of Alpine history, see Mathieu 2019. I would like to thank Jon Mathieu for providing me a draft of his work.

6.   Viazzo 1989. For a retrospective analysis on this research path cf. Viazzo 2000; Fornasin 2017.

7.   Mathieu 2009.

8.   Navarra 2002b; Zannini, Gazzi 2003; Zannini 2005.

9.   Fornasin, Zannini 2002, p. 18.

As Andrea Zannini rightly observed,[10] an assessment of the anthropic pressure on this territory in the nineteenth century must begin with a particular datum: in his work on the history of the Alps between the sixteenth and twentieth centuries, Jon Mathieu – comparing the demographic trends of 26 Alpine districts – found that the province of Belluno in the nineteenth century had an average increase per year of 0.72 per cent, a level of population growth exceeded only by the French department of the Maritime Alps.[11] This growth was achieved within a model of high demographic pressure, differing considerably from the model proposed by Viazzo, but also from the situation in the neighbouring Alpine area of Carnia during the same period, which was excluded from Mathieu's analysis since it belonged to the province of Udine that stretched across the Friuli plain to the Adriatic.[12]

Given the peculiarities of the case, therefore, it is appropriate to take into consideration the evidence analysed in the aforementioned essay by Zannini, to which I refer in order to provide details on the birth and mortality rates and marriages in the province of Belluno and its various districts.

First of all, it should be noted that up until 1875 – the year normally associated with the beginning of mass migration – these growth rates correspond to the wider population trend. Secondly, the transition of the demographic regime should not be placed, as previously thought, in the decade after the annexation of these territories to the Kingdom of Italy, but rather in the years immediately following the great crisis of 1816–1817.

Finally, it is important to analyse the data on the basis of the districts that made up the province. Even given that the growth affected all the districts of Belluno, there were significant differences between each district, in terms of both the rate and the chronology of growth.[13] In fact, there were many factors that could influence demographic trends, as has been shown by research on contiguous

10. Zannini 2005.
11. Mathieu 2009, pp. 28, 37. See also Mathieu 1998.
12. Breschi, Gonano, Lorenzini 1999.
13. Tables 1–2.

Chapter 2

Table 1.

Population of Cadore during the nineteenth century.

Municipality	1802	1807	1821	1846	1853	1862	1871	1881	1901
Auronzo	2,454	2,454	2,684	3,534	3,852	3,832	3,942	4,130	4,045
Comelico Superiore	2,175	2,232	2,328	2,923	3,202	3,556	3,335	3,573	3,733
Danta	301	290	310	333	364	418	433	558	584
Lorenzago	603	682	753	866	952	976	939	1,065	1,055
Lozzo	1,000	1,004	971	1,336	1,599	1,659	1,645	1,720	1,806
San Nicolò	473	644	490	620	675	660	592	588	552
San Pietro	1,046	1,132	1,160	1,460	1,579	1,652	1,841	2,082	2,402
Comelico Inferiore	1,331	1,474	1,375	1,656	1,951	2,085	2,239	2,413	2,705
Sappada	*875*	*875*	1,458	1,144	1,268	1,255	1,149	1,178	1,251
Vigo	1,294	1,299	1,368	1,678	1,827	1,987	2,023	2,232	2,265
Tot. Auronzo district	*11,552*	*12,086*	12,897	15,550	17,269	18,080	18,138	19,539	20,398
Borca	602	1,012	783	929	1,087	1,126	1,123	1,125	887
Calalzo	1,078	1,288	1,038	1,178	1,659	1,474	1,271	1,181	1,324
Cibiana	670	667	666	986	1,036	982	1,099	1,107	1,225
Domegge	1,401	1,696	1,898	2,022	2,429	2,391	2,356	2,235	2,294
Ospitale	350	400	422	638	787	782	883	893	815
Perarolo	748	759	723	1,085	1,190	1,326	1,491	1,578	1,383
Pieve di Cadore	2,079	2,093	2,255	2,458	3,195	3,367	3,335	3,384	3,319
San Vito di Cadore	1,380	1,124	1,131	1,371	1,561	1,560	1,498	1,490	1,326
Selva	962	994	1,009	966	1,152	1,044	912	896	875
Valle	1,775	2,108	1,938	2,506	2,947	2,702	2,422	2,314	2,503
Vodo	1,696	1,749	1,737	2,057	2,240	2,173	1,958	1,975	1,553
Zoppè	347	335	358	407	466	689	368	426	535
Tot. Pieve di Cadore district	13,088	14,225	13,958	16,603	19,749	19,616	18,716	18,604	18,039
Tot. Cadore	*24,640*	*26,311*	26,855	32,153	37,018	37,696	36,854	38,143	38,437

Source: Zannini 2005, pp. 221–222, 226 (the data in italics are estimated).

Table 2.

Population of the province of Belluno during the nineteenth century.

District	1802	1807	1821	1846	1853	1862	1871	1881	1901
Agordo	14,361	14,505	14,419	19,509	21,898	22,712	23,086	22,724	25,030
Auronzo	*11,552*	*12,086*	12,897	15,550	17,269	18,080	18,138	19,539	20,398
Belluno	30,408	32,040	28,987	36,023	39,959	43,322	46,297	46,337	53,472
Feltre	26,268	25,506	23,576	29,555	32,913	33,606	37,939	38,168	43,033
Fonzaso	13,547	13,795	13,265	16,479	18,218	18,564	19,737	17,651	20,909
Longarone	7,411	7,582	7,373	9,395	10,576	11,329	11,369	11,117	11,919
Pieve di Cadore	13,088	14,225	13,958	16,603	19,749	19,616	18,716	18,604	18,039
Total	*116,635*	*119,739*	114,475	143,114	160,582	167,229	175,282	174,140	192,800

Source: Zannini 2005, p. 211 (the data in italics are estimated).

villages.[14] However, it is striking that the highest overall growth rate over the nineteenth century was to be found in the orographically most inaccessible district of Auronzo (+ 77 per cent). This growth rate – and that in the other district of Cadore, Pieve di Cadore (+ 38 per cent), which, if not so high, was still substantial – raises two issues or, rather, a single issue that can be analysed from two different points of view. How was it possible to sustain such high growth in an area considered geographically 'hostile' like upper Cadore? And what was the impact of this intense and prolonged demographic growth on the ways of using the available resources?

Agricultural limitations and an integrated economy

The available sources for estimating the resources become more numerous during the nineteenth century. Quantitative sources especially multiplied in this period, a symptom of the spread also in the Veneto area of that 'quantifying spirit' that was gaining force in Europe.[15]

One particular source has been much used to account for the agrarian situation in the Venetian territories at that time. This is what is commonly known as the 'new Lombardo-Venetian census', though it was begun during the previous French domination when the work for the new cadastre was initiated with the decree of 12 January 1807. The work that led to its implementation took about forty years: the complete mapping of the territory was begun by the French and finished after the return of the Austrians; then the census campaigns took place between 1826 and 1828, in which the preparatory deeds were drawn up and the land classified; then the valuation rates were approved in 1843; and finally the new cadastre was implemented for the provinces of Venice, Padua and Rovigo in 1846 (and for Treviso, Verona and Belluno in 1849, Vicenza in 1850 and Udine in 1851).[16]

As with any source, this cadastre must be used critically. First of all, as with any type of cadastral document, there is a 'gap' between the

14. Navarra 2002a.
15. Frangsmyr, Heilbron, Rider 1990.
16. Berengo 1963, pp. 25–63; Tonetti 2003.

purposes for which it was created – which were of a fiscal nature – and the uses made of it in the historiographical field – for example, the analysis of crop distribution and land ownership.[17] There are also specific problems with the Lombardo-Venetian cadastre, which Marino Berengo referred to: uneven data collection; errors in valuations; the practice, found precisely in the area that most interests us (the district of Auronzo), of re-using the descriptors proposed for the main town for smaller communities during the classification process.[18]

Despite these limitations, the documentation produced during the cadastral campaign is the first that provides an overview of each department of the Kingdom, and at the same time a comparison of the results between the various departments. And the aggregated data for Cadore outlines correlations in the area clearly enough to dispel any interpretative doubt.[19]

The total area of land in the two Cadore districts was 113,430.8 hectares. Having taken out wasteland, there remained 82,657.4 hectares of agro-silvo-pastoral land. The total area of cultivated land was 2,891.3 hectares, 2.54 per cent of the total area of the two districts and just 3.5 per cent of the agro-silvo-pastoral surface.

This data is thrown more sharply into relief if we consider two further points. The first is that this cultivated area was not evenly distributed. There was some unevenness between municipalities but, generally, the area cultivated in the district of Pieve di Cadore was proportionally greater than in the high Cadore belonging to the district of Auronzo.

The second point concerns the 'composition' of this cultivated surface. Land classified as 'under the plough' was only 261.8 hectares, concentrated in the municipalities of Borca and San Vito di Cadore. The remaining 2,629.5 hectares were cultivated almost exclusively with human labour, since they were placed in the categories of 'cultivation by hoe' and 'cultivation by spade'.

For a more detailed analysis of Cadore farming, the cadastral documents can be studied alongside the data collected in certain agricul-

---

17. For a critical evaluation of this source, cf. Moreno, Raggio 1999, pp. 95–98.
18. Berengo 1963, pp. 44–45.
19. Table 3.

tural surveys. The first of these was carried out in the area by Marco De Marchi and Giacomo Antonio Talamini (the latter being the parish priest of Borca) as part of the much larger investigation conducted by Filippo Re on the state of agriculture in the Kingdom of Italy and published in the *Annali dell'Agricoltura del Regno d'Italia*. This investigation, carried out during the French occupation, marks the starting point of the present research.[20] As for the end point, after Italian unification, mention should be made of the data presented by the president of the Belluno Chamber of Commerce, Riccardo Volpe.[21] Between these two chronological markers, as well as the cadastral documentation and the other published sources, there are also the first reports of the Belluno Chamber of Commerce, which have been analysed and published by Antonio Lazzarini.[22] And to these must be added the reports or pleas that curates, parish priests and public officials sent regarding individual village communities. These sources make it possible to identify the characteristics of the Cadore agricultural sector during the first three quarters of the nineteenth century.[23]

This heterogeneous evidence confirms that Cadore conformed to a frequent characteristic of Alpine agriculture, namely small units of land ownership, often fragmented into non-contiguous parcels, situated at different altitudes and functioning within a farming system oriented towards self-sufficiency.[24] In this context, direct management of the land predominated, since, in many municipalities, even the largest farm units were under ten hectares. Such fragmentation constrained the labour force, mainly the female workers, to diversify across the growing cycles of several products that required different altimetric and ecological conditions.

20. *Annali dell'Agricoltura del Regno d'Italia compilati dal Cav. Filippo Re*, 12 (1811), pp. 193–207; and *Annali dell'Agricoltura del Regno d'Italia compilati dal Cav. Filippo Re*, 17 (1813), pp. 133–57.

21. Volpe 1871; Volpe 1880. On Volpe, see Larese 2005.

22. Lazzarini 2004b; Lazzarini stresses the limits of this documentation, especially as concerns the statistical data.

23. For the analysis of Cadore agriculture, I shall refer to these publications and the cadastral sources: ASVe, *Atti preparatori*, bb. 219–28.

24. Cf. Coppola 1989.

Chapter 2

Table 3.

Surface areas of different categories of land in Cadore, mid-nineteenth century.

Municipality	Ploughed land	Hoed land	Spade-cultivated land	Meadow	Wooded meadow	Meadow with resinous trees	Water meadow	Pasture	Wooded pasture	Pasture with resinous trees	*Tall woodland*	*Coppiced woodland*
Auronzo	-	195.5	.	1,191.9	12.2	10.6	21.1	1,120.7	807.6	1,944.7	*17.1*	*501.9*
Borca di Cadore	99.5	0.0	-	577.4	-	-	-	433.1	9.0	22.9	-	-
Calalzo	-	120.3	-	357.8	-	-	-	556.9	-	204.0	*29.4*	*208.8*
Cibiana	-	41.6	-	243.3	1.2	6.3	-	67.3	622.3	1.5	*20.5*	*23.6*
Selva di Cadore	-	114.6	-	475.4	-	9.6	-	784.1	565.5	-	-	*123.2*
Comelico Superiore	-	246.0	-	791.8	-	-	128.8	2,448.1	306.8	200.9	-	-
Ospitale	-	26.7	-	127.6	7.9	-	-	580.2	1,104.2	-	-	*290.0*
Danta	-	35.1	-	177.2	-	-	71.9	32.9	-	-	-	-
Domegge	-	229.9	-	1,003.9	-	-	-	765.2	711.7	-	*20.4*	*214.6*
Perarolo	-	38.4	-	150.3	-	11.7	-	411.9	399.8	172.1	-	*280.4*
Lorenzago	-	86.4	-	614.3	-	-	-	127.8	-	-	-	*279.2*
Lozzo	-	108.0	-	374.5	-	-	6.4	1,299.5	-	-	*23.5*	*197.3*
Pieve di Cadore	-	255.9	-	823.6	-	-	1.0	955.0	-	403.3	-	*261.9*
San Nicolò	-	89.5	-	311.0	-	-	58.0	611.5	-	-	-	*200.9*
San Pietro	-	133.3	-	273.6	-	-	31.3	2,006.0	-	-	-	*73.7*
Comelico Inferiore	-	190.7	-	426.4	-	-	25.6	1,649.6	-	-	-	*307.9*
San Vito	162.3	26.6	-	840.4	-	-	-	1,432.3	142.5	288.5	-	-
Sappada	-	0.0	174.9	255.5	-	-	-	1,355.5	-	-	-	*13.0*
Valle	-	183.6	-	668.4	-	-	-	424.1	300.8	197.5	-	*294.0*
Vigo	-	180.6	-	442.8	-	-	6.3	2,427.5	-	221.5	-	*256.2*
Vodo	-	151.9	-	915.3	-	-	-	881.5	744.9	90.6	-	*85.2*
Total	261.8	2,454.6	174.9	11,042.4	21.3	38.2	350.4	20,370.7	5,715.1	3,747.5	*110.9*	*3,611.8*
% over agro-silvo-pastoral land	0.32	2.97	0.21	13.36	0.03	0.05	0.42	24.64	6.91	4.53	*0.13*	*4.37*
% over total area	0.23	2.16	0.15	9.73	0.02	0.03	0.31	17.96	5.04	3.30	*0.10*	*3.18*

Note: In italics the categories that make up the forested areas in the strict sense.

Source: My own summaries based on the data collected in Scarpa 1963. Surface area unit hectares.

The setting. Cadore in the nineteenth century

Municipality	Resinous woodland	Protected resinous woodland	Leafy resinous woodland	Uncultivated land	Uncultivated land with woody plants	Uncultivated land with resinous trees	Forest area in the strict sense	Agro-silvo-pastoral land	Wasteland	Total area
Auronzo	3,205.0	-	1,209.0	231.8	824.3	-	4,933.0	11,293.4	10,044.9	21,338.3
Borca di Cadore	462.1	-	-	214.9	-	-	462.1	1,818.9	851.3	2,670.2
Calalzo	275.2	-	-	291.4	-	95.0	513.4	2,138.8	2,138.2	4,277.0
Cibiana	325.2	6.4	-	188.7	-	-	375.7	1,547.9	488.3	2,036.2
Selva di Cadore	464.3	-	-	319.6	-	-	587.5	2,856.3	335.6	3,191.9
Comelico Superiore	2,869.7	-	-	1,090.4	-	-	2,869.7	8,082.5	1,052.4	9,134.9
Ospitale	552.1	-	-	650.4	-	-	842.1	3,339.1	559.1	3,898.2
Danta	456.5	-	-	-	-	-	456.5	773.6	6.7	780.3
Domegge	506.8	-	117.4	234.1	-	-	859.2	3,804.0	1,245.1	5,049.1
Perarolo	495.7	-	-	1,073.0	144.9	-	776.1	3,178.2	979.2	4,157.4
Lorenzago	616.1	-	-	82.6	-	-	895.3	1,806.4	838.8	2,645.2
Lozzo	480.5	-	-	64.2	133.5	-	701.3	2,687.4	310.7	2,998.1
Pieve di Cadore	1,322.4	-	-	1,182.1	-	-	1,584.3	5,205.2	1,427.7	6,632.9
San Nicolò	821.6	-	-	-	-	-	1,022.5	2,092.5	293.8	2,386.3
San Pietro	2,195.0	-	-	-	-	367.3	2,268.7	5,080.2	195.8	5,276.0
Comelico Inferiore	3,060.0	-	-	-	813.4	142.0	3,367.9	6,615.6	2,900.0	9,515.6
San Vito	344.3	-	-	417.2	13.3	-	344.3	3,667.4	2,407.8	6,075.2
Sappada	1,477.9	-	-	504.2	-	-	1,490.9	3,781.0	2,090.2	5,871.2
Valle	532.5	-	-	827.1	-	164.6	826.5	3,592.6	355.0	3,947.6
Vigo	1,411.7	-	-	427.1	29.5	-	1,667.9	5,403.2	1,509.2	6,912.4
Vodo	508.7	12.8	-	439.7	62.6	-	606.7	3,893.2	743.6	4,636.8
Total	22,383.3	19.2	1,326.4	8,238.5	2,021.5	768.9	27,451.6	82,657.4	30,773.4	113,430.8
% over agro-silvo-pastoral land	27.08	0.02	1.60	9.97	2.45	0.93	33.21	100		
% over total area	19.73	0.02	1.17	7.26	1.78	0.68	24.20	72.87	27.13	100

This pronounced fragmentation of property also influenced the orientation of production in agriculture. The best lands were kept for the production of cereals, in particular maize, barley and rye, according to proportions determined by the altitude. Average returns per unit area were subject to numerous microclimatic and geographic variables (exposure to the sun, slope of the land, humidity etc.), but remained low even in the best areas at the bottom of the valleys, while the poorest areas were only just productive.[25]

At the beginning of the nineteenth century, the introduction of the potato represented an important innovation and, within a few decades, it became a staple food in the population's diet.[26] It is difficult to say whether the great famine over the two years 1816–1817, whose effects in Cadore were among the most dramatic in the whole of Lombardy-Venetia, played a decisive role in its spread.[27] However, the potato was already the staple food of the area when, in 1847, blight ruined the entire crop, leaving the population fully exposed to the cereal crisis of 1846–1847.[28]

However, even in years with favourable conditions, the picture that emerges is that of residual agriculture, in which cereal production, and agricultural production as a whole, was largely unable to meet the needs of the population for more than three or four months of the year.[29]

At times the quality and reliability of the statistical data may be questioned; and then there is also the difficulty of quantifying the

---

25. In the municipality of Sappada, some land parcels were registered as arable even if the estimated yield was less than the seed, see Sacco 2002, p. 168.

26. On the introduction of the potato, see *Annali dell'Agricoltura del Regno d'Italia compilati dal Cav. Filippo Re*, 17 (1813), p. 134; Fabbiani 1985, p. 98. At the beginning of the 1840s, the potato was attested to be a staple food in Sette 1843, pp. 193–94.

27. On the famine in Veneto, see Monteleone 1969. The famine was the main cause in the spread of the potato according to Maresio Bazolle 1986–1987, II, p, 72.

28. Brunello 1979b, p. 134.

29. This period of food self-sufficiency is reiterated in all the pleas that Cadore communities sent to the government: see some examples in ASVe, *Governo veneto*, 1815, XXXIV, b. 406. See also some questionnaires carried out in the early stages of the cadastral campaign: ASVe, *Censo stabile, quesiti risposte circostanze locali*, b. 27 (for the district of Auronzo); ASMi, *Studi, parte moderna*, b. 1173, f. 7 (for the district of Pieve di Cadore).

needs of the peasant households in a situation where the majority of the foodstuffs passed directly from production to domestic consumption. However, it is clear that the exploitation of the cultivated land could not enable the local population to be self-sufficient, especially during a period of strong demographic growth as in the nineteenth century.

To clarify this last point, it is helpful to analyse the situation in Cadore within the wider Alpine context of which it was a part. From an economic point of view, the Alpine zone has been described as 'a fundamentally homogeneous system characterised by strong markers that can be found everywhere, but affected by subtly varied, sometimes polyvalent subsystems'.[30] The standard version of this model, which developed during the early modern period up to the second half of the nineteenth century, is of an integrated economic system in which diverse sectors combined to bridge the chronic food deficit.

Within this common model, important differences could emerge according to the weightings of the different supplementary sectors in the respective mountain areas. Leaving aside for now the assessment of the other segments that made up the primary sector, there were three main activities that produced income: migration, manufacturing activities and mining.

Among these, the most widespread in the Alps – and certainly the most studied – was the practice of migration. This has been analysed particularly for the late nineteenth century, when it assumed distinct characteristics and forms compared with previous periods. However, in Cadore, as in most Alpine areas, migration had already existed for centuries, even if for earlier periods it is more difficult to know fully the destinations, the numbers involved or the forms of migration.[31]

A significant part of this movement was linked to the thousands of crafts and itinerant trades. Every valley and every district specialised in some profession:

> the tinkers and coppersmiths of the Comelico, the ice-cream makers of Pieve di Cadore, the sweet-pastry chefs and sellers of baked apples and

30.   Coppola 1991, p. 204. See also Panjek, Larsson, Mocarelli 2017.
31.   Lorenzetti, Merzario 2005.

pears of Zoldano, the chair makers of Agordino, the painters of sacred images of Paluzza and Treppo Carnico, the domestic servants of Cavazzo, Lauco and Zuglio, the knife grinders of Paluzza, Paularo and Ligosullo.[32]

This type of migration was directed primarily towards Venice which, in terms of its size and importance, remained one of the main goals of migration from the Venetian Alps at least until the nineteenth century.[33]

Another type of migration was related to the activities in which the migrants were already engaged in their places of origin. In Cadore, more widespread than migration linked to the transhumance of herds or seasonal agricultural work was that linked to the timber market, in terms of both cutting operations and the transport of timber.[34]

It is difficult to quantify the extent of these migratory flows. At the beginning of the nineteenth century, Marco De Marchi, responding to the questions of Filippo Re's agrarian survey, wrote that half the population of Cadore spent four to eight months outside the district, though it is not clear if the author was referring only to males or to the total population.[35] In any case, these are very high numbers, confirmed in the following decade by the cadastral documentation. On the basis of this last source and some quantitative surveys, it is also possible to state that this phenomenon was more pronounced in the district of Pieve di Cadore than in that of Auronzo and that in the former internal migration prevailed, while in the latter it was migration abroad.[36]

At the same time, a gradual change took place in the character of the migration from Belluno province. The beginning of this transformation was caused by the construction of the Alemagna road, which linked the Tyrol to Venice via Cadore. The road was built in five years between 1823 and 1828 (with work continuing until 1832) by the Varese company of Antonio Tallachini, which made extensive

32.   Lazzarini 1981, p. 244.

33.   Lazzarini 1998.

34.   Cf. Perco 1988; Ferigo 2008.

35.   *Annali dell'Agricoltura del Regno d'Italia compilati dal Cav. Filippo Re*, 12 (1811), p. 206.

36.   Lazzarini 1990, p. 203.

use of local skilled workers. Over the following years, Tallachini won other contracts for the construction of roads, bridges and aqueducts in the Austrian Empire, and continued to use the workers of Belluno province, obviously appreciating their skills. Thereby a new type of migration was initiated, linked to the construction sector. Following Tallachini and other entrepreneurs, migrants spread towards central and eastern Europe as these areas developed economically.[37]

Although, unlike what happened in the Prealps and the Veneto plain at the end of the nineteenth century, this migration continued to have a mainly temporary character, gradually it took on more distinct characteristics compared with what was widespread in previous centuries. The destinations changed, as did the work undertaken, the makeup of the migratory flows (with the increase of female and child migration) and the time spent away from the place of origin (which often became many years). Overall the phenomenon became more significant, in terms of both numbers of people and total weight within the mountain economy. This latter point should be placed alongside the overall decline of other traditional occupations in the final decades of the nineteenth century.[38]

If the practice of migration became progressively more important as a source of income, so that by the end of the century it was the main economic choice for very many families in the area, the same cannot be said of the two other typical sectors of the Alpine economy – mining and manufacturing activities. As for the first of these, there were deposits of lead sulphide and zinc carbonate at Auronzo, but the mines played a limited role in the economy of the area and were certainly unable to create related industries. This was unlike the situation in the nearby Agordino valleys (especially the Imperina valley), although the sector here was contracting by the nineteenth century.[39] As for manufacturing, the only profitable branch of industry which could provide employment to the Cadore population was that linked to the timber trade.

37.   Vendramini 2002, pp. 10–18.

38.   Lazzarini 1990.

39.   Vergani 2003, pp. 232–36.

For a complete economic picture, it is therefore necessary to return to the other activities that, together with the exploitation of cultivated land, made up the primary sector. And in this respect, too, the situation in Cadore is an exemplification of a wider Alpine model: agriculture was based on the complementarity between the few small pieces of private property suitable for sowing or scything – 'often less than a hectare and with the parcels not even contiguous' – and the great common possession of the woodlands and Alpine pastures.[40]

The complexity and importance of uncultivated lands

Let us start with a story. At the end of 1823, a letter was received at the directorate of state property that warned of some illegal cuts that were being made in the 'Pera wood' located on the mountain of the same name in the territory of Sottocastello, a hamlet of Pieve di Cadore, on the border with the Friuli municipality of Cimolais.[41]

The state authorities knew that cuts were due to be made in that area. The first request to fell some trees had been submitted by the owner of the land, the vestry of the church of San Lorenzo, to the forestry inspector of Cadore in a letter sent on 16 June 1822. In the letter, the area was referred to as 'the mountain pasture called Pera', and permission was requested to fell some trees that were in poor condition (pine, larch and beech) in order to encourage its development as pasture land, 'to which use only is it suited'. On 10 August, in submitting the request to the offices of the state property of Belluno, the forestry inspector Francesco Perucchi described the mountain as 'an inhospitable place situated amongst the highest rocks', whose only possible use was grazing for sheep and goats; 'but that leaves no possibility of timber products'. On the basis of this information, the cut was granted by the offices of the state property of Belluno on 5 November and confirmed ten days later by the director of state property, Domenico Aita:

---

40.   Coppola 1989, pp. 499–500. See also Netting 1981.

41.   The documentation on these events is in ASVe, *Direzione Generale del Demanio*, Presidio, b. 559, f. 1156.

he gave first priority, however, to the evaluation and marking of the trees necessary to determine the tax that was due to the forest authorities, for which the inspector Perucchi was responsible.

The cutting licence was issued to the vestry in the following May and the cutting works were contracted to Michele Della Patta Pozzi of Cimolais, who began work in the autumn. This was the situation on 31 December 1823, when Domenico Aita, advised of the complaint, ordered the forestry inspector Perucchi to immediately suspend the illegal cuts made in the 'forest of tall trees called Pera or the valley of Santa Maria, which is well-stocked with trees' and to produce a detailed report on the situation as soon as possible.

The first report from Cadore was sent on 9 January 1824. It began with an unsolicited excuse, recalling that the cut had been approved both by his direct superiors in the office of the state property of Belluno and by the heads of the directorate in Venice. However, Perucchi declared that he had suspended the cut and asked to be able to go to the municipality of Cimolais, in the Friulian district of Maniago, to ascertain the extent of the offence.

Only on 29 March, almost three months later, was Perucchi able to supply more details, giving as his reason for the delay the harsh terrain and heavy snow that had put a stop to every operation. The report speaks of 700 trees felled, from which 1,100 lengths of wood of various sizes had been obtained. The timber had already been sold by Della Patta Pozzi to the timber merchant Daniele Centazzo of Maniago and was still being transported on the Celina river, near Montereale.

In Venice, this report confirmed some reservations that had already emerged concerning the work of the Cadore inspector. First of all, the snows he used to justify the lost time had certainly not prevented the trespassers from beginning to transport the illegally cut timber. Moreover, from a series of inconsistencies in Perucchi's reports it was clear, and was confirmed in subsequent investigations, that not only did the forestry inspector of Cadore not know of the existence of a forest that was in the same municipality as his inspectorate, but he had clearly authorised the cut without first carrying out an inspection in the area, as prescribed by the forest regulations. Finally, it seemed that the sum of money taken by Perucchi for granting the cut was greater than that communicated to the offices of the state property.

At that point the investigation was transferred to the Pordenone forestry inspector, Antonio Melche, who was asked to assess the real extent of the offence and the actions of the people involved: the vestry, the contractor and the loggers who had made the cut, the merchant who had bought the goods and, last but not least, his colleague from Pieve di Cadore.

In the report that was sent to Venice once the interrogations and investigations had been completed, various points emerge that will reappear again and again in the following chapters: the difficulty of effectively controlling this remote and forbidding territory; the unreliability – often stemming from their complicity – of the local officials of the forest administration; and the dubious relationships between the timber merchants of the urban centres in the foothills and some of the local agents. However, for now it is important to highlight another point. In what had been variously described as 'mountain pasture land', 'woodland' and 'mature forest', a total of 1,500 trees had been cut, more than double the figure estimated in the report of March 1824 following the discovery of the offence; and these were trees that were far from being in poor condition, as they had been described in some of the reports prior to the cut. However, in defending himself from accusations in this regard, Perucchi played a good hand in pointing out that, according to the documents available to the forest administration, the area was used as pasture, with the sporadic presence of shrubs.

This is one of many examples in the papers of the forestry magistrates of that time that shows the complexity inherent in defining and delimiting the wooded areas.[42] These events highlight the difficulties in concretely applying that geometric conception of the territory that lay behind the silvicultural theories of the period.

Further examples of these difficulties in defining and quantifying the woodlands are to be found in the statistics drawn up during the

---

42.   Cf. Armiero 2007, pp. 238–39; Ceschi 1999, pp. 15–30.

The setting. Cadore in the nineteenth century

Figure 4.

Wood transport in the Alps (1829), engraving by Ludwig von Martens. Source: Private archive (B. Pellegrinon).

nineteenth century concerning the extension of the forest patrimony in the Veneto region.[43]

The main statistical findings were published in the second half of the century, and the data was usually organised on a provincial basis. For the province of Belluno (which included the Cadore area), which was the only completely mountainous province and the one with the highest percentage of forest cover, the results vary considerably, even within the span of a few years and within the writings of the same authors. Over the course of less than a decade (1871–1873–1880), the secretary of the Chamber of Commerce, Riccardo Volpe, estimated the forest area to be 89,000, 101,000 and 127,000 hectares respectively, compared to a total provincial area of 330,000 hectares (therefore with very significant proportional variations). In 1879, the forestry inspector Pietro Soravia reported to the Ministry of Agriculture, Industry and Commerce that, within a span of seventy years, the provincial forest area had increased from 85,000 to 132,000 hectares. This was a prodigious increase (equal to 55 per cent), especially if we consider that it had taken place in a period in which contemporaries were constantly complaining about the damage caused by excessive deforestation. Yet, just five years earlier, a report by the same inspector, Soravia, estimated the forest cover of the province to be around 69,000 hectares, a notably lower figure than that of his starting point supplied a few years later.

Even the results contained in the official statistics of those years appear very contradictory: the ministerial statistics 'Castagnola' (1870) assign to the province of Belluno 101,000 hectares of forest area, while 'Majorana', just five years later, lowers the estimate to 68,000 hectares. However, what is most disconcerting when comparing such diverse data is that they are derived from the same source – that is, the cadastre initiated by the French and finished by the Austrians.

Yet, for the young science of silviculture, a precise knowledge of the forest area was a necessary prerequisite for any kind of action to protect or exploit the forest resources. Attempts to take such action

---

43. The following data has been analysed in Bajo 1882, pp. 116–18; Lazzarini 2013, pp. 11–13.

were not lacking.[44] Already during Napoleonic rule, an investigation had been carried out into the forest lands of the kingdom, the first complete one ever done for the Veneto area, since the Serenissima had limited itself to counting the oaks to be reserved for the Arsenal.

Some registers were also produced regarding the common woods, one of which was drawn up by the conservator to the Belluno woods, Gaspare Doglioni, whose jurisdiction extended well beyond the current borders of the province, including Primiero and most of the Friulian mountains too.[45] This document is full of information on the woodlands of the area, organised according to the division, canton and municipality where they were situated. It lists the following for each woodland: the size, value, quality (coppice or tall trunk), dominant species and method of cultivation; the distance from rivers or streams on which the timber could be transported (and this shows that knowledge of the forest patrimony was primarily functional to its commercial exploitation); easements and the constraining limits of these, titles or claims related to these easements. There was also a column in the register in which the reference to the cadastral map number should have been indicated, but that is completely empty since, as Doglioni explains in his concluding remarks, the necessary cadastral documentation was not yet available; and this fact limits the reliability of the numerical data.

Investigations on the matter were resumed after the return of the Austrians, with the compilation of new registers on the state of the common woodlands.[46] The registers were drawn up according to a similar model to that adopted by the Napoleonic administration. The data already available were integrated with reference to the cadastral maps, information on the cuts made during the previous years and information on any buildings in the woods or surrounding areas. Also in this instance, the forest inspectors were aware of the unreliability of the reported figures and explicitly commented on it. Often

---

44.   See the project for the implementation of a forestry cadastre in ASVe, *Governo veneto*, 1819, XXIX, b. 1483, f. 3.

45.   ASVe, *Ispettorato Generale ai Boschi*, r. 198.

46.   For the province of Belluno: ASVe, *Ispettorato Generale ai Boschi*, r. 207.

the description of the forest districts was accompanied by comments that revealed deforestation, or that the territory in question should be considered to a large extent as pasture, wooded pasture, wooded meadow, bushy terrain or uncultivated land of some kind.[47] In short, the terrain was very varied, with the result that any arbitrary definition risked creating complications like those that arose during the cutting operations on Mount Pera.

The criterion that I shall use to quantify the extent of woodlands in the Cadore area is that identified by Giorgio Scarpa as a result of an analytical study of the cadastral documentation – and which is subject, therefore, to the limitations already mentioned regarding this type of source. According to this criterion, only those lands classified as woodland in the strict sense are considered as part of the forest area, excluding therefore the terrain that was more ambiguously defined (for example wooded pasture).[48] The conclusion is that, based on the cadastral documentation, 27,451.6 hectares can be defined as woodland in the strict sense. This is 24.2 per cent of the total area of Cadore and 33.21 per cent of the agro-silvo-pastoral area. This was an area ten times larger than that of arable land and proportionately greater in the district of Auronzo, in particular in the valley of Comelico, where it covered more than half the total agricultural area, and where the woodlands were reported to be in a better state.

Again with regard to the definition of the woodlands, there were some points that did not necessarily refer to the condition of the lands surveyed, but rather to the ways in which they were used. In both registers, and for all municipal districts, the method of cultivation is indicated using these formulas: 'Nature is the sole cultivator' or 'Nature provides without the work of man'.[49]

Yet the territories in question had been the subject of intense human activity, the documentary evidence for which is evident at least from the early Medieval period and continually attested over the fol-

---

47. Bianco 2008b.
48. Scarpa 1996. See also Lazzarini 2007. Table 4.
49. On the use of these categories as a political project by the nineteenth-century state administrations, see Ingold 2009.

The setting. Cadore in the nineteenth century

Table 4.

Surface areas of the woodlands in the Venetian provinces in the mid-nineteenth century.

Province	Tall leafy woodland	Resinous woodland	Coppiced woodland	'Protected' woodland	Total woodland area	Cliffs, rocky outcrops, wooded pasture	Total forest area in the widest sense	Total area	% of woodland /total area	% of forest area in the widest sense/total area
Belluno	1,405	31,117	29,031	311	61,864	41,873	103,737	324,210	19.08	32.00
Padua	379	4	4,965	0	5,348	219	5,567	217,888	2.45	2.55
Rovigo	12	0	553	0	565	258	823	113,791	0.50	0.72
Treviso	8,703	0	7,742	0	16,445	2,083	18,528	245,077	6.71	7.56
Udine	17,981	17,193	51,538	1,273	87,985	29,990	117,975	663,343	13.26	17.78
Venice	1,887	0	2,006	0	3,893	679	4,572	294,098	1.32	1.55
Verona	707	689	23,002	127	24,525	9,929	34,454	305,804	8.02	11.27
Vicenza	38	12,977	32,647	191	45,853	22,237	68,090	288,707	15.88	23.58
Total	31,112	61,980	151,484	1,902	246,478	107,268	353,746	2,452,918	10.05	14.42

Source: My own summaries based on the data collected in Lazzarini 2013. Surface area unit hectares.

lowing centuries. Regardless of their knowledge of the territory, the forestry inspectors must have been aware of the fact that the Cadore populations, over and above their few marginal pieces of cultivated land, aimed to exploit the immense forest resources. Moreover, those same registers contained numerous examples in this regard. The most recent commercial cutting operations were indicated for many districts, and the main easements to which the woodlands were subject were specified in all districts. These rights were usually listed for each hamlet, in continuity with those of the previous *regoliere* administrations. The most relevant were those relating to the local consumption of wood – that is, the right of the population to obtain from the local woodlands free firewood (for domestic heating and cooking) and free wood to work with (to produce tools) and to build with (to construct or repair houses and community buildings).[50]

Furthermore, forest lands were subject to various customary practices, which helped to meet the needs of the population according to the model of an integrated economy as outlined earlier: hunting; the gathering of food or medicinal products (berries, herbs, mushrooms,

50.   ASVe, *Censo stabile, quesiti risposte circostanze locali*, b. 27.

acorns, walnuts and hazelnuts etc.); the extraction of resin, tannin (for the tanning of hides) and turpentine (from larch trees); the use of the lower branches of the trees as fodder and the collection of dead leaves as bedding for the animals.[51]

In this sense, the idea that nature was 'the sole cultivator' stems from the limited categories adopted for the compilation of the questionnaires. These categories were typical of the silvicultural theories of the period, according to which the only conceivable methods of cultivation were those prescribed by the new forest science, which was understood primarily in terms of a forest economy.[52] In the legislation, defining a place meant attributing specific functions to it, incompatible with those valid for other territories. In other words, in the forest legislation of those years, and in the silvicultural writings that inspired it, even where 'woodland' was written, the intended meaning was 'timber'.

On the contrary, the woodlands were multifunctional areas *par excellence* within the customary agrarian systems, so much so that Diego Moreno speaks of the 'multiple use of resources' in discussing the ability of the rural population to exploit the forest resources thanks to a wealth of skills deriving from their close ties with the territory. Along these lines, some methodologically innovative studies have enabled us to jettison the image of a natural forest as it was proposed by the sources produced by the forest magistrates and rather to consider it as an 'artefact', constantly being redefined by anthropic action.[53]

There were various ways of using the forest resources, but the one in which the contrast between official forest theory and the customary practices of the local population emerges most clearly was pastoralism. For the forestry specialists of the period, animals in general – and small ones in particular – were the main 'enemies' of the woods and the principal cause of their decay. Where there was woodland there could not be grazing. In this regard, defining the boundaries of a wood, for the authorities, meant distinguishing between legal practices and those

---

51. Cf. Volpe 1880, pp. 102–07; Bettega, Pistoia 1994, pp. 19–21. For some examples on the tannin production, see ACA, *Atti di amministrazione*, 1818, b. 57, 5 Oct. 1818.

52. Bianco, Lazzarini 2003, p. 94.

53. In particular, see Moreno 1990.

other practices that, having crossed that border, became illegal.[54]

The dichotomous relationship between the forest as a source of fodder and its silvatic uses, as identified in the forest legislation of the period, lost its significance in everyday practices where, very often, woodland and pasture were complementary. First of all, this was because nomadic grazing was also practised in those lands considered forest, even though the rural statues did put in place some restrictions.[55] In addition, in the Alps, the band where most of the forest cover was situated was usually a bridging area between those lands closest to the villages, where cultivated land gradually gave way to meadowland and the first pastures, and land situated at high altitudes, usually above the tree line, where there were the broad Alpine pastures, called *monti*. These territories, which usually contained some farmhouses, were collectively enjoyed by one or more village communities. Here, in the summer months, the local livestock was driven to the pasture by shepherds chosen by the respective communities. In this way, most of the workforce was 'spared' for agricultural work in the valleys or for migratory work.[56] Moreover, these high-altitude pastures were much larger than required by the area's livestock. Therefore, some pastures were rented out to foreigners in exchange for monetary sums or foodstuffs.[57]

On this issue, some studies have shown a further level of complementarity between the woodlands and pastures in the eastern Italian Alps of an entrepreneurial character. Often the tenants of the pastureland surplus to the requirements of the communities were the very timber merchants who were acquiring cutting rights in the woodlands close to those same pastures. The joint lease of the mountain pastures and of the woodlands – or at least of the logging rights in the woods – allowed the merchants to have animals at their disposal to facilitate the transport of timber. The needs of the two sectors were met in another comple-

54.   Corti 2006. For the French Alps, cf. Simon, Clément, Pech 2007.

55.   See the report Perucchi sent to the forestry administration summits in ASVe, *Ispettorato Generale ai boschi*, 1815–1817, b. 130, f. 2.

56.   Da Deppo 1990; Perco 1993. On alpiculture as 'a form of exploitation that consumed space but saved labour', see Mathieu 2009, p. 52.

57.   Barpi 1876.

mentary way: the wood created during the forest work permitted the maintenance of huts and provided the fuel needed for the processing of milk; dairy products supplemented the food of the woodcutters, with lower transport costs compared to foodstuffs from the valley floor.[58]

We have seen the multifunctional role that the woodlands played in the Cadore economy in relation to the different activities associated with them. However, it is important now to look beyond the valleys of Cadore, in order to understand the economic value of these resources within that complex commercial sector called the timber industry.

The timber industry

As we have seen, there is much evidence showing the meagre state of Cadore agriculture; equally abundant is the evidence identifying the processing and trade of timber as the main economic opportunity for the region. In a report sent to Venice in August 1841, the provincial delegate of Belluno described the municipality of Comelico Superiore in this way: 'At more than three thousand feet above sea level there are situated the four villages into which the municipality is divided, that is Padola, Dosoledo, Candide and Casamazzagno, under an inclement sky, surrounded by a few hoed lands on a steep slope, where nothing but potatoes, little barley and oats can ripen.' Yet, continued the delegate, the municipality 'is one of the most important and rich in the province for its extensive, flourishing high forest that provides work and many other resources for the inhabitants'.[59] So much so that one contemporary proposed an interesting comparison for the firs in the area: 'These are, in fact, our ears of corn, our mulberries, our vines'.[60]

The woods of Comelico were among the most extensive and rich in the whole of Cadore, but similar descriptions can be found for many other municipalities, particularly for those in the Auronzo dis-

---

58.   Cf. Coppola 2000, p. 247; Occhi 2006, pp. 52–53; Lorenzini 2011, pp. 104–07.
59.   ASVe, *Governo Veneto*, 1840–1844, XXVII, b. 6241, f. 50/207.
60.   Bettina 1869, p. 9.

trict, both before and after the 1840s.[61] After all, the timber coming from those woodlands had already been traded for centuries, along the travel routes determined by the Piave river and its tributaries that crossed the Cadore territory (the Ansiei, Boite and Padola), on which most of the goods were transported.

The forest resources of Cadore met all the main supply needs in this ever expanding market, especially in the final decades of the eighteenth century, when there was a surge in prices over most of Europe.[62] As for firewood, the main wood was beech. Sometimes it was transformed into charcoal, in order to facilitate its transport or to meet the needs of particular industrial sectors, but more often it was marketed directly in bundles of standard size called *taglioni* and *borre*. Between the sixteenth and seventeenth centuries, the trade in firewood and charcoal represented the largest share of Cadore's exports, but it was gradually replaced, over the following centuries, by the much more lucrative trade in timber for construction and industrial uses.[63] This timber mainly came from conifers such as white fir, spruce and larch, which were usually cut into standard size assortments – particularly the cut of 4.17 metres called *taglia* – before being immersed in water for transport. These trees were especially plentiful in the area of upper Cadore and were renowned, so much so that, according to Riccardo Volpe, in 1838 a joint English-French commission judged the wood of Cadore as the best in the world from a qualitative point of view.[64]

As already mentioned, it is not easy to assess the extent of these various trades. Smuggling was too extensive; the range of products and arboreal species traded was too vast; and the quantitative evidence in regard to the quality, dimensions and value of the goods is too vague. It must also be remembered that Cadore, as well as being a production area, was also a transit zone for timber coming to Venice from the

---

61. For some examples, see the reports in ASVe, *Direzione Generale del Demanio, Provincie Venete*, 1820–1824, Belluno amministrazione e annualità, b. 91, 8 Oct. 1818; and ASVe, *Ispettorato generale ai boschi*, 1850–1854, b. 395, 19 Sept. 1850.
62. Radkau 1990.
63. Agnoletti 1993.
64. Volpe 1873, p. 7.

northern German-speaking valleys.[65] For the early modern period, one of the most cited documents is the nineteenth century transcription of a notarial deed quantifying the duties on the export of Cadore timber in 1597. The document is incomplete, since one of the three registers is missing and, naturally, it does not take into account smuggled goods. Approximately 160,000 pieces of timber of different sizes are found to have been exported from Cadore by river transport, a figure that must be considered a flawed estimate.[66] Over the following centuries, the available data indicates a progressive increase in traffic, estimated at around 200,000–300,000 pieces of timber a year in the eighteenth century and 300,000–400,000 pieces in the mid-nineteenth century.[67]

More reliable evidence attesting to the continuous increase in the use of wood in industry is the number of sawmills. Most of the Cadore sawmills were built on the short stretch of the Piave river between the towns of Perarolo and Longarone. Near Perarolo, located at the confluence of the Boite river and the Piave, a rake weir was built, called a *cidolo*, which allowed the passage of water but blocked the logs, thus permitting the collection of all the timber that had floated down from the upstream territories. The logs thus collected were separated according to owner and sent on to the sawmills located in the stretch of river immediately after the weir.[68] After sawing, the timbers were usually loaded onto rafts and sent on their way towards the Veneto plain[69].

Around fifty or sixty mills were operating in the area by the end of the sixteenth century.[70] But by the beginning of the nineteenth century, a report sent by the prefect of Belluno to the Ministry of the Interior at Milan attested to 150 active sawmills that annually cut around 400,000 logs of larch and fir into planks, constituting the main manufacturing activity of the entire department.[71] There was then further growth dur-

---

65. Occhi 2002.
66. Published in Fabbiani 1959, pp. 7–9.
67. Agnoletti 1993, pp. 82–84.
68. For a technical description of the sawmills of the area, see Wessely 1993.
69. Zangrando 1993.
70. Agnoletti 1996, p. 1034.
71. ASMi, *Commercio, parte moderna*, b. 9.

ing the century, since by 1871 there were 182 sawmills operating in Cadore and in the Piave stretch downstream from Perarolo.[72] In the previous decade, evidence indicates that more than 10,000 people were employed in the cutting, transport and processing of timber in the province of Belluno (one seventeenth of the population).[73]

Further evidence of the commercial value of the Cadore woods and of the extent of the cuts made therein is the numerous infrastructures built to facilitate the initial stages of transporting the timber (yarding and free-floating) that preceded the sawing.[74] The first stage consisted in transporting the trunks from the cutting site – where they underwent some preliminary processing – to the riverbank. The most used constructions for the downward journey of the trunks were semicircular channels built of wood, called *risine*, which reduced friction and eased the sliding of the logs.[75] In cases where the cutting areas were located beyond the watershed with respect to the river, the trunks had to be first brought up to the crossings by means of wagons or sledges pulled by oxen. The storage pens were placed along the banks of the watercourses that crossed the area, but not all of them had sufficient water to start the flow. Most of the timber was floated down in spring, in order to make the most of full streams following the melting of snow. To facilitate the start of the floating, barrages were built at various points on the watercourses, called *stue*, which created artificial basins. If necessary, the collected water, into which the trunks that were to be transported had been thrown, was released with the opening of the barrier, in this way starting the flow of the goods. A timber merchant described the dramatic opening of a *stua* in the Vanoi valley in these words:

> That great mass of timber, that had been herded before the barrier and surrounded by an immense volume of water, suddenly moved with an unprecedented roar all at one point: the pale flanks of the valley became

72. Volpe 1871, p. 154.
73. Guarnieri 1862, p. 178.
74. Ronzon 1990.
75. Soravia 1988.

all reddened with the impetus of the timbers, which were all jolted up
and then began to crash down ...[76]

The channels and weirs were placed strategically to service the largest
possible area of forest. The construction and maintenance costs were
extremely high. In some cases, they are still visible today, and their
presence alone was clear evidence of the intensity of cutting operations in the area.[77]

The budgets of the forestry magistrates can also convey a rough idea
of the magnitude of the Cadore timber trade in the early nineteenth
century. According to the legislation issued by the French, for every
official cut carried out in the woodlands, including those done in the
common woods, a tenth was to be paid to the forest administration
(then reduced to eight percent by a regulation of 1837).[78] According to
the data collected by forestry inspector Baldassarre Buja, in the decade
1836–1845, the gross amount obtained from the woodlands in the
district of Auronzo alone amounted to about 4,000,000 Austrian lire.[79]
Eleven years later, another forestry inspector, Pietro Bajo, claimed that
the revenues from forest taxation in the Cadore division corresponded
to more than double those obtained overall in the rest of the Austrian
Veneto region;[80] and this evidence comes from an area where, as we
shall see, tax evasion in the forestry sector was so widespread that it
was directly practised by the municipal administrations.

From this huge trade the village communities gained a basic income, since they owned in various ways the majority of the forest

76. Negrelli 2010, p. 399.
77. Agnoletti 1996, p. 1038.
78. Governmental notification 1 Sept. 1837 n. 27599–2789, in *Regolatore amministrativo
    teorico-pratico, ad uso degli impiegati amministrative in genere*, VIII, Stabile Civelli Giu-
    seppe e Comp., Milan 1846, p. 325.
79. Buja 1847, p. 11.
80. Bajo 1958, p. 12. Regarding forest taxation, ASVe, *Direzione Generale del Demanio,
    Provincie Venete*, 1820–1824, Massime, amministrazione e boschi, b. 83 includes the
    budget of the Veneto forestry administration for 1820. It is data too specific to be
    considered statistically representative. Nevertheless, it is useful to stress that 58% of
    the forest administration's provincial revenue – mainly consisting of tenths of cuts in
    public forests – came from only four municipalities of the Comelico area (Comelico
    Superiore , Comelico Inferiore, San Nicolò and San Pietro).

The setting. Cadore in the nineteenth century

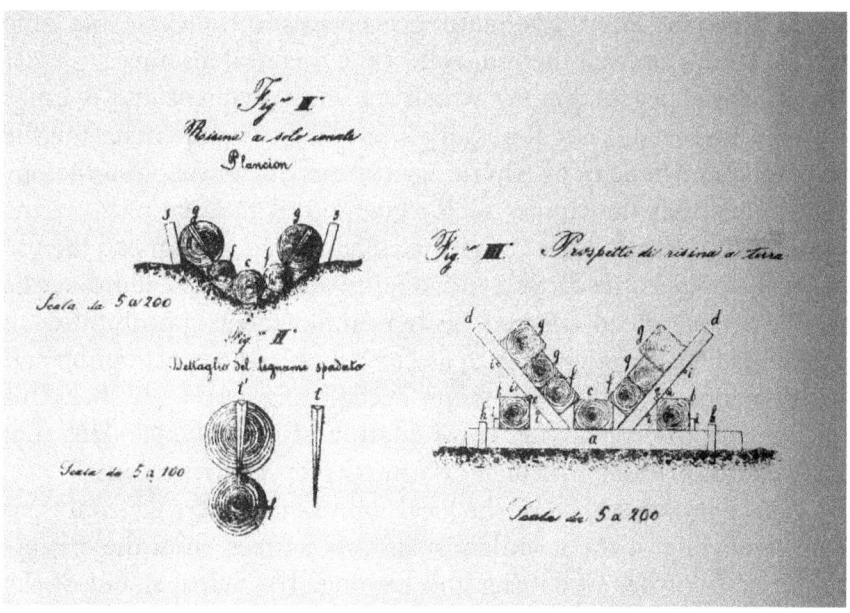

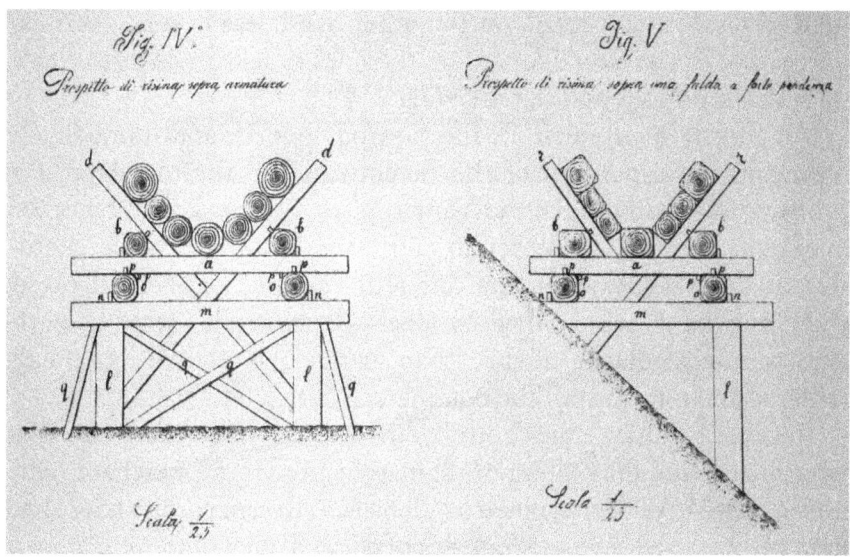

Figure 5.

Depictions of risine. Source: Soravia 1988.

lands. Thus, the granting of cutting licences and the leasing of large wooded areas allowed them to collect the financial resources to meet their main expenses, among which the most frequent and onerous was the importation of foodstuffs necessary to compensate for the structural deficiencies of Alpine agriculture. There were also the opportunities that the timber sector guaranteed to large parts of the population. Usually, leases contained clauses that guaranteed the use of local labour in the cutting and logging operations. In addition, the timber supply chain ensured further employment opportunities in various collateral activities such as, for example, the construction and maintenance of the infrastructure needed to transport timber. This encouraged the spread and consolidation of professional skills that allowed occupational mobility also into other Alpine regions.[81]

Yet the profits earned by the local communities derived from their sole ownership of the woodlands; and, sometimes, from the organisation of the work of cutting and logging. The management of the complex cycle that transformed the timber of those forests into commercial products for retail, on the other hand, was beyond their capacity. The timber merchants were the ones to take to charge of this, with the enormous associated benefits.

As already mentioned, in the previous period, and immediately following the expansion of the Serenissima on the mainland, the timber trade destined for the Veneto plain was controlled by urban operators, above all by Venetian patricians. In the following centuries, at different times in the different commercial areas involved, these merchants were joined by local operators who acted as partners or intermediaries of the urban merchants, and who gradually replaced them to control the commercial cycle.

This last requisite – the control of the entire commercial cycle – was what guaranteed the highest profit margins; and those merchants who took control have been defined as 'globalists'. Recent studies have shed light on the activities and strategies of these figures, who were among the most complex and important in the business world that operated between the Alps and the Veneto plain in early modern times. Ac-

81. Pozzan 2013, pp. 129–42.

cording to a typical model of the period, these were family businesses, able to operate in diverse supply areas (which could belong to different jurisdictions) and with available capital to finance large investments, the returns from which would only come decades later.[82]

These characteristics implied – and also favoured – at least two other features. Firstly, the timber trade was the pivot around which revolved many other activities, which often turned out to be functional to the main one: for example, the extension of credit, both to private individuals and to institutions that boasted titles on woodland (communities, feudal lords, states). To this must be added other commercial activities along the routes to and from the cutting areas. As for incoming trade, independently managing the supply of foodstuffs led to a considerable reduction in costs, both because it provided direct sustenance to the woodcutters and because it met the needs of the mountain communities that were rich in forests but lacked fields for cultivation. As regards outgoing trade, the rafts that left from Perarolo or the other river ports, as well as being a commodity in themselves, were also one of the fastest means of transport to reach the urban areas of the plain. They could therefore be loaded with coal, metals or other merchandise from the mountain territories.

Territorial control was also fundamental in order to access the advantages deriving from complete management of the production and commercial cycle. The main global merchants, in fact, managed trade that extended from the Alpine chain to the Adriatic coast, often operating over several river systems and across different political-administrative contexts. Therefore, the success of these activities presupposed a constant presence along the trade routes or, at least, at the main junctions (the cutting areas, storage points, river ports, customs stations, trading centres etc.). This was done through a vast network of intermediaries, strategic marriage alliances and client relationships with the local elites. To consolidate this network of relationships, they also made numerous property investments in the areas involved, since the principal operators needed multiple residences at the main points of commercial activity. As for the families coming from the

82.   A review of these works is Zannini 2011.

Alpine valleys, their 'formal' transfer to the plains and integration into the patrician world of the main cities of the mainland 'did not involve any loosening of relations with the regions of origin'.[83]

Most of the studies on the area that exported to Venice focus on companies active during the domination of the Serenissima. However, it seems that the following entrepreneurial characteristics were typical of the sector at least until the second half of the nineteenth century: family-based organisation, control of the entire commercial cycle, diversification of investments, the central role of credit, patronage ties with local elites, multiple residences.

The story of the Micoli Toscano family, exhibits many of these characteristics: already active in the eighteenth century in the Tagliamento river basin, during the nineteenth century the family extended its activities to become one of the main companies operating in the central-northern Adriatic.[84] The best known example, however, is that of the Feltrinelli family, which began to get involved in the sector in the mid-nineteenth century, operating from the municipality of Gargnano, on Lake Garda, and became, within a few decades, one of the main Italian entrepreneurial dynasties, moving from a regional to an international position, during a period of profound change within the timber trade.[85]

In such a rich and complex market, only a few of the many occasional and local agents involved in the production cycle succeeded in consolidating their position to fully exploit the opportunities for social ascent that the timber trade offered. Of all the areas that supplied Venice, it seems that Cadore was among the first where families active in the local market were able to expand to become global operators, even in other cutting areas; and it seems that this happened more frequently in Cadore than elsewhere.[86] As early as the sixteenth and seventeenth centuries, the Fabris, Gera, Poli, Pellizzaroli and Vettori families were the first to make this journey; they

---

83. Corazzol 1997, p. 202.

84. Bianco, Lazzarini 2003, pp. 42–49. Cf. also the case of the Lazzaris family in Zangrando 1991; Pavan 2017.

85. Segreto 2011.

86. For their presence in Tyrol and Carnia, cf. Occhi 2006; Bianco 2002a.

were followed over the succeeding centuries by the Cadorin, Coletti, Lazzaris and Viel (or Wiel) families. In the second half of the nineteenth century, the main families operating in the Venetian market were from the upper Piave valley.[87]

Evidence of success at the local level is to be found in the form of the imposing villas in Venetian style that some families built in their areas of origin. These are also the most obvious sign of the profound social stratification that commercial activities linked to the timber trade introduced into the area.[88] This was even more pronounced before the second half of the nineteenth century, when, following repeated fires, regulations were gradually imposed to build all houses in masonry; until then, the typical dwelling of most of the population was built of wood.[89]

The example of the Gera family illustrates the process well. Originally from the town of Candide (Comelico Superiore), by the end of the sixteenth century they had acquired Venetian residency and, in the following century, they were recognised Venetian citizens *originari* and also held some public offices.[90] Their ascent continued in the following century when the family, which had moved to Conegliano, was ennobled. However, in accordance with the commercial model outlined above, they maintained close ties with their area of origin throughout their time in the forestry sector, which lasted until the end of the nineteenth century. Already in the mid-seventeenth century, the family owned the *stua* on the Padola river, the most important one in Cadore, since it served a particularly rich area of forest and guaranteed to its owners a toll on all the goods brought down from there by river.[91]

In 1818, Vittore Maria Gera agreed with the municipality of Comelico Superiore to rebuild the *stua* in stone. In exchange for the

87. Fabbiani 1959; *Tariffa dei legnami in magazzino coll'aggiunta della misura del metro col piede veneto ed altri ragguagli* 1865. The term 'origin' must be understood in a context of frequent inter-Alpine mobility, as described in Corazzol 2016.

88. Da Ronco 1905; Da Ronco 1906; Eiche Clere, Riva de Bettin 1994; Bianco, Lazzarini 2003, p. 20. Cf. the German case described in Warde 2002, p. 185.

89. Gellner 1991.

90. Vianello 1993, p. 305. On this and other families, cf. Fabbiani 1970.

91. Fabbiani 1959, p. 19.

work, which according to the Belluno nobleman and poet Francesco Miari cost over 120,000 Austrian lire and was designed by the same Gera, the municipality of Comelico Superiore loaned some woodlands to the family business.[92]

The relationships that the Gera and other Cadore families active in the timber trade maintained with the most influential institutions and officials at the local level were not exclusively formal in nature or limited to issues related to the leasing of woodlands and the maintenance of facilities needed for logging and floating timber. The ties that linked the various family firms both to each other and to the local notables most influential in the management of public affairs were usually articulated on several levels (business relationships, ties of patronage and familial connections).

The complexity of these links, and their influence on the dynamics of administrative change initiated at the beginning of the nineteenth century, are issues that need to be analysed in more depth through the notarial documentation, as has been done for earlier periods, or through the few available company and private archives. It is, however, possible to make some tentative observations thanks to an important correspondence between three members of this Alpine elite in the early decades of the nineteenth century: Giovanni Battista Lupieri, who was from Luint (Carnia), Liberale Monti from Candide (Comelico Superiore) and Giuseppe Solero from Sappada.[93]

The letters cover many topics, passing back and forth between private and wider collective events. To the youthful interests in dance, music and poetry were soon added political discussions, particularly during the Napoleonic experience, which aroused great hopes among the three friends. The constant military upheavals of those years are described at both the continental and local levels; not least because Lupieri, as a doctor, was a member of the conscription commission and was repeatedly asked to favour the exemption of members of some of the leading families of the area. With the Restoration and

---

92. On the woods: ACCS, *Raccolta cartolare*, b. 68, f. 1–4. On Vittore Maria Gera, cf. Miari 1819; BCF, *Biblioteca storica*, F 8.1d/5, *Raccolta di cose patrie*.

93. Agarinis Magrini 2000.

the return of the Austrians, a certain disillusionment emerged, but this did not prevent the three from continuing to fulfil public duties in their respective communities, without however abandoning their youthful ideals, to the extent that in 1839 both Lupieri and Monti commissioned identical portraits of Napoleon for their homes.

Themes relating to the professions of the respective authors also recur in the letters. For example, there are discussions of the most common diseases in the area and the first vaccination campaigns, which related to the medical activity of Lupieri; and Giuseppe Solero particularly dwells on the reports of the famine of 1816–17, having just taken on the management of an agricultural estate.

The correspondence is also rich in information about the notables of the area, as all three authors themselves belonged to this class. Lupieri was the son of landowners and was also related to the Micoli Toscanos. Although he originated from a valley in Carnia, where he also held administrative positions, he was the doctor of the main Cadore families. Liberale Monti was a lawyer and local official, as was his father Osvaldo, one of the best-known figures of the ruling elite of Cadore between the eighteenth and nineteenth centuries, so much so that he was sent as ambassador of the Council to Paris and Passariano, where he met Napoleon Bonaparte. Liberale married a girl of humble origins, much to Solero's bewilderment. The latter thus informed Lupieri of the wedding:

> A monstrous marriage, dictated by blind, senseless love, strengthened by a bestial passion and fulfilled out of human regard, I don't know, I say, if a happy, uninterrupted continuation of reciprocal affection, love, trust and peace is possible. God willing, I wish him well with all my heart. It will be nice to see a peasant woman, only used to using rakes and conversing with animals, being continually introduced to lords, meeting with them and holding them in conversation, courted and complimented as a result of such a metamorphosis.[94]

Giuseppe Solero belonged to a wealthy family from Sappada, which had made its fortune through trade in timber and cereals. He married Enrichetta Jacobi, the last heiress of a family of lawyers and registrars from Pieve di Cadore. His three sisters married scions of the

94. Agarinis Magrini 2000, p. 66.

wealthiest families of Comelico (the Gera, Pellizzaroli and Vettori families) while his uncles by marriage were from another illustrious family of Comelico, the Zandonella dall'Aquila.[95]

These were only their closer family ties, but in the correspondence among the three friends many members of the elites of Cadore and the Friulian plain (where the Solero family moved in 1816, near to San Vito al Tagliamento) are frequently mentioned, whether in reference to a hunting trip or a commercial agreement, to a business trip or a courtesy visit, a marriage or a baptism.

The status of these heterogeneous figures varied greatly: from a lawyer or official, whose influence did not extend beyond the borders of a town, to the most prominent members of the Friulian nobility and the Lombardo-Venetian government. Therefore, if this correspondence highlights the inevitable social fluidity that the main players within these peripheral territories were forced to countenance, it also makes evident the possibilities that were open to those who, with their wealth and connections, were able to interact with the supra-local political and economic structures and therefore act as mediators between the centre and the periphery.[96]

---

95. On the Solero family, see also Armano 2015. On the Zandonella dall'Acquila family, see Da Ronco 1903.

96. Cf. Blok 1974.

3.

OLD USES, NEW ABUSES

Full moon

It is time to analyse the impact of the new legislation in this Alpine area and to understand the reactions provoked by the application of the provisions introduced during the Napoleonic administration, beginning with those that made up the forestry regulations.

As early as January 1812, only a few months after the issuing of the operative guidelines of the forest law of May 1811, the prefect of Belluno informed the finance and interior ministries that it would be impossible to apply the new regulations in the Cadore area, since 'the special circumstances of those places, and the types of cultivation in those woodlands are in diametrical opposition to the new rules'.[1] The issue was raised again a year later in a prefectural report in which the main causes of friction between the legislation and local needs were identified.[2]

The first and most urgent issue concerned the selection of trees to be cut down during the forest works. The forestry agents were put in charge of this task, but only after naval agents had visited and exercised their right to reserve certain trees for shipbuilding. This was what the law envisaged. The problem was that in Cadore, 70,000 trees had to be felled by the end of spring 1813 (the prefect indicated May/June), and the strength of the forestry officer workforce was completely inadequate. Exacerbating the difficulty was the fact that until the end of April there was a heavy blanket of snow in the appointed areas, further slowing down work.

A second issue concerned the felling itself, and then the transporta-

---

1   ASMi, *Agricoltura, parte moderna*, b. 45, 27 Feb. 1813 (with a reference to another report dated 23 Jan. 1812).

2   On these events, cf. Lazzarini 2008a. Antonio Lazzarini has kindly provided me the new shelf marks for the documentation that he consulted. For this – and much more – I am deeply grateful to him.

tion of the felled trees. The decree of 5 June 1811 n. 131 prescribed that auctions for the cutting concessions in the public woodlands should be based on the 'living tree'. In other words, merchants had to buy trees still standing in the woodland and then to manage or to subcontract the work of cutting, preparing and transporting the timber.[3]

The prefect warned that this method would lead to the ruin of the entire region, since in most of the municipalities lease contracts contained a clause to ensure the use of local labour in forestry work. In the district of Auronzo, where the principal woodlands were situated, this work involved, directly or indirectly, the entire population. Indeed, each household had the right to have at least one of its members employed in the forest work. In this way each family could benefit from the proceeds of these activities, often being paid in foodstuffs.[4] According to the prefect, not enough merchants were prepared to face the risks involved in contracting the work out to an external workforce; and even if they were able to proceed in this way, it would have devastating consequences for most of the local population.

The final dispute concerned cutting methods. In line with the most widespread theories proposed by the emerging science of silviculture, the new legislation recommended the 'regular section' cut. In Cadore, on the other hand, a 'single cut' method was traditionally used, where the trees to be felled were each identified according to criteria of commercial maturity.

The traditional method involved dividing the trees into various cutting classes corresponding to the diameter of the lower part of the trunk. Each class of cut carried its own commercial price, but the price was not proportional to the volume of the tree. It was undervalued for trees with a diameter of less than XII ounces (41.8 cm) and overvalued for those of a higher class. From the practical point of view, this did not prevent abuses, but it discouraged the felling of less mature trees, because if a tree was even a few millimetres short of the diameter of the higher cutting class, its inclusion in the lower class meant a considerable material loss. As has been noted, the un-

3   *Bollettino delle leggi del Regno d'Italia*, I, Milano 1811, pp. 511–39.

4   In that period mainly corn: ACA, *Atti di amministrazione*, 1817, b. 55.

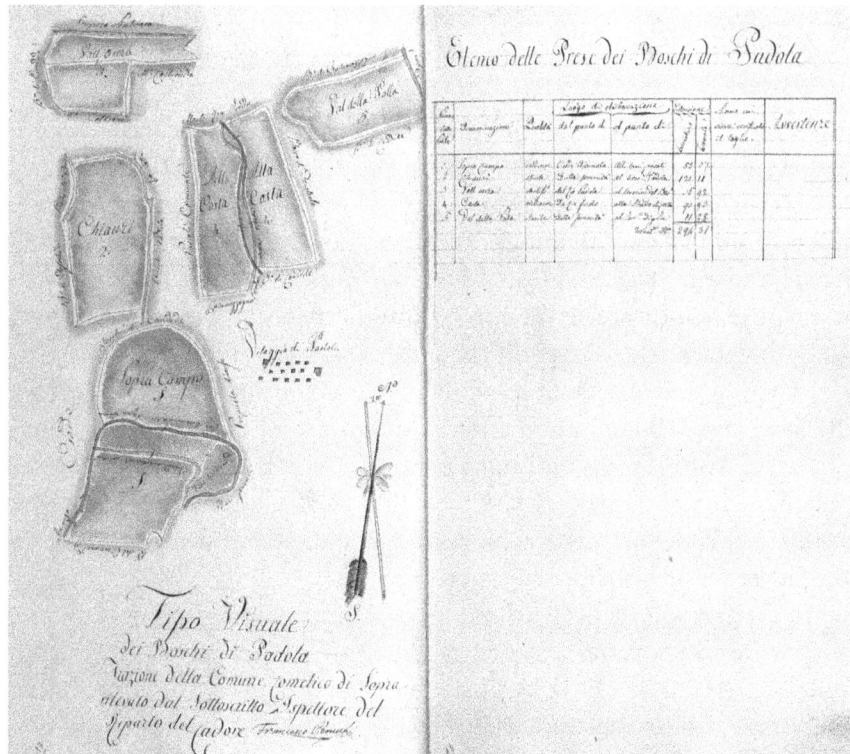

Figure 6.

Forestry map for the 'regular section' cut method, early nineteenth century. Source: BSC, digital archive.

doubted merit of this method was that it fixed both the rules for the management of the woodlands and the parameters for the economic evaluation of the logs.[5]

On this last point, the support of the prefect for the Cadore demands was explicit:

> The woodlands of the department, and in particular those of Cadore, are now at the highest degree of prosperity, and their flourishing state cannot be attributed to anything other than the method by which they are currently utilised ... Conversely, if the section cut method is introduced,

for every hundred trees that are cut in a given area of land, only one will
be mature; the others will not be suitable either to be used for shipbuilding, or to be cut into smaller sizes, or even to be used for firewood.[6]

Therefore, the prefect of Belluno asked that enough forest inspectors be sent to complete the selection of the trees between May and
June; that the visit of the naval agents be carried out promptly; that
there should be a total derogation from the requirement to sell 'living
trees'; and that the traditional cutting method should be continued
in Cadore, and that the section cut method should be abandoned.

A few days after a copy of the letter was sent to the Interior Ministry, with a note attached in which the prefect warned of the 'serious
disorder we will encounter if the directorate of state property does
not agree to the proposed modifications, which take account of the
peculiar circumstances of the woodlands of Cadore and the other
lands of this department, which are quite different from those of all
the other woodlands of the Kingdom'.[7]

In Milan, the capital of the Napoleonic Kingdom of Italy, the
authorities were moved to act by the ominous signals coming from
the department of Piave; in a directive dated 18 May they decided to
meet the Cadore requests. The selection of trees was deemed necessary, but to speed it up they were willing to increase the number of
staff by using the municipal guards and to select the trees destined
for the navy at the same time as the ordinary ones. The 'regular section' cut was confirmed, but with the qualification that it would only
be applied to mature trees. Finally the obligation to carry out an auction of 'living trees' was revoked.

This compromise solution was only temporary, imposed by a situation that was becoming more and more tense as the felling was
delayed due to the bureaucratic exigencies of the new legislation, and
there was insufficient time to renegotiate or formalise a permanent
agreement. In the autumn of that year, the Austrians regained control of the territory that they had been forced to abandon eight years
earlier, ending the French occupation of the area.

6   ASMi, *Agricoltura, parte moderna*, b. 45, 27 Feb. 1813.
7   ASMi, *Agricoltura, parte moderna*, b. 45, 4 Mar. 1813.

Old uses, new abuses

There is a lack of information about how the forest cuts were organised in the tumultuous biennium of 1814–1815. Some reports indicate that the woodlands of the area came under heavy pressure due to the exigencies of warfare and the needs of the population, harshly tested by the combination of economic hardship and the resumption of military operations.[8] A level of normality returned only at the beginning of 1816, with the restructuring of the forest sector in the Kingdom of Lombardy-Venetia by the Austrians. As already mentioned, this reorganisation was restricted to bureaucratic structures, almost all the staff employed under the French being retained and the forest law of 1811 remaining in force.[9]

The problems relating to the Cadore area were immediately brought to the attention of the heads of the new government. The aforementioned Francesco Perucchi, who had been appointed head of the newly established Forestry Inspectorate of Cadore, presented a memorandum on the state of the woodlands in the area, the criteria for their use adopted in previous centuries and the most appropriate ways to apply the forest legislation of 1811.[10]

We have already noted the dubious reliability of Perucchi as a public official and his suspected connivance in illegal cutting operations. It is now necessary to consider two other characteristics that allow us to understand his work and his assessments better. He was born in Pieve di Cadore (in the village of Nebbiu) in 1781, and had also been employed within the Cadore Community in the three years before its abolition (1803–1806). Furthermore, Perucchi had been active in the timber trade. This means that he had a good knowledge of the traditional community management of the woodlands and, at the same time, excellent empirical knowledge of the main production and commercial operations related to the timber supply chain.[11]

These points clearly emerge in the memorandum that the inspector

---

8   This was the opinion of the conservator Gaspare Doglioni: ASVe, *Governo veneto*, 1815, XXXIV, b. 406, 3 Mar. 1815.

9   Lazzarini 2009, pp. 111–94.

10   ASVe, *Ispettorato Generale ai boschi*, 1815–1817, b. 130, f. 2.

11   For Perucchi's c.v., see Lazzarini 2009, p. 176.

sent to the heads of the forestry administration at the beginning of 1816. This began with a historical reconstruction of the legal status of the Cadore woodlands. The author then proceeded to analyse the traditional cutting methods, the criteria for selecting the trees to be cut and the rules and officials in place to govern the forest works. Finally, with regard to the implementation of the forestry legislation, Perucchi suggested some modifications. He favoured a derogation from the directive requiring an auction of 'living trees', another from that which forbade grazing in the woods (although he wanted to confine goats to the mature woodlands), and case by case selection of the cutting method (regular section or individual selection), based on the condition of the woodland.

On 19 March, the directorate of state property in Venice replied to Perucchi that, given the importance of the issues raised by the Cadore inspector, it was appropriate to postpone any decisions on the proposed changes to a more suitable time.[12] However, in the following months, the force of events constrained the government to attend to those same issues.

At the end of May, due to delays that had occurred in the selection of trees reserved for shipbuilding, cutting operations in the Auronzo district had still not been authorised. On 20 May, the officers of state property of Belluno communicated to their superiors in Venice that the cutting licences could not be put off any longer 'in order to prevent the much feared and fatal consequences of a desperate people'.[13]

Ten days later, the chancellor of Auronzo, Marco Bognolo, at the request of a municipal deputy of San Pietro di Cadore, reminded the provincial delegate of the urgency of the forest works, since these were the only means of meeting the liabilities of the municipality and of guaranteeing the subsistence of the local population.

Since there was no progress over the following days, on 12 June thirteen deputies of the district of Auronzo delivered a plea to the chancellor, who forwarded it through the provincial delegate to the government in Venice. The authors complained that bureaucratic red tape had wasted the most appropriate time to make the cuts, in the

---

12   ASV, *Ispettorato Generale ai boschi*, 1815–1817, b. 130, f. 2.

13   ASVe, *Senato di Finanza*, 1816, IV, b. 18, f. IV/10.

days preceding the June moon. And this was not the first time the problem had arisen. Indeed, ever since the new forest law had been introduced, delays in the granting of licences had got worse every year, exacerbating discontent among the inhabitants. The authors re-iterated that the latter were together the sole legitimate owners of those woodlands from which they derived the main source of their subsistence. If then the legislation set a right of precedence for the needs of the navy, the deputies did not object, so long as this did not postpone the start of forest works, since delays only increased the pressure on the woodcutters.

This last aspect highlights clearly the contrast that was emerging between the new forest model – inspired by silvicultural science and adopted by the governmental authorities – and the traditional practices on which the exploitation of the woodlands was based at the local level. From a 'bureaucratic' point of view, the organisation of forestry work was based on predetermined and universally valid deadlines: these applied to cutting requests, selection visits, licensing concessions and so on. However, this timetable was very different from the empirical one adopted by rural populations and regulated according to natural cycles rather than bureaucratic stamps.

The timelines laid out for the forest and naval agents to complete the selection of the trees may have been suitable for the woodlands of the foothills, but they did not fit the needs of the high mountain ter-ritories, such as the Cadore region, where the snow cover often lasted until late spring and slowed down the selection process. Likewise, silvicultural theories did not take into account moon phases when considering when to make the cuts. There had been some debate on the merits of the respective seasons, but neither Henri Duhamel de Monceau nor any of the other authors involved in the subject over the previous decades had given consideration to the role of moon phases in forestry work.[14] At the local level, on the other hand, it was essential to fell conifers in the days closest to the full moon in order to facilitate the debarking of the trees. This is well illustrated by a timber merchant who had been contacted by the Venetian Senate,

14   Di Bérenger 1965, pp. 478–79 (originally published between 1859 and 1863).

more than sixty years earlier, for information on the subject:

> this is done because at that time the tree is 'in love', and the bark comes
> off almost by itself, and the wood is in its greatest vigour; so, when the tree
> is cut and left on the ground as it is for about fifteen days, the branches
> extract the 'mood' [the sap] and, stripped of its bark, the trunk quickly be-
> comes dried and lightweight, which improves the wood and makes it less
> difficult and expensive to handle and to transport to its destination ...[15]

Therefore, the traditional Cadore system followed natural pat-
terns and answered to nature's deadlines. The whole cycle culminated
in the spring after the cut (usually in May), when the trunks were
sold to merchants just as the snows were melting, increasing the river
flows, which in turn aided in rafting the timber.

This system, developed over time in accordance with environmental constraints and possibilities, served the needs of an integrated
economy based on pluriactivity, typical of Alpine areas, since it did
not overlap with the short agricultural season or with that part of
the year during which a substantial part of the population engaged
in migratory work. The continuous delays to the authorisation of the
cuts by the Venetian authorities had procrastinated the work until the
summer, when the demands of agricultural work were more intense.

Even though the chancellor of Auronzo and the provincial delegate supported the petition and delivered it to the central government with the utmost urgency, Venice did not reply with the diligence
expected by the petitioners. Thus, as the July moon approached, the
inhabitants of Comelico Superiore decided to proceed independently with the cuts.

The news of the crime reached the forest inspectorate of Pieve on
14 July. An investigation was immediately ordered, and municipal
foresters and two representatives of the municipal deputation were
appointed to this task. Four days of investigations revealed that, between 8 and 10 July, about 4,430 trees had been illegally cut down in
the various woodlands of the four villages that made up the municipality of Comelico Superiore.[16]

---

15   Quoted in Lazzarini 2006b, p. 30 n. 27.

16   ACCS, *Corrispondenza*, 1817–1818, 14–17 July 1816.

The suspects were the villages' inhabitants, who had entered the woodlands en masse in order to reassert their rights in the face of the increasing interference of the forestry administration. The action replicated methods already adopted in previous centuries, including a typical model of peasant protest: land invasion.[17] The cuts, in fact, had not been done indiscriminately. The trees had been felled according to the traditional Cadore criteria: only fir trees between fifty and sixty years old and with a diameter between ten and twelve ounces had been felled (the measure most frequently adopted in the traditional Cadore system).[18]

Faced with a fait accompli, the local state representatives (the chancellor and forestry inspector) found themselves caught between a rock and a hard place. The first choice was to enforce the existing law, as their public office – and their superiors – obliged them to do. The second was to act on their growing awareness that these protests were not the work of a few reckless transgressors, but that there was discontent which involved almost all the inhabitants of the area. They recognised that the root of this disquiet was the myopic government failure to grant certain exemptions from the application of the forest law. This thinking was increasingly apparent in the reports sent to Venice:

> Since I could not avoid the obligation to report to my superiors ... on the illegal cuts carried out by the inhabitants of this municipality, the much praised superiors have noted this event with great displeasure ... and have explicitly ordered me to find the leaders and the main perpetrators of such arrogant and insubordinate actions, and to communicate their names to the competent courts, commanding them to proceed with the full force of their office, to crack down on these arbitrary acts and teach these people how to honour the orders and will of their superiors. These are the precise words with which the aforementioned dispatch to me was written, and thus you, municipal agent, can understand that although I have tried as best as possible to justify these reprehensible actions carried out by these people to the praiseworthy royal delegates,

---

17   For similar cases under the Venetian domination, see Bianco 2000b. Land invasion is a typical form of peasant protest, especially as concerns lands considered common resources by rural population (independently by their official legal status): see the model proposed in Hobsbawm 1974; and also Guha 1990.

18   ASVe, *Direzione Generale del Demanio, Provincie Venete*, 1815–1819, b. 15, f. 6.

they deemed it necessary to apply the full force of the law against the perpetrators of the offence.[19]

In this letter, which I have transcribed almost in its entirety, chancellor Bognolo requested the municipal agent of Comelico Superiore to inform him of the identities of the instigators and principal promoters of the illegal cut. The tone is more displeased than inquisitorial; when the repressive action is mentioned it is always attributed to his superiors, and the chancellor seems almost to apologise for being the instrument of its imposition.

Therefore, it seems reasonable to imagine that Marco Bognolo was not particularly disappointed to tell his superiors that the inquiry had failed to identify the protagonists of the protest. All those interrogated had claimed that 'the inhabitants, by mutual agreement, pushed by their extreme needs, by the hunger to which they were prey, and by the fear that the desired authorisation would either never arrive, or not arrive in time to be put into effect, all went to the woods together to cut, without being induced by any particular encouragement or incitement'. And when the chancellor pointed out the criminality of the committed actions, he was met with the response that 'they have only cut what is their sacred and unquestionable property; which property has been somewhat violated by the forest administration, when it persists in denying the people the right to rely on and to make use of these resources which are essential for their subsistence'.[20]

Forest Inspector Perucchi sent a similar report to his superiors and suggested that it would be advisable to proceed with the work to secure commercial trunks, since the trees had already been cut down; and when this plan was approved by the provincial officers of state property, Perucchi was 'pleased' to communicate the news to the municipality of Comelico Superiore.[21]

From then on, Venice assumed a more direct role in the saga. On 8 October, the directorate of state property proposed a compromise solution designed to invoke at least partial respect for the law in for-

---

19   ACCS, *Corrispondenza*, 1817–1818, 14 July 1816.

20   ASVe, *Senato di Finanza*, 1816, IV, b. 17, f. 1.

21   ACCS, *Corrispondenza*, 1817–1818, 30 July 1816.

estry matters, while simultaneously pardoning *de facto* the lawbreakers. This fudge was about the only option available to the authorities, unless they wanted to prosecute the entire population of the municipality. The ruse was to inform the government that the cut had been authorised on 1 July, but that the notification had not arrived in time in Comelico Superiore. Therefore, although the formal procedure had not been observed, the cut could be considered formally authorised. This was enough for the government to close the matter. Abuses had been condoned and, although municipal officials were considered co-responsible for what had happened, this was more an issue for future reference than moral sanction.[22] However, in fact the matter was far from concluded, since the following spring the story repeated itself almost identically.

On 22 May 1817, a deputy of the municipality of Comelico Superiore informed chancellor Bognolo of grave delays in the granting of the cutting licences. On this occasion, Marco Bognolo chose to entirely disregard institutional protocol.[23] After all, he believed that he had taken all possible precautions against such delays. He had already had the cutting requests prepared in August 1816. In March 1817, he had convened the municipal deputies and the representatives of the villages of the municipality of Comelico Superiore in his office to declare themselves responsible for the observance of 'all the laws and regulations in force in the forestry sector'.[24]

Therefore, according to the chancellor, the forestry administration was solely responsible for the situation. He argued that 'one can only believe that the forestry administration was established for the benefit of the woodlands, and therefore for the welfare of their owners; however, its decisions operate decisively in the opposite direction to this very useful purpose'. His conclusion was just as polemical:

> there is certainly no forest official, even among the most knowledgeable, who will not learn much from the rough Cadore woodcutters, about eve-

---

22   ASVe, *Senato di Finanza*, 1816, IV, b. 17, f. 1.

23   ASVe, *Senato di Finanza*, 1817, IV, b. 90, f. 9.

24   ACCS, *Corrispondenza*, 1817–1818, the convocation: 19 Mar. 1817, the declaration: 24 Mar. 1817.

rything concerning the conservation, cultivation and growing of trees, and about all the operations and practices related to forest work.[25]

Bognolo's dispatch arrived in Venice at the start of June, attached to a report from the provincial delegate written in full support of the recriminations of his subordinate.

At this point, the government decided to raise the matter with the director of state property, Domenico Aita.[26] In his response of 25 June, Aita dismissed the accusations made by the provincial delegate and the chancellor and lauded the virtues of the forestry magistrates. In his opinion, the delay in cutting operations was attributable to the population and to the Cadore municipalities, who had opposed the division of the woodlands into sections, as had been prescribed in the 1811 forest law, and without which 'no cut can take place'.[27] Aita specified that the 'section cut' method was something different from a simple clear-cutting, as some officials of the Cadore forestry department had wrongly believed it to be. Nevertheless, he praised the utility of this and other precepts of the forestry economy, 'which, precisely because they have been recently introduced in these provinces, inevitably encounter great obstacles in the inveterate local customs, in the popular prejudices, and in the ridiculous application of erroneous and illogical doctrines'.[28]

In a choice between respect for the forest laws and the containment of social tension, the government preferred the latter. At a meeting on 19 June it arranged that, in the event of delays, the provincial delegation could issue the necessary cutting authorisations and, at a meeting on 29 July, it blamed the conduct of the directorate of state property.[29]

Moreover, the general directorate of state property had already authorised exemptions from the standard 'section cut' method, so that it increasingly resembled the traditional Cadore system, derogating from the maximum number of twenty *allievi* per hectare as set by the 1811

---

25   ASVe, *Senato di Finanza*, 1817, IV, b. 90, f. 9. Quoted in Lazzarini 2008a, pp. 168–69.

26   ASVe, *Senato di Finanza*, 1817, IV, b. 90, f. 9.

27   ACCS, *Corrispondenza*, 1817–1818, 5 Mar. 1817.

28   ASVe, *Senato di Finanza*, 1817, IV, b. 90, f. 9. Quoted in Lazzarini 2008a, p. 169.

29   ASVe, *Senato di Finanza*, 1817, IV, b. 90, f. 9.

law.[30] A further exemption was granted regarding the method used for allocating the work of cutting, preparing and transporting the timber. Given the particular characteristics of the high Cadore area and the centrality of the forest work to the survival of the local population, municipalities were allowed autonomy in the preparation of the trunks and their transportation to counting points along the river banks using their own system, called *lavoranzie.* This system remained in force until the annexation of these territories to the Kingdom of Italy. It stipulated that each village could organise a team of woodsmen, selected from among all the families interested in participating in forest work, under the direction of a manager elected by these same families.[31]

Unofficial accounts

In the meantime, another battle front had opened up between the forest authorities and the municipalities of the area. This time, however, the conflict did not cause whole villages to mobilise and did not produce extraordinary gestures such as the massive abusive cuts of the summer of 1816. It was a less obvious controversy, but no less important, since it concerned an issue that was sensitive for all parties: municipalities, local populations, forest magistrates, government authorities. This was the forest tax.

The French, and then the Austrian legislatures maintained that the forest sector should be financially self-sufficient. In this respect, it is indicative that, until the second half of the nineteenth century, the forest administration was answerable to the Ministry of Finance rather than the Ministry of Agriculture, despite the latter being more appropriate.[32]

---

30   The *allievi* are the plants that were not cut down in a cutting area to allow reproduction of the forest. The derogation had already been granted in the French period: ASMi, *Agricoltura, parte moderna*, b. 45, 18 Mar. 1813.

31   See the guidelines for the participation in forest works in ACA, *Atti di amministrazione*, 1818, b. 56, 27 Mar. 1818; ACCS, *Corrispondenza*, 1839, 30 Sept. 1839. For a general description of the *lavoranzie* system ASVe, *Ispettorato generale ai boschi*, 1835–1839, b. 213, f. 27.

32   Lazzarini 2009, p. 154.

There were essentially two sources of income from which to meet the high management costs: revenues from fines for forest offences and, above all, those deriving from the tax on cutting rights. The latter corresponded to one tenth of the net value of the timber obtained from any cutting concession in a public woodland, including the work carried out in the common woodlands.[33] This was for the protection of the forests and for their better economic exploitation, the main purposes for which the forest inspectorates had been established, as explained by the director of state property, Domenico Aita, in a letter addressed to the municipalities of the Auronzo district.[34] However, the view of the local populations on the legitimacy of the tax was quite different. It was perceived as a tax imposed to support a magistracy which, as we have seen, was considered only a hindrance to the smooth functioning of the forest works.

Already in 1812, just one year after the issuing of the new forest legislation, the municipalities of Cadore asked to postpone the payment of the tenth from the time of drafting contracts to the next May fair, when most of the forest products were sold to the merchants and taken down river. The actual payment had then always been delayed such that, after the restructuring of the forest administration by the Austrians, it was decided to settle the outstanding debts owed by the Cadore municipalities to the directorate of state property with a series of extraordinary cuts to be carried out in the spring of 1817.[35]

Thus the debt burden seemed to have been definitively resolved and the collection of the tenth took place with regularity during the first years of Austrian rule. However, at the beginning of 1819, rumours about the illegal actions of the municipal administrations of the district of Auronzo in carrying out forest work became more and more insistent.

According to the available documentation, the first formal accusation was presented to the Venetian government on 6 February

---

33 Decree 28 Sept. 1811 n. 236 *Bollettino delle leggi del Regno d'Italia*, II, Milano 1811, pp. 934–40. From 1837, the tax was reduced to eight per cent, see governmental notification 1 Sept. 1837 n. 27599–2789.

34 ASVe, *Direzione Generale del Demanio, Provincie Venete*, 1815–1819, b. 15, f. 31.

35 ASVe, *Direzione Generale del Demanio, Provincie Venete*, 1815–1819, b. 15, f. 6 and f. 95.

1819.[36] From that moment, practically every district and provincial office with minimum competency on the matter produced reports aimed at sanctioning such behaviour. Even so, as was written at the conclusion of the investigation, 'for some the sense of duty, for others the fear of being compromised provided strong incentive to putting forward resolute denunciations and representations'.[37]

In the following weeks, the numerous reports that reached Venice presented a picture of systematic violation of forest tax regulations by all the municipalities of the district, with the likely complicity of various other local magistrates. In addition to the various deputies of the municipalities involved, the main suspects were the chancellor, Marco Bognolo, his successor Talamini (from 1819, district commissioner), the head of the municipal foresters Giovanni Battista Corte and, once again, the forestry inspector Francesco Perucchi. Given the questionable loyalty of all those able to carry out the investigations on the spot, the provincial director of state property, Carlo Malgrani, was sent to the district as a government commissioner. He had for a long time been an official in the directorate of state property, where he had served during the previous periods of Austrian and French rule; and he was considered immune to any compromise with the Cadore interests, since he had recently been transferred to Belluno from the office in Udine, where he had served for the previous eighteen years.[38]

Malgrani's investigations lasted for over a year, from March 1820 to June 1821, and his findings outlined a well-tried system of widespread lawlessness. Overall, between 1815 and 1820, the municipalities of the Auronzo district had evaded the payment of 60,086 lire due to the directorate of state property for the tenth, which corresponded to illicit timber sales with a net value of more than 600,000 lire.

---

36   ASVe, *Senato di Finanza*, 1819, III/3, b. 266.

37   ASVe, *Direzione Generale del Demanio*, Presidio, b. 559, the final report is dated 20 June 1821. Apart from some specific details, I take information on the event from here. Also interesting is the slip of the tongue made by the author of a joint response that the municipal deputies of the district of Auronzo sent to the authorities on 24 Apr. 1819. In denying any wrongdoing in the payment of the tenth for the previous year, he also referred to 1817: ACA, *Atti di amministrazione*, 1819, b. 58.

38   ASVe, *Presidio di Governo*, 1815–1819, XII, b. 142, f. 6/I.

Chapter 3

Every municipality of the district managed two separate budgets. The first was the official one, from which were obtained the estimated and final accounts that were submitted to checks by the authorities. The second one, as Commissioner Malgrani explains, was defined as a 'register of the *regola*' and was compiled in secret and then bequeathed when the municipal deputies were being replaced. This latter one contained higher revenue and expenditure figures than those legally recognised. The higher revenues were generated in two main ways: (a) through the sale of trees, the cutting of which had not been authorised by the forestry administration; (b) through providing a different estimate of the costs for the cutting, preparation and transport of the timber which, as we have seen, were managed directly by the municipal administrations. As for undeclared expenses, they consisted of two main items: (i) the purchase of grain to be distributed to the inhabitants in greater quantities than permitted by the government authorities; (ii) gratuities for the municipal deputies and other local officials.

This had all become possible as a result of the dubious behaviour of the main state officials at the local level, even if Malgrani declared that he did not have sufficient evidence to determine whether the conduct of Chancellor Bognolo and Forest Inspector Perucchi was the result of ineptitude or connivance with the municipal administrations, while suspicions about Commissioner Talamini seemed unfounded.[39]

---

39   The work of Francesco Perucchi and Marco Bognolo was sanctioned by the commissioner at the directorate of state property, Guido Avesani, in a letter dated 14 Mar. 1822: ASVe, *Direzione Generale del Demanio*, Presidio, b. 559. Regarding Bognolo, it should be added that, over the following years, his career seemed to take on more the features of the gangster than of the district commissioner. In San Pietro, where he 'operated' between the late 1820s and early 1830s, he managed to be accused of every embezzlement and abuse of office imaginable: he altered the minutes of municipal meetings as he pleased to foment discontent between the municipalities of the district, he pushed to have his protégés appointed to the municipal administrations, he took over rooms reserved for public functions for his own lodgings, he arrested people in order to extort money for their release and demanded bribes for every task within his office (the granting of passports and stamp duties, authorisation of river passages and so on). As for his private life, this matched his behaviour in public: he preferred married women, and by one of them he had a son. The most striking episodes of this exceptional career are summarised in ASVe, *Governo*, 1835–1839, XXXV, b. 5085, f. 8/5.

As in the case of the abusive cuts made on Mount Pera, Perucchi did not hesitate in replying to the accusations made against him by his superiors. The inspector reiterated that the forest division assigned to him was too large, and the surface area and economic value of the woodlands under his supervision was too great. Faced with these vast duties, the staff at his disposal was minimal and the inspector was often constrained to delegate numerous tasks to the municipal foresters. The latter were appointed from the inhabitants of the municipalities, and therefore could not be relied upon to oppose abuses committed by most of their fellow citizens or even by their own officials. This was all the more the case given their low salary, which was in itself an incentive to find other, less lawful, sources of livelihood.[40]

On this point, the government agreed with the issues raised by the forest inspector of Cadore and arranged to assign him an assistant. The forestry apprentice Francesco Erasmo Coletti was assigned to this role, succeeding Perucchi in the following decade.[41] The government also consented to the request of the municipalities of the Auronzo district to be able to postpone payment of the tenth until the timber had been sold to the merchants rather than payin at the time of felling.[42]

There was also discussion of a possible withdrawal of the exemption, granted a few years earlier, from the forest regulation that stipulated an auction system for the cutting and logging works. However, the government commissioner Malgrani firmly opposed this point. He declared that, having had concerns over the common management of the forest works when he first came to Cadore, he had now changed his mind after seeing the flourishing state of the woodlands in the area thanks to the cutting criteria traditionally adopted at the local level. According to Malgrani, it was a method that was certainly burdensome for the forest administration, but that had many good qualities. The main advantage was 'that the commoners, co-owners of the woodlands, being jealous to preserve their property as far as possible in order to pass it on to future generations', take great care not to damage

---

40   ASVe, *Direzione Generale del Demanio*, Presidio, b. 559, 22 June 1822.

41   ASVe, *Ispettorato Generale ai boschi*, b. 669, f. 20.

42   ASVe, *Senato di Finanza*, 1821, XI, b. 488, f. 5/8.

trees that are too young when carrying out the cutting and logging work, thus guaranteeing a better regeneration of the forest area.[43]

As for the total sum owed from evasion of the forest tax in the years up to 1820, the municipalities were offered a compromise, a less burdensome sum than the 60,000 Austrian lire previously demanded. However, the municipal authorities did not pay the debt, so that the outstanding amount was still due in 1863.[44] Finally, as regards the perpetrators of the fraud and their likely accomplices, from the documents available in the archives of the Venetian courts, it seems that none of the local officials were brought to trial for these offences.

The cow of the poor

Another cause of disputes between the forest authorities and the populations of the mountain areas concerned the relationship between woodland and pasture. As has already been emphasised, in customary agrarian regimes these two environments were characterised by a strong complementarity. The forest areas, especially the less dense ones, were often used also as grazing land, in order to maximise the use of the scarce productive land in the valleys for cultivation and production of fodder.[45] Furthermore, the woodlands provided a raft of products used for raising animals. In addition to the obvious need for wood for the construction of winter shelters for animals and to shape the tools needed for the manufacture of dairy products, the collection of dead leaves allowed the provision of litter for livestock, while the lower branches of trees were often used as alternative forage.

Already under the *ancien régime* there was awareness of the damage that pastoral activities could bring to the woodlands. Both the rural statutes and Venetian legislation contained constraints and prohibitions in this respect. However, the statutory provisions made at local

---

43   ASVe, *Direzione Generale del Demanio*, Presidio, b. 559, 20 June 1821 and 9 Aug. 1822.

44   ASVe, *Luogotenenza*, 1862–1866, 41, b. 1549, f. 2/34. ACA, *Amministrazione*, 1854–1888, I, b. 266.

45   Moreno, Poggi 1996. For other regions, see the definition of 'wood pastures' and 'savanna' proposed in Rackham 1982; Rackham 1996.

Figure 7.

Ex voto; Saint Nicholas, the patron saint of the raftmen, intercedes with the Virgin Mary to help a drowning man; nineteenth century. Source: Museo degli Zattieri del Piave, Codissago.

level aimed at optimising the complementarity between these two activities. On the other hand, as regards the woodlands attached in various ways to the rural communities, the prohibitions repeatedly mentioned in the Venetian legislation must be seen more as a recognition of the phenomenon than as a concrete attempt to limit its spread.[46]

A very different attitude took hold during the final decades of the eighteenth century. This period was characterised by the extensive debate on deforestation that I have already discussed. Within this new context, pastoral activities were considered one of the main reasons for the contraction of the forest area. However, if pasturing per se was defined as harmful to the woodlands, the problem was considered more

---

46   See the previous chapters and also Lazzarini 2004a.

or less serious depending on the type of herd, according to a scale that set the economic value of the species beside the environmental damage. The grazing of cattle was partially tolerated – or at least not harshly opposed – even in areas adjacent to woodlands, while the most severe criticism was directed towards the grazing of small animals, especially goats, which were often described as the scourge of the woodlands.[47] One of many people interested in the issue at that time was Cesare Beccaria, a notable exponent of the Italian enlightenment, who in a memorandum to improve the use of the common woodlands in Lombardy, advised imposing a limit of only one goat per family.[48]

As for the other guidelines on forestry policy proposed by the new science of silviculture and, more broadly, by those engaging in the scientific debate of the second half of the eighteenth century, it was the Napoleonic administrators who adopted these points and made them their own at the start of the nineteenth century. Indeed, the assessments written in the specialist journals of the period were used and repeated with the same terms and forms of expression in the reports drawn up by the prefects of the Kingdom of Italy in the early nineteenth century. The prefect of the department of the Piave, for example, thus expressed himself in a letter to the Ministry of the Interior in December 1806:

> It may seem paradoxical to your excellence, when I inform you that the villagers are seeking to destroy with their own hands the source of their wealth and their only means of sustenance ... They put themselves at the mercy of hordes of goats by allowing them to enter the woodlands; these goats climb up into the large trees, tearing the bark, causing them to become diseased and often to die, or devouring the tender buds as they appear.[49]

There is no doubt that the actions of the French administration were inspired by the silvicultural proposals of the previous decades, and indeed were based on them. However, it is in the concrete implementation of these precepts that the limitations of this approach to the forest question emerge, particularly in the mountain areas. The

---

47   Armiero 2000.

48   Vecchio 1974, p. 21.

49   ASMi, *Agricoltura, parte moderna*, b. 22, 21 Dec. 1806.

decree of 27 May 1811, in its very formulation, is a case in point, since there is a clear discrepancy between the strongly assertive – and groundbreaking – aspirations of the new legislation and the room for derogation – or mediation – which it also guaranteed when the regulation was introduced.

The regulation of grazing is addressed in the fourth title of the law, that concerning the rights of use to which public woodlands were subject, since for the legislators this problem was part of the more complex issue of the customary use of the common land, as claimed by the local population.[50] Articles 30–35 regulated grazing rights in the public woods, with particular reference to common woodlands. Articles 30–32 regulated grazing in general. In short, it was the task of the forest administration to allocate to each municipality, or to the inhabitants who claimed special rights in this matter, the areas where livestock could be grazed; but only in those woodlands where, because of the age and species of the trees, no damage could be caused by the animals. There followed Article 33, which stated, verbatim:

> Under no circumstances will anyone who has pasturing rights be permitted to send or lead to pasture in the public woodlands – state or municipal – as well as in the private woodlands, woolly animals, such as goats, lambs and rams. The same prohibition applies also in uncultivated areas and on the moors at the end of the woodlands.[51]

This was a total prohibition, therefore, applying not only to woodlands, regardless of their nature, but also to lands adjacent to them. Yet, Article 35 (Article 34 specified the penalties) indicated the criteria for derogating from the rules as previously laid out, with specific reference to Article 33.

The difficulties and ambivalences inherent in the fight against the grazing of goats emerge also from the deliberations of the French, and then Austrian, officials of the directorate of state property. The most articulate reflection on the issue was that of Giuseppe Gautieri, a Lom-

---

50 Another example of continuity with the writings of the previous decades: 'as far as the mountain areas are concerned, the problem of grazing is often seen as part of the wider issue of the common lands' – see Vecchio 1974, p. 37.

51 *Bollettino delle leggi del Regno d'Italia*, I, Milano 1811, pp. 424–25.

bard official of the directorate of state property under both the French and the Austrians, and author of various writings, including a renowned manual for forest employees.[52] Gautieri devoted a volume of over 330 pages to the specific issue of grazing goats, and here the assessments of both the man of science and the government official stand out clearly. Indeed Gautieri, as well as being a mid- to high-level official, was also an example of an educated elite, very much a product of the agrarian academies, a profile that was not uncommon in that period.[53] To a greater extent than other authors of that circle, 'one sees in Gautieri an official who speaks from personal and daily experience, an expert who knows well which species of tree suffer more and which suffer less from the nibbling of animals; and therefore he does not push for a general drive to banish livestock, something almost impossible to carry out'.[54]

The preface of his work, a dedication to Antonio Psalidi, the director of the state property of Milan, reads more like a dystopic novel than a scientific treatise:

> The picture I present to you is rather loathsome, but true ... Goats defended by cunning and powerful watchmen threaten to drive away the cows and sheep from the mountain. The woods are destroyed by the goats, and the mines lie disused in the bosom of the earth, the ovens and forges no longer smoke, and the miners, the diggers, the charcoal burners, the smelters and other workers, exhausted from hunger, are constrained to emigrate from the mountain. The mountains are subject to landslides, the trees are weakened from the cold on the slopes, the riverbeds are silted up and unable to contain their waters, which are already overflowing and flooding the countryside below, the snow and glaciers spread and creep lower, the huts of the mountain people are burnt down by lightning, the crops on the plain are withered, the houses are unsafe...[55]

However, the tone of the writing became much less Manichean

---

52   Gautieri 1812. See also Gautieri 1817.

53   Gautieri 1816. Curiously, under the name of the author appear the two particular distinctions: 'General Inspector to the Woodlands' and 'Member of many academies and literary societies'; although I am inclined to believe that the choice is determined more by vainglory than by any awareness of this possible interpretation of his work.

54   Vecchio 1974, p. 207. On Gautieri, see also Gené 1833.

55   Gautieri 1816, pp. not numerated.

when discussing the grazing of goats.[56] Although he listed the numerous kinds of direct and indirect damage caused by the goats and their 'destructive tooth', Gautieri was aware that 'to the poor the goat is often necessary' and 'to the mountain man, for whom the maintenance of the goats costs nothing or very little during the eight or nine months when he lives with them on the mountain, it is clear that this animal brings him a considerable advantage'.[57] Therefore, Gautieri reiterated the advisability of banishing the goats from the woodlands, but placed the problem within a more comprehensive policy of state intervention in mountain areas, which should aim to encourage a reconversion of pasture farming to the grazing of sheep, or at least some species that would cause less harm (for example, Angora goats).

Gautieri also noted in his writing the limited effectiveness of the prohibitions hitherto placed on the grazing of goats in mountain areas. He listed numerous prefectural reports from which it emerged that not even the new French legislation had been able to contain the problem.[58] This did not change with the return of the Austrians; from the reports coming from the various districts, it seems that directives of the central government had a limited effect in this sense, whereas the practical application of Article 33 of the 1811 law depended on how determined the various forest inspectors were and also on power relations at the local level.[59]

Of the territories placed under the control of the Venetian government, the province of Belluno, after that of Vicenza, was the one

---

56 These opening words have probably prompted some scholars to misunderstand Gautieri's attitude towards the grazing of goats, attributing to him a rather intransigent position, whereas in fact his proposals were among the most conciliatory of the time; cf. Sansa 1997; Corti 2006. In this regard, note the much more rigid attitude assumed by Melchiorre Gioia in his departmental investigations, for whose bibliographic and archival details I refer to Sofia 1997.

57 Gautieri 1816, pp. 323–24.

58 Gautieri 1816, pp. 267–73.

59 Some examples in Corti 2006. For the Cadore area, see the answers provided by the municipal administration of Comelico Superiore to a questionnaire sent to the municipalities of the province of Belluno by the conservator to the woods, Gaspare Doglioni. These show that the forest law of 1811 had not caused any change at the local level regarding the management of goat grazing: ACCS, *Corrispondenza*, 1815–1816, questionnaire dated 2 Oct. 1815, answers dated 30 Oct. 1815.

where, according to the authorities, the grazing of goats had assumed epidemic proportions and caused the greatest damage.[60] The issue also concerned the Cadore area, but the districts most affected by the phenomenon were the pre-Alpine ones, in the south of the province. In 1818, for example, following the continuing devastation caused by the grazing of goats and sheep in the woodlands of Feltre district, the area's forestry inspector decided that the full application of Article 33 was necessary to preserve the woodlands of his area from further damage. The news of this decision provoked such protests that the inspector was prompted to do a U-turn 'so as not to compromise public order'.[61]

At that point, the real risk of an increase in social tension pushed the government to directly manage the affair for the entire province. The report presented by Domenico Aita on that occasion summed up the essential points of the issue:

> Although the directorate [of state property], considering only the welfare of the woodlands, would wish to prevent the introduction of grazing animals of the forbidden species into these areas, and especially goats, it is forced to confess that the sudden exclusion of these would be both impossible and harmful. Impossible because whatever the level of surveillance, it would never be possible to get such large numbers of these unruly animals to respect the forest land ... harmful because leaving so many animals without food would cause incalculable damage to both the private owner and the public economy.[62]

These arguments are also candidly made in the few documents that reveal the attitudes on this issue of the weakest sections of the mountain population. Often the petitions sent to the authorities and signed by many heads of families emphasised that the desire to graze goats was not a voluntary choice for the majority of the population but a necessity, since few families were wealthy enough to own cattle, and only the possession of a goat, the 'cow of the poor', could ensure an adequate food supply for the most needy.[63]

---

60 ASVe, *Senato di Finanza*, 1825–1829, XI, b. 773, f. 1/9; ASVe, *Magistrato Camerale*, 1830–1834, XXIV, b. 286, f. 1/2; ASVe, *Magistrato Camerale*, 1830–1834, XXIV, b. 550, f. 1/5.

61 ASVe, *Senato di Finanza*, 1824, XI, b. 672, f. 1/2.

62 ASVe, *Senato di Finanza*, 1824, XI, b. 672, f. 1/2.

63 ACCS, *Corrispondenza*, 1839, 20 Apr. 1838.

It is not easy to assess the real effectiveness of the legislation regarding loose pasturage and its relative importance within a more comprehensive conjunctural transformation, which was already underway throughout the Alps and which included among its characteristic features the transition from predominantly ovine-goat farming to dairy cow farming. This process took place at different times and to varying degrees in the various subregions that made up the Alpine chain, but it accelerated during the nineteenth century, when institutional and administrative changes combined with significant economic and social factors.[64]

A similar point must be made regarding the other major subject of legislation on this issue, the grazing of sheep. The law of 25 June 1856 abolished the *pensionatico*, a grazing easement that people or legal bodies enjoyed on others' lands during the winter period and that they gave to the shepherds during the months when the flocks came down to winter on the plains.[65] This practice was increasingly opposed by developments within agronomic science, which considered it as harmful to agriculture as loose pasturing was to the forest economy. The effects of the abolition of the *pensionatico* did not directly affect the mountain areas, such as the province of Belluno, where there were very few territories subject to this servitude, but it indirectly involved them since in some communities transhumant pastoralism played a central role in providing income for many families.[66]

Which sustainability?

So far, these events have been described from the perspective of a relatively limited area such as Cadore. However, we can also consider

---

64 For an overview on animal farming in the Alpine economy, see Mathieu 2001. For the analysis of these dynamics at the local level, see Zannini, Gazzi 2003.

65 On the *pensionatico* and the debate preceding its abolition see Berengo 1963; Novello 1996.

66 An example in this sense is the community of Lamon, in the south-western part of the province of Belluno: see Conte 2001, p. 43. For the distribution of this easement in the Venetian provinces: ASVe, *Prefettura delle finanze*, 1852–1856, XVIII, b. 563, f. 37/23.

them from a broader perspective, as the progressive imposition of models of centralist management of the forest resources, inspired by the new science of silviculture. This phenomenon took hold in most European states between the eighteenth and nineteenth centuries, and was subsequently imposed, during the nineteenth century, in the colonial territories gradually acquired by the major European powers.

Recent historiography has identified in the spread of this new approach to resource management – first of all within scientific thinking and, over time, also at the institutional level – a constitutive phase in the development of theories of environmental conservation and, perhaps, of proto-environmentalist thinking.[67]

Retrospectively, what made this development one of the first examples of concern for environmental conservation was the concept of sustainability. This notion is widely used today in public debate and in academic thinking on ecological issues, but it has its roots in the 'sustainable yield' approach developed by German silviculture for the exploitation of forest resources. Today, the most cited definition is that proposed in 1987 in the report of the so-called Brundtland commission: 'Sustainable development is development that meets the needs of the present without compromising the ability of future generations to meet their own needs'.[68] The idea introduced two centuries earlier by the emerging science of silviculture was to develop a system of management of woodland areas able to ensure the maximum production of wood mass without compromising the continuity of cuts over the long term. In both cases, these are very generic formulations leading to controversial – or misleading – interpretations. In fact, it is difficult to define the criteria for evaluating a sustainable management of resources and, above all, to establish who is responsible for identifying these parameters.[69]

Let us examine, for example, the issue of goat grazing and the dam-

---

67   Jacoby 2001, pp. 4–6; Radkau 2005; Dargavel, Johann 2013; Guha 2016, pp. 59–65

68   WCED 1987, p. 43.

69   For a critical analysis of the concept of sustainability, cf. Worster 1993, pp. 142–55; Radkau 1996, p. 66; Stuber 2008. With a different approach, Paul Warde has contextualised the silvicultural idea of sustainability in a broader framework: see Warde 2018.

age it caused to young trees and to the reproduction of woodlands. Perhaps the tones adopted in the writings of the eighteenth and nineteenth centuries were overemphatic, but there is no doubt that the massive presence of this animal in wooded areas harmed their sustainability as understood by the main forestry experts. However, the goat assumed a very different role from the point of view of the economic and social sustainability of many mountain communities, which derived essential resources for their subsistence from goat farming.

The issue was raised by Arrigo Serpieri among others, with regard to a notorious 'anti-goat' law issued by the fascist regime in 1927, about which he stated: 'in these conditions, even the sacred protections of forests, even the war against goats is becoming cruel'. And, a few years later, reflecting on the forest policy to be adopted for the mountain regions, Serpieri noted the risks and contradictions of an approach that did not support policies of environmental sustainability alongside social and economic policies:

> I believed, and I still do, that we cannot implement in our mountains the same forest policy as France or Germany because our forest policy cannot be disconnected from the integral needs of mountain economy and life. We cannot defend and enlarge our forests, although these measures would be fundamental for their protection, against mountaineers and their lives.[70]

Regarding the application of theoretical reflections on forest issues at the local level, it is possible to highlight the ambiguous – and sometimes misleading – use made of such apparently objective, scientific notions; the various significations that the social actors involved could assign to the woodlands and their 'sustainable use'; the ongoing negotiations in which the silvicultural precepts were steadily mediated; and, finally, the active role played by the local population in redefining these precepts and in influencing the development of silvicultural thinking.[71]

It is possible, for example, to understand in this sense the ideological assumptions that fuelled the eighteenth and nineteenth century

---

70 Both the quotations are in Armiero 2011, pp. 117, 133.
71 Hölzl 2010.

debate on deforestation. In the publications of the period a contrast predominates between a customary management (usually associated with community forms of land use), considered ruinous for the survival of the woodlands, and a rational approach to management, based on scientific principles, thanks to the contribution of disciplines such as mathematics, statistics and cartography. At the turn of the eighteenth and nineteenth centuries, this debate favoured the adoption of legislation inspired by the new science of silviculture in most European states.

However, the only reliable data to justify the widespread alarm about the extent of deforestation was the increase in timber prices, which was caused by several factors (population growth, transport costs etc.). On the other hand, as regards fears about the disappearance or general retreat of the woodlands, this perceived phenomenon was not based on reliable statistics.[72] Moreover, even when the data of the new cadastres of that period became available – and the Lombardo-Venetian one was among the most advanced – its interpretation by contemporaries was contradictory.

It should be remembered that the various attempts to quantify the extent of the wooded areas of the province of Belluno, all based on the Lombardo-Venetian cadastre, produced conflicting results that ranged between twenty and forty per cent of the overall area of the province. To get a more reliable picture of the extent of the forested areas, it was necessary to wait for the landscape photographs taken at the end of the nineteenth century and the first aerial images taken in the twentieth century. The decades astride the nineteenth and twentieth centuries seem to be the period when the forested area reached its lowest extent in many European countries. Yet, if we accept this fact, we must also consider the bankruptcy of the forest policy adopted in the nineteenth century and inspired by silvicultural thinking.[73]

In fact, the actions of the forest administrations of the early nineteenth century were not driven by concern for deforestation, nor by other environmental considerations, but by the search for an economic sustainability of forest resources that would allow them to

---

72   Warde 2006b, p. 34; Sansa 2012.

73   Tello 2009, p. 624; Zannini 2012b, p. 509.

meet market demands and state requirements. One example is sufficiently indicative. During the early years of the Austrian forest administration in Lombardy-Venetia, projects already sketched out in previous decades were relaunched, providing for the systematic replacement of beech trees with conifers of greater economic value (fir and larch) in some state woodlands of the mountain areas (Cansiglio, Somadida and some forests of the Carnic Alps). The intervention, only partly implemented at that time, today would 'cause not only environmentalists to shudder but also foresters, long oriented towards a silviculture based on naturalistic principles'.[74]

Likewise, we should not completely dismiss the charges made by the silvicultural experts of the period against the rural population, which was always held as being mainly responsible for the degraded state of the forests.[75] However, some clarification is in order. There were two main reasons why an area of woodland could become broken down: the need for wood and the need for land. In the latter case, the choice was motivated by the convenience of converting that area to another form of use such as agriculture, and by the advantages deriving from this conversion. In the Veneto area, this happened in many parts of the plain and in the foothills, both before and during the centuries of Venetian rule, and especially in the period following the War of Candia, when the Serenissima had supported the privatisation and cultivation of much common land (1646–1727).

This was not the case in Cadore. In this area, as in most of the eastern Alps, the woodlands were still in the nineteenth century the main source of subsistence both for local institutions and for a large part of the population. Although there were innumerable abuses and intensive exploitation of resources, all of which grew during the nineteenth century alongside anthropic pressure, the accusations, so frequent in agronomic writings, that describe the rural population as intent on deliberately destroying their main means of survival, appear designed to

---

74 On the Carnic Alps: Bianco, Lazzarini 2003 (quotation at p. 94); on Cansiglio: Lazzarini 2002b; on Somadida: ASVe, *Direzione Generale del Demanio, Provincie Venete*, 1815–1819, b. 14, f. 43.

75 On the risk of idealising certain preindustrial systems of resource management, see McNeill 1992, p. 354.

serve particular interests.[76] In fact, not only was there a presumed economic rationality in place that tried to limit profit in order to perpetuate the return, but it is also important to remember that the system of exploitation of forest resources had been developed and practised over a long time through a profound empirical knowledge of the territorial context. This had allowed the population to become aware both of the potentialities offered by the exploitation of the woodlands and of the environmental constraints that limited this exploitation.[77] Interesting evidence of this awareness emerges from the toponymic analysis of some wooded areas as recorded and described during the cadastral survey carried out in Cadore and the rest of Belluno province:

> For example, at Selva, in the woodland called 'Colmarchie' every activity was forbidden because it protected the houses from avalanches. Again, in the 'Piei di Sopra' woodland, all cutting was prohibited in order to protect the village of Borca. Likewise the 'Bandito' woodland of Fonzaso was so called because it was forbidden to cut there, again for the safety of the village, threatened by avalanches and boulders. And then there was the 'Gliausel' beech wood, functional to the security of the village of Villa Piccola di Auronzo.[78]

Moreover, that the traditional management systems of the Cadore woodlands were far from irrational and that local practices were far from being the only cause of deforestation emerges from the considerations and comments of those very forestry (and state) officials who were in charge of introducing the silvicultural innovations that would have allowed the replacement of customary systems of woodland exploitation.

We can dismiss the commendatory tones with which Francesco Perucchi described the forestry activities of the Cadore population, since his superiors suspected him of connivance with respect to various forestry offences. And this would also apply to the chancellor Marco Bognolo who, in May 1818, in response to a government investigation into possible improvements to the common lands, stated that in the

---

76   Radkau 2008, p. 149.

77   Vecchio, Piussi, Armiero 2002, pp. 150–54.

78   Scarpa 1996, p. 171. Other examples in ASVe, *Ispettorato Generale ai Boschi*, 1824, r. 207 (the most common toponym was 'wood over the houses').

woodlands of his district no improvements were conceivable since

> these woodlands, due to the essential role of their products, are regarded
> as sacred property, and it is impossible to describe the zealous attention
> and the meticulous care with which they are guarded and managed. For
> this reason one can calmly maintain that the forest administration is su-
> perfluous in my district, and indeed could be detrimental to the prosperity
> and welfare of those same woodlands.[79]

And yet, even the provincial director of state property, Carlo Malgrani, who had been sent to Cadore because he was considered a stranger to the area, praised the cutting systems traditionally used in the area as the most suitable to ensure the regeneration of the woodlands. However, the most significant affirmation of the validity of the cutting method practised in Cadore came from Adolfo di Bérenger, who is considered the founder of the Italian school of silviculture, some decades later. Born in Bavaria in 1815 to a noble French family in exile, Bérenger graduated from the forestry school of Mariabrunn (near Vienna), but carried out his entire professional career in Italy. After a brief period of service in Parma, he entered the Lombardo-Venetian forest admin-istration, where he remained until the annexation of the region to the Kingdom of Italy, holding various positions including that of forestry inspector of Cadore between 1849 and 1856.[80]

From a brief, and in some ways unjust, comparison between Franc-esco Perucchi and Adolfo di Bérenger, the evolution of the staff that made up the Lombardo-Venetian forest administration becomes evi-dent. Francesco Perucchi can be considered a typical example of the employees who became part of the forest system in the early nine-teenth century, a period when, due to political instability and a lack of adequately trained personnel, a basic practical knowledge of the subject and a certain bureaucratic experience were sufficient to ac-cess a position, even at high levels, within the forest administration. In this sense, Perucchi, who had been a timber merchant and active in other branches of the local administration, also exemplified the

79   ASMi, *Censo, parte moderna*, b. 916, 13 May 1818.
80   For a profile of Adolfo di Bérenger, see Agnoletti 2001. On his office in Cadore:
     ASVe, *Ispettorato generale ai boschi*, 1845–1849, b. 330, f. 59.

Chapter 3

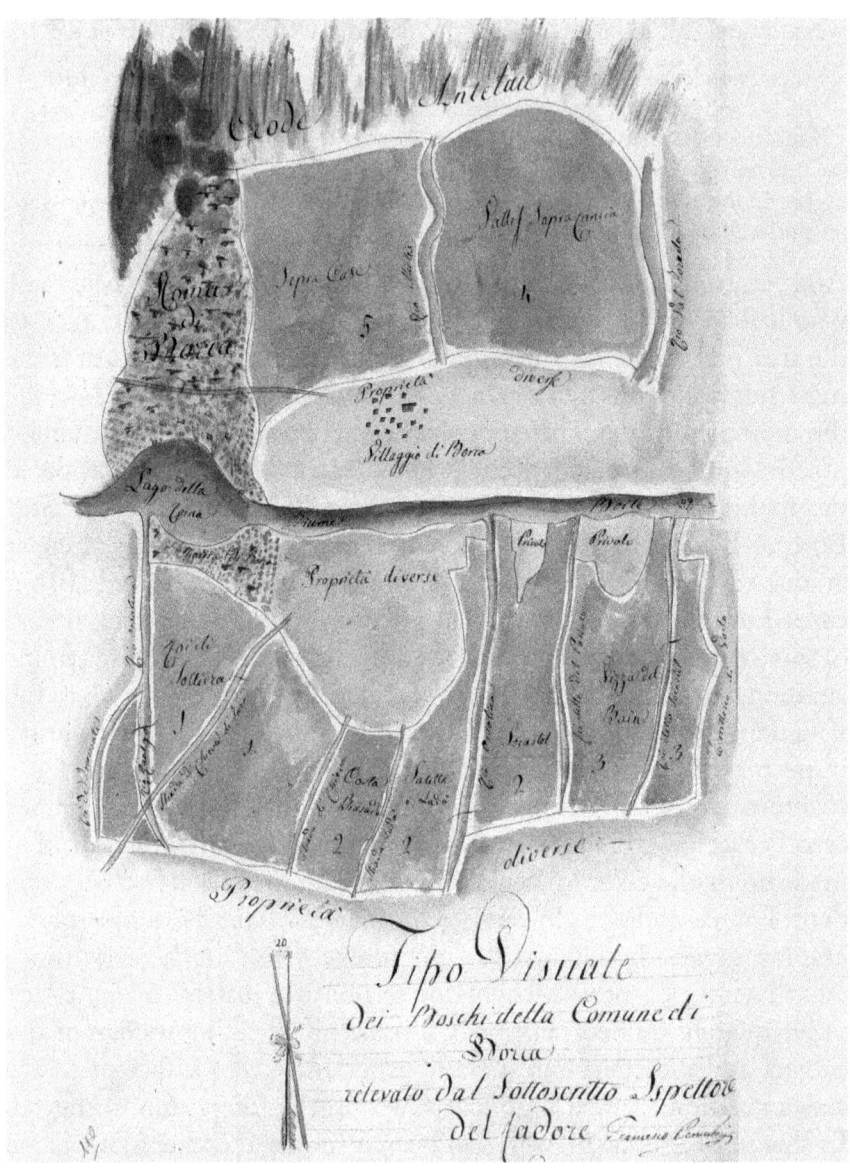

Figure 8.

Bosco sopra le case [wood over the houses] near the village of Borca – example of a protected woodland toponym, early-nineteenth century map. Source: BSC, digital archive.

contradictions between the awareness of the increasing importance of the forest sector on the part of the heads of government and the lack of scientific training of the staff assigned to work in this sector.

In the following decades, the situation slowly changed as the gradual turnover of personnel was managed according to criteria that favoured the recruitment and promotion of staff with adequate theoretical training (even if abuses very often continued). At first, graduate engineers from the University of Padua were recruited. These came with a good technical and scientific training, but were not necessarily trained in forestry. Then, from the end of the 1830s, those who had graduated from the forestry school at Mariabrunn were given priority.[81]

Adolfo di Bérenger is certainly the best-known example from this later period, although he was better educated and more able than his colleagues. Indeed, it is difficult to find someone of equal prestige, not only in Veneto, but also in the whole of nineteenth-century Italian forestry. His path, however, helps us to understand the direction in which he took silviculture in the new state when he became director of the first forestry school set up by the Kingdom of Italy at Vallombrosa, near Florence.[82]

Bérenger was trained within the German silvicultural world and, even in his mature works, the theoretical references most cited in his writings are from the greatest exponents of the German school. In fact, the only experts really taken into account by the Lombardo-Venetian forestry administration were German.[83] And given his vast scientific expertise, Bérenger does not hesitate to criticise harshly the abuses committed by the rural populations, timber merchants and even local

81   Lazzarini 2009, pp. 111–94.

82   Di Bérenger's theories also influenced the founding father of American conservationism, George Perkins Marsh, who was friendly with Bérenger during his years in Italy and who praised Bérenger's book, *Studii di archeologia forestale*, as the 'most learned work ever published on the social history of forestry': see Hall 1998, p. 94.

83   The volumes bought for the library of the forest administration headquarters were indicative of this trend: almost all the books were in German, so that it was necessary to purchase an Italian-German dictionary, ASVe, *Prefettura delle finanze*, 1857–1861, XXX, b. 947, f. 9/2.

officials in the sectors in which he found himself operating.[84] At the same time, however, in his reflections it is possible to observe a gradual move towards a more hybrid form of forest science, with the assimilation and codification of empirical practices that Bérenger, like other forest experts working in very different territorial contexts, held to be as valid as the theoretical precepts of his training.[85]

Bérenger's many years of service were carried out for the most part in mountain areas; and, in the light of the very particular historical and environmental characteristics of the Italian peninsula, especially its mountain regions, he came to understand that Italian forestry policy could not be based on a simple re-presentation of theories elaborated in – and for – very different territorial contexts.

As regards the high-timber woodlands, for example, Bérenger always opposed the use of the clear-cutting method of German forestry and felt that the traditional cutting method based on single cuts (with the integration of sectional division) yielded the best results economically and in terms of forest conservation, as he had observed in woodlands of the Veneto mountain regions during his appointment in that area.[86] Another example of Bérenger's pragmatic attitude emerges in his reflections on the role of lunar phases in determining the most suitable times for cutting operations, which had caused so much tension in Cadore during those first few years when the new legislation was implemented. While reiterating that the most eminent forest scientists (Duhamel, Heyer, Sauer, Shübel) doubted the effects usually attributed to the phases of the moon, Bérenger added a qualification:

> However, it is wise not to reject wholly such grave opinion, consecrated by the authority and consent of the centuries, and rooted in the traditional elements of the rude science of the people. With all due respect to the validity and force of modern theories, they are not enough to refute such constant convictions held by both peoples and writers.[87]

---

84   Cfr. ASVe, *Ispettorato generale ai boschi*, 1850–1854, b. 410, f. 43; ASVe, *Prefettura delle Finanze*, 1862–1866, XXVIII, b. 1445, f. 2/40.

85   Rothman 1994; Whited 2000; Sansa 2009; Hölzl 2011.

86   Lazzarini 2008a, p. 170. The reference is to di Bérenger 1871.

87   di Bérenger 1965, p. 479.

4.

CONTESTED FORESTS

A forest of numbers

At the beginning of 1816, at the same time as the structural reorganisation of the forest system, the replacement of the 1811 legislation was proposed, since its limitations were realised even by some of the Napoleonic officials brought into the new administration. Over the following decades, various options were attempted: preliminary studies of different kinds were commissioned, committees were set up on the subject, bills were drafted, already existing regulations were put forward (for example the one issued in 1852 for the hereditary territories of the Habsburg Empire). However, as mentioned earlier, all this produced a lot of paperwork without any legislative outcome.[1]

There were various reasons for the failure of the project, despite the heads of government wanting its resolution. The interested parties were too many and too varied: the political and financial ministries of Venice and Milan (which often had conflicting interests), the navy (which until the 1840s retained special rights over public forests), and Vienna (which never allocated an adequate budget for a comprehensive reform package).[2] The issue on which I shall focus is another question, often raised in the field of forestry policy, the solution to which was considered a prerequisite for the implementation of any reform programme in this area: 'the question of the ownership and property of woodlands that through endowment had been left to the municipalities'.[3]

---

1   The main attempts were made in the 1820s, 1830s and 1850s: ASVe, *Magistrato Camerale*, 1830–1834, XXIV, b. 288, f. 29/14; ASMi, *Agricoltura, parte moderna*, b. 6. On the introduction of the law issued for the hereditary territories of the Habsburg Empire: ASVe, *Luogotenenza*, 1852–1856, LXX, b. 623, f. 1/8.

2   Cf. Lucia Coletti 1988; Lazzarini 2013.

3   ASVe, *Magistrato Camerale*, 1830–1834, XXIV, b. 288, f. 29/14. A similar assessment in ASVe, *Direzione Generale del Demanio. Provincie Venete*, 1815–1819, b. 6, f. 2.

Chapter 4

As early as November 1815, just a few months after the formal establishment of the Kingdom of Lombardy-Venetia, the question of common land had been brought to the attention of the central administration by a memorandum addressed to the new sovereign and signed by Alvise Baccanello, who had held the office of 'superintendent of *beni comunali*' before the fall of the Serenissima. This was an unusual report, presented as a *curriculum vitae* in order to obtain preferment. In it, Baccanello traced the main steps taken by the Venetian administration regarding common land; he indicated the magistrates responsible in this area and illustrated the difference between *beni comunali* and *beni comuni* (defined by him as '*comunitativi*'). Overall, the author concluded, these lands constituted 'an immense property, which could in any case offer striking resources' to achieve 'those increases in population, agriculture and livestock, which could easily be achieved from a different organisation of the lands in question'.[4]

A table was attached to the memorandum indicating the common lands registered during the time of the Republic of Venice; those sold; the proceeds from the sales; and the composition of the remaining 201,033 hectares of land ('mountainous', 'lowland', marsh or woodland), 173,482 of which were located in the provinces that formed the Austrian Veneto. The figures proposed by Baccanello were the same ones that he had presented in a table drawn up in 1790 for the Venetian administration, and referred only to property considered *beni comunali* under Venetian law.[5] Although the memorandum did not produce the desired effect regarding Baccanello's career (I have not found any subsequent preferments in favour of Alvise Baccanello), the new government took seriously the issues addressed in it.

Since the basic objective of any initiative was to establish the exact extent of these lands, their composition (woodland, pasture, marshland etc.), their distribution within the Kingdom's provinces and the ways in which they were used, the documentation preserved in the archives of the Venetian magistracy cited by Baccanello was gradually integrated with that produced by the cadastral administration.

4   ASVe, *Presidio di governo*, 1815–1819, XVI, b. 146, f. 1/4.

5   The table is published in Simonato Zasio 1993.

The result was a report presented to the government at the end of 1819 on 'the state of the common lands located in the Austro-Venetian provinces based on the cadastral registers, sales and grants of usufruct present at the offices of the magistrate of the *beni comunali*'.[6] Although the overall extent of the land surveyed was more than double that proposed by Baccanello (366,309 hectares), the appendix of the table warned about the reliability of the data since, on various occasions, it had not been possible to specify the extent of the land and its legal nature.

The main problem was that the cadastral surveys, instead of resolving the controversies, ambiguities and continuous disputes over common lands that appeared from the reading of the Venetian documents, simply superimposed themselves on them; proprietary forms and institutions that no longer had legitimacy in the post-Napoleonic legislation were transposed onto the 'modern' documents.

In a preliminary questionnaire on the state of agriculture sent to the municipal administrations by the cadastral committee, the seventh question asked 'what municipal woodlands and what private woodlands' were present in the district of the municipality. The deputation from Auronzo replied that these lands, which it called simple wooded pastures, 'had always been the common property of the community, previously referred to as freehold, now called municipal land'. The response of the other municipalities of the district was even more ambiguous (the quote is from Comelico Superiore, but the formula is similar elsewhere):

> in this district there are no municipal woods, but rather consortium woods, the exclusive property of the original men or families of these villages ... These woodlands are for the sole use of these families, who also maintain the bridges, roads and churches of their respective villages, for which purpose the aforesaid inhabitants conduct the necessary administration.[7]

These formulae are confirmed some years later in the compilation of the cadastral introductory information on the respective mu-

---

6   ASMi, *Censo, parte moderna*, b. 916, 31 Dec. 1819.

7   ASVe, *Censo stabile*, Quesiti risposte circostanze locali, b. 27.

nicipalities in 1826–27. Again, this quotation is from the file of the municipality of Comelico Superiore – and in particular from the municipal district of Casamazzagno – but it exemplifies solutions adopted for the whole district:

> There are no municipal woodlands. There are woods that are the property of the consortium of original men of the village of Casamazzagno, and other woods of the consortium of original men of the village of Candide with Spalù, and these enable them to maintain their houses and farm buildings, as well as the bridges, embankments and roads of the municipal district.[8]

The same references to shared rights and use are found for pastureland. These descriptions would not have been out of place if they had been made in the previous century. The woodlands are defined as '*consortili*', not the property of the municipality but of the 'original men', and their use is assigned on a family basis. However, they contradicted the entire legislation enacted from the Napoleonic period onwards, and in particular that Italian decree of 25 November 1806, the first article of which stated 'The property that at the time of the former Venetian republic was administered by the so-called "bodies of the original inhabitants", now defunct, is held by – and if not, is to be held by – the administrations of the respective municipalities'.[9]

In this situation, the decision of the Austrian government to bring into force the Italian decree of 25 July 1806 – which prescribed that all uncultivated common lands not needed by the inhabitants for grazing their animals should be rented or leased out in perpetuity – did not significantly affect the municipal patrimony.[10]

In fact, there remained a basic ambiguity in the definition of the lands considered municipal by the legislature (and common by the local populations).[11] On the one hand, the ownership of this property

---

8   ASVe, *Censo stabile*, Atti preparatori, b. 226.

9   *Bollettino delle leggi del Regno d'Italia*, III, Milano 1806, p. 1026.

10   *Raccolta degli atti di governo e delle disposizioni generali*, Imperial Regio Governo di Milano, I/2, 1820, p. 31.

11   As already mentioned, when I refer to these disputed lands in general terms, I shall use the expression 'common land(s)', even if, from an official point of view, they were considered municipal lands.

by the municipality, understood as an administrative body, was denied in order to uphold the freehold rights of one (or more than one) restricted group of inhabitants, the 'consortium of original inhabitants', which re-emerged also in the cadastral documents. On the other hand, in those areas where the property had previously been granted in usufruct by the Serenissima to the communities, there existed a quite different situation: the ownership of the municipality was denied in favour of an alleged ownership of the land by the state. In such a situation, any attempted intervention over common land provoked appeals and disputes, and even conflicting arguments found apparent legitimacy through convenient interpretations of the available documents.[12]

However, the situation was destined to change decisively within a few months when, in December 1820, a new report on the common land was presented to the Central Congregation of Venice, signed by the Friulian count Pietro Maniago. This was destined to influence profoundly the policy of the Austrian government in the following decades.

The noble Friulian lawyer Pietro Maniago (1768–1846) had been appointed to the Central Congregation in the summer of 1819 after three years of involvement with the provincial congregation of Udine.[13] A few days after his appointment, he was given the task of preparing a new report on common land in the Venetian provinces, at the request of the Viceroy, Archduke Ranieri.

This task absorbed Maniago until the end of 1820: his report was finally presented at the session of the Central Congregation on 27 December. It is difficult to imagine a better debut, since the reading of the report aroused much admiration amongst Maniago's colleagues who, in delivering it to the government, commended it warmly; as, more recently, did Marino Berengo who called it 'masterly'.[14]

Indeed, the author of the report had already distinguished himself

---

12 See the examples in Pitteri 2005.

13 On Maniago, see Tonetti 1991; Gianni 2011.

14 Berengo 1963, p. 129. The report is conserved in ASVe, *Congregazione Centrale*, 1844, b. 451, f. 3.2.1.

in Udine and, in the following years, he became known as one of the most competent and prepared officials of the Austrian administration. His opinion was also often sought on issues of forestry policy, where he did not shy from clashing with the general directorate of state property, showing a considerable knowledge of the most recent developments in silvicultural science.[15]

The Maniago report and the heyday of agrarian individualism

From the attachments still available, it seems that Maniago prepared his report using the same sources as had been used in the report of the previous year, i.e. the documentation of the Venetian period and the first results of the cadastral campaign. However, he seems to have conducted a more comprehensive examination and used a broader definition of common land, since he identified an overall area of more than 487,862 hectares, equal to about a fifth of the entire territory of Veneto and much higher than that proposed the previous year.[16] These lands were mainly concentrated in the provinces of Udine (256,118 hectares) and Belluno (126,016 hectares), where they represented, in both cases, about forty per cent of the provincial area.

In order to understand Maniago's point of view on the issue of common land, it is important to consider both his social status (he was a major property owner) and his geographic provenance (he was from the Friulian plain). In fact, unlike the other Venetian provinces, Udine was the only province where common lands of considerable size were still present even in the lowland areas. They were lands usually reserved by the inhabitants of the respective villages for the loose grazing of their livestock; throughout the year or, more often, between the end of September and the feast of St. Mark (25 April), the

---

15   Bianco, Lazzarini 2003, pp. 112–18; ASVe, *Magistrato Camerale*, 1830–1834, XXIV, b. 288, f. 29/14.

16   The sources used for the report are in ASVe, *Governo*, Allegati, 1821, b. 114; the statistical records in ASVe, *Governo*, Allegati, 1839, b. 278. See Tables 5–6.

Contested forests

Table 5.

Pietro Maniago's survey on common land in the Venetian provinces (1820), general overview.

Province	Belluno	Padua	Rovigo	Treviso	Udine	Venice	Verona	Vicenza	Total
Surface area	312,729.9	195,277.3	102,857.6	233,929.1	615,199.5	234,229.5	269,197.2	276,325.3	2,239,745.4
Population	109,152	233,588	124,199	211,082	306,037	137,070	216,863	266,311	1,604,302
Surface area of municipalities with common land	311,742.9	39,003.6	11,366.9	106,958.8	585,953	68,746.9	107,037.6	191,307.8	1,422,117.5
Population of municipalities with common land	108,990	54,642	10,210	9,8521	287,804	40,662	89,479	173,660	863,968
Common land owned by the municipalities	70,922.0	2,901.7	319.7	8,279.2	125,969.8	10,357.9	8,105.3	60,356	287,211.6
Common land owned by the state	55,093.3	0	0	13,249.3	130,148.2	791.5	1,237.3	131.2	200,650.8
Total	126,015.3	2,901.7	319.7	21,528.5	256,118	11,149.4	9,342.6	60,487.2	487,862.4
Value of the common land owned by the municipalities	388,688	542,004	84,621	119,559	1,116,917	158,455	225,459	974,468	3,610,171
Value of the common land owned by the state	223,073	0	0	167,724	1,082,239	26,208	44,467	8,187	1,551,898
Total	611,761	542,004	84,621	287,283	2,199,156	184,663	269,926	982,655	5,162,069
Revenue from rented lands	44,079	68,698	4,845	21,859	131,509	9,447	68,105	204,944	553,486
Projected revenue from lands not rented out	120,394	8,154	0	17,832	134,209	3,116	4,885	20,876	309,466
Total	164,473	76,852	4,845	39,691	265,718	12,563	72,990	225,820	862,952
Families with animals	14,246	3,136	425	8,720	33,856	1,895	6,729	16,749	85,756
Families without animals	5,998	8,030	1,659	7,963	19,462	9,886	12,896	19,379	85,273
Total	20,244	11,166	2,084	16,683	53,318	11,781	19,625	36,128	171,029
Animals	144,926	18,627	5,040	64,064	209,057	10,970	19,263	130,304	602,251
Surface area of municipalities without common land	987	156,273.7	91,490.7	126,970.3	29,246.5	165,482.6	162,159.6	85,017.5	817,627.9
Population of municipalities without common land	162	178,946.0	113,989.0	112,561	18,233	96,408	127,384	92,651	740,334
Families with animals	71	13,892	6,682	9,508	1,915	3,981	8,701	7,583	52,333
Families without animals	4	18,603	15,874	10,165	1,115	17,062	17,364	10,237	90,424
Total	75	32,495	22,556	19,673	3,030	21,043	26,065	17,820	142,757
Animals	464	79,483	51,186	64,867	12,108	30,645	27,310	52,090	318,153

Source: ASVe, *Governo*, Allegati, 1839, b. 278. Surface area unit hectares; monetary unit Austrian lire.

latter being the date that marked the start of the agricultural season.[17] These were lands and practices that had already in the second half of the eighteenth century been coveted by the landed elites, and also targeted by the most influential agronomic experts (two categories that frequently corresponded to the same socio-economic group).[18] Such attitudes continued during the nineteenth century and are well exemplified in the pages dedicated to the issue of common land in

17   Brunello 2011, p. 7.
18   Cf. Bianco 1997; Bianco 2003; Cittadella 2012.

Chapter 4

Table 6.

Pietro Maniago's survey on common land in the Venetian provinces (1820), overview of the province of Belluno.

District	Agordo	Auronzo	Belluno	Feltre	Fonzaso	Longarone	Mel	Pieve di Cadore	Total
Surface area	47,683.5	60,970.5	53,953.9	40,059.8	19,252.7	27,365.3	15,543.6	47,900.6	312,729.9
Population	14,419	11,439	19,032	21,935	13,265	7,373	7731	13,958	109,152
Surface area of municipalities with common land	47,683.5	60,970.5	53,953.9	40,059.8	19,252.7	26,378.3	15,543.6	47,900.6	311,742.9
Population of municipalities with common land	14,419	11,439	19,032	21,935	13,265	7,211	7,731	13,958	108,990
Common land owned by the municipalities	3,390.3	30,850.4	1,172.8	3,596.3	1,891.6	4,945.3	6,148.8	18,926.5	70,922
Common land owned by the state	5,355	0	13,443.1	16,685	6,075.6	11,998.4	1,536.2	0	55,093.3
Total	8,745.3	30,850.4	14,615.9	20,281.3	7,967.2	16,943.7	7,685	18,926.5	126,015.3
Value of the common land owned by the municipalities	21,266	214,252	4,292	37,717	3,899	16,470	57,047	33,745	388,688
Value of the common land owned by the state	78,239	0	28,376	71,206	26,989	14,082	4,181	0	223,073
Total	99,505	214,252	32,668	108,923	30,888	30,552	61,228	33,745	611,761
Revenue from rented lands	9,782	2,842	2,932	14,124	3,626	3,129	7,469	175	44,079
Projected revenue from lands not rented out	998	93,800	407	5,929	579	790	5,500	12,391	120,394
Total	10,780	96,642	3,339	20,053	4,205	3,919	12,969	12,566	164,473
Families with animals	2,441	1,726	1,837	2,697	1,833	896	749	2,067	14,246
Families without animals	637	280	832	1,652	1,130	343	763	361	5,998
Total	3,078	2,006	2,669	4,349	2,963	1,239	1,512	2,428	20,244
Animals	13,768	13,411	20,537	24,863	36,322	6,983	14,018	15,024	144,926
Surface area of municipalities without common land	0	0	0	0	0	987	0	0	987
Population of municipalities without common land	0	0	0	0	0	162	0	0	162
Families with animals	0	0	0	0	0	71	0	0	71
Families without animals	0	0	0	0	0	4	0	0	4
Total	0	0	0	0	0	75	0	0	75
Animals	0	0	0	0	0	464	0	0	464

Source: ASVe, *Governo*, Allegati, 1839, b. 278. Surface area unit hectares; monetary unit Austrian lire.

the periodical *L'Amico del contadino*, the mouthpiece of the Friulian liberal landowners published by Count Gherardo Freschi between 1842 and 1848.[19] Maniago's report is a particularly good example of this attitude towards agrarian individualism.[20] Indeed, his project was not confined to surveying the common land present in the Venetian provinces, but also indicated what was the most desirable form of manage-

19   Gaspari 1993, pp. 205–15. On Freschi, see Zanier 1998.
20   Berengo 1963, p. 129.

ment. Already in his introduction he stated, according to a formula widely used at the time, that the common lands 'precisely because they belonged to everyone, belonged to no one'.[21] It followed that they would only be adequately safeguarded and exploited in private hands, as the history of those nations that were most advanced in agriculture seemed to suggest; and such a view was also taught in the main studies of agricultural economics.

Privatisation did not necessarily have to take place through the sale of land, which would inevitably have favoured the big land-owners. Depending on local circumstances, the type of property and its legal position, it might be convenient to sell, to form a emphyteusis or to rent out the lands, even if it was preferable to grant them to people able to cover the costs required to develop them. A single exception (optional) to privatisation was planned for Alpine pastures.

However, Maniago's project to transform agriculture in the spirit of capitalism through the privatisation and cultivation of the common land sprang from an assumption, the details of which the author was probably not aware. Such a conversion of land use could appear feasible – and probably also perform a function of economic optimisation – for the common land of the Friulian plain (the social costs might be another matter). Yet the situation in this area, though significant in itself, did not correspond to that in the other provinces (or to the northern part of the same province of Friuli). In these areas, the lands that under the Serenissima had been defined as common land of the plain were very limited, while there were huge areas of alpine woodland and pasture that appertained to the municipality.

Indicative, in this sense, are the tables produced by Maniago, and the observations attached to them. The author's basic theory was that the size of the common land in an area was in inverse proportion to the size of the population and the number of animals that could be kept there. The references to other European countries or to the writings

---

21 ASVe, *Congregazione Centrale*, 1844, b. 451, f. 3.2.1. This assessment was widespread among the ruling classes of that period, cf. Mocarelli 2013, p. 194; Matteson 2015, p. 64.

on the subject concerned examples where the privatisation of common land had encouraged cultivation of the land or its scything for hay.

Maniago's proposals were more confused regarding situations where this conversion was not possible or easy, as with woodlands, for example. The ideological approach of the author emerged clearly here. On the one hand, he affirmed the advisability of also privatising the woodlands, to prevent them from being used too freely and to ensure that the new owners were committed to limiting thefts of wood. On the other, he took the opportunity to model the areas in which the forest cover was fuller: 'for example Cadore, where the woodlands are better kept and in better condition than in the other mountain villages. The reasons can be analysed and used for educational purposes in similar places elsewhere'.[22] And yet almost all the Cadore woodlands shared that common management so abhorred by the Friulian count.

Nevertheless, the report was undoubtedly the culmination of liberal thought on these issues in the Veneto region. It is remarkable for its extensive cultural references and for its knowledge of the policies of other European states; for its precision (never attained before) in identifying the common land; above all, for the lucidity with which the author distinguished between the different historical and legal forms that, since the beginning of the nineteenth century, had been brought together to form the property of the municipalities. For these reasons, the arguments within it constantly informed Lombardo-Venetian policy on these issues over the following decades.[23]

At the end of the 1820s, after the cadastral campaign of the 1826–28, when the preparatory property deeds had been drawn up and the classification of the land had been carried out, the central government discussed the possibility of new legislation on the matter. The intention was to address the issue in an organic way; on the one hand to put an end to disputes over the ownership of the common lands (a problem that only existed for the territories that had previously belonged to the Serenissima); on the other, finally to achieve the

---

22   ASVe, *Congregazione Centrale*, 1844, b. 451, f. 3.2.1.

23   Bonan 2017.

desired privatisation of these lands.[24] Given the requirements of this project, a natural collaborator was identified in Pietro Maniago who, appointed a government councillor in 1828, oversaw for years the delegation (called *referato*) to the municipal administration.[25]

After various discussions involving the heads of the Milan, Venice and Vienna administrations, an initial plan was drawn up for the privatisation of the common land in November 1836. The document began with these words:

> [The Emperor Francis I] convinced that with the royal property in the hands of the municipalities it can never be brought to achieve that income, nor subjected to those improvements, of which it is capable, and that the public and private good of the Municipalities requires, convinced that this common possession becomes a source of multiple and unavoidable abuses and that the Municipalities are not qualified to enter into those speculations that the current flourishing state of agriculture calls for, following the example and the principles that have determined us to yield to private trade through the alienation of the royal property of the State and of the Administrations ...[26]

There followed the draft of the law, consisting of nineteen articles. The project was discussed in the government meeting of 13 April 1837. The rapporteur, the Ragusan count Matteo Luigi Zamagna, declared himself against the bill for two reasons. The first was the absence of any distinction between the types of common land, since there were exemptions from the law only for some grazing land encumbered by easements and municipal buildings. The second reason arose from his belief that a project of this magnitude could not be achieved within the three-year period envisaged by the legislation under discussion. Both objections were accepted and led to a reformulation of the bill. The new version was approved on 16 April 1839 and announced on 10 July the same year.[27]

The final resolution of 16 April 1839 consisted of only eight articles and, apart from the additions proposed in the aforementioned

24   ASVe, *Magistrato Camerale*, 1830–1834, XXIV, b. 286, f. 1/7.
25   Tonetti 1997, p. 234.
26   ASVe, *Governo*, 1835–1839, XLIV, b. 5303, f. 68/94.
27   The law is published in *Legislazione in materia di Regole e di usi civici* 1998, pp. 26–27.

government meeting, remained faithful to the intentions clearly stated in the preface of the previous project. Article 1 stated that the alienation (the transfer of common land into private hands will always be referred to in this way) was mandatory where a municipality was burdened by debt. Article 2 responded, if only partially, to one of the suggestions of the councillor Zamagna and specified that the alienation must be carried out with 'solicitude' for the common land defined as uncultivated. Despite the requests of some delegations, including that of Belluno, the government initially chose not to propose any taxonomy to clarify the meaning of uncultivated land.

Article 4 stipulated that the purchasers of common land would have to bear any predial taxes or easements that were attached to the land. Article 5 indicated the possible forms of alienation: privatisation could take place through a contract of sale or emphyteusis. Where the municipality deemed it appropriate, the division of the property between the community members was also possible (either definitively or leasehold). A community member was considered to be someone who was domiciled in a municipality, was registered at the registry office and paid local taxes. Article 7 urged the competent authorities to promote the sale of common land, while Article 8 established the procedure for complaints.

If these articles were to encourage the privatisation of the common land, in line with the intentions of the legislature, then the remaining Articles 3 and 6 had to guarantee the conditions for this to happen within a well-defined legal framework. In other words, they had to put an end to the controversies that had blocked any intervention on the matter in previous decades. Article 3 stated that, in order to prevent any obstacles that might impede the orderly sale of the common land in the Veneto provinces, the sovereign renounced any direct dominion over property administered by the municipalities. To complement this provision, Article 6 reaffirmed the decree of 25 November 1806. With these two steps, the legislature sought to overcome the continuing ambiguity between the *beni comuni* and the *beni comunali* inherited from the Venetian legislation, assigning full ownership of all lands considered to be common to the municipal administrations.

In delivering the law to the district commissioners, the central government showed a certain awareness of the risks and uncertainties to which they were exposing themselves with the introduction of such a provision: 'it is easy to foresee that many obstacles will arise, and that much energy, perseverance, patience and deference will be needed to overcome them'.[28] And this misgiving proved to be dramatically true in the following months, particularly in Cadore, where the news of the law caused the explosion of tensions that had been escalating during the previous decades.

Local modernisation and its costs

As we have seen, the local communities and Cadore administrators had stuck fairly closely together in disputes with the forestry administration regarding the application of certain forestry regulations, such as the payment of the tenth or cutting methods. This was in order to try to maintain their relative autonomy in the management of forest resources and to have some of the privileges that had been granted during the Venetian period re-established. However, the social tensions caused by administrative modernisation also reverberated at the local level, gradually radicalising the conflict over the management of common land. These tensions found a new institutional forum in the municipal councils and assemblies.

Under the old regime, the political contest at the local level, which was primarily a contest for control of the enormous common resources, had focused on the narrow forum of the Cadore Council. In this context, even if the main factions were able to mobilise large sections of the population through ties of family or patronage, the main players were few and the methods of co-option were relatively simple within this small circle of families. The suppression of the Community and of the Council, and the assignment of common resources to the municipal administrations had shattered the existing forms of local political power. The situation was further complicated

---

by the establishment of the municipal legislation introduced after the return of the Austrians. This led to a much wider popular participation in the local administrations in those areas characterised by an accentuated land division, such as the Alpine regions.

Some clarification may be helpful at this point. In fact, the legislation regarding the municipalities that was introduced on 12 April 1816 was for a long time highly regarded. This reputation can be traced back to four letters written by Carlo Cattaneo and published in the journal *Il Diritto* in the summer of 1864. These opposed the adoption by the new unitary state of the Piedmontese municipal system, which Cattaneo considered detrimental to local autonomy.[29] Cattaneo contrasted this system with the municipal legislation of the Kingdom of Lombardy-Venetia, which originated in the Theresian reform introduced in December 1755 – though only in the Lombard provinces – and which was then reissued, with a certain continuity that was overemphasised by Cattaneo, for the whole of Lombardy-Venetia in 1816.

Subsequent research has shown that the democratic aspects of the Lombardo-Venetian municipal system were more formal than substantial, and that Cattaneo was expressing a specific political polemic rather than writing comparative essays in law.

First of all, the constraints placed on the planning of municipal budgets left very little room for autonomy to the municipalities, and the management of the budget was almost completely imposed and controlled by the administration of the government appointee.[30] On this point, it is important to remember that the Theresian municipal legislation was part of a comprehensive programme of state modernisation, the most significant parts of which were tax reforms and the making of the new census. In this context, municipal expenditure was expected to be sustained primarily from the yields of common land. If these exceeded expenditure, then the surplus could be used to reduce personal tax and the land surcharge.[31]

29   Cattaneo 1972, pp. 398–422.

30   Tonetti 1992, p. 179; Della Peruta 1999, p. 385.

31   Rotelli 1974, p. 180.

Secondly, it is necessary to consider the definition of the electoral body and the criteria for representation that the Lombardo-Venetian legislation articulated in the two distinct forms of the assembly and the council. In the municipalities governed by an assembly, the chancellor of the census (afterwards the district commissioner) had to convene, twice a year, an assembly of all predial taxpayers, to which was added a representative of those who paid only personal tax. The assembly had to discuss and approve the draft budgets of the municipalities, and elect the municipal committee to take charge of the local administration. The committee was composed of three members, one of whom – the political deputy – was to be drawn from the three largest taxpayers of the municipality and may be seen as a kind of mayor. The major towns and cities were organised according to the council model, composed of sixty members in Milan and Venice, forty members in the royal cities and provincial capitals and thirty in the other municipalities. Having initially been appointed by the government, a third of the members of a municipal council were replaced each year by the provincial congregation from a list of candidates, containing twice the number of names as of available seats, proposed by the municipal council itself. In all those municipalities that were not capitals or royal cities (which enjoyed a more extensive representation), the councils also nominated a committee made up of three members.[32]

As was noted by Marco Meriggi, the Lombardo-Venetian municipal legislation, in its concrete application, led to different outcomes in the various environmental, social and economic contexts in which it was applied. On the plains, where the land was owned by a few large landowners, the local administration was controlled by a small circle of wealthy aristocratic and bourgeois landowners, who often resided in the main urban centres and entrusted their duties in smaller centres to the tenants of their farms. The situation gradually changed as property became more fractional with increased altitude, and the difference narrowed between the number of households and the number of landowners in a municipality. In Alpine areas, charac-

32 Rotelli 1974.

terised by extreme fragmentation of the small amount of cultivable land, the municipal legislation produced the unintended result of a hugely increased participation in local political life.[33]

The real vibrancy that characterised the assemblies of mountain municipalities should not, however, be understood in the strictly democratic terms bestowed by Cattaneo. Another great protagonist of the Risorgimento, Ippolito Nievo, provides a more realistic picture of political confrontation at the local level in his description of the municipal assembly of a village in the Friulian Prealps:

> And I will just describe to you how the municipal meeting was divided between the *Pianigiano* and the *Montagnuolo* parties in their dispute over the appointment of the deputies; the one side gained support from the younger ones, those with higher outgoings, while the other was support-ed by the old constipated ones, poorer and more numerous. Nor were words lacking on either side: from the idealistic dreamers, the indulgent peacemakers and those who were just stubborn and deaf; while others tried to get their way with cunning flattery or with false praise. With everyone kicking under the table, a certain amount of discord was also spread among those mountain speakers ...[34]

Descriptions that were perhaps less colourful in tone, but just as explicit in underlining the ungovernability of these assemblies, were presented to the government during an administrative enquiry at the beginning of 1819, in which the district commissioners and the provin-cial delegates of the mountain areas expressed their opinions in various ways on the desirability of reducing popular participation in the local administration. In the summer of 1819, the government took a first step in this direction, announcing that all municipalities governed by an assembly convened from more than 300 taxpayers should instead adopt the form of a council. In 1835 this threshold was abolished and it became possible to adopt the form of a council even if there were fewer than 300 taxpayers on the cadastral registers. The purpose of this inter-vention was to contain the tensions arising from another measure, this time of a socio-economic nature, adopted by the government four years

33   Meriggi 1987, pp. 60–80.
34   Nievo 2010, pp. 231–32.

later. This was the law of 16 April 1839 to privatise common land.[35]

In lowland areas such as, for example, the southern part of the province of Udine, referred to by count Maniago in his plans for privatisation of the common land, this legislation reflected the joint interests of both the central administration and local elites in the pursuit of agrarian individualism.

However, this was not the case in Cadore, for reasons which, in my opinion, were shared by other mountain areas. In a situation of marked land fragmentation, such as in Cadore, even in those municipalities governed by a council, there was a very disparate collection of people active in the municipal administration.[36] Those who could be defined as notables constituted only a small part of the active citizenry, and often did not even make up the entire committee. Many of the conflicts that emerged in the municipal assemblies do not seem to have derived from social differences, but from antagonisms of a personal or familial nature, as well as specific private quarrels of an economic nature.[37]

Moreover, during the first years of the Austrian administration, the complexity of interests involved in the management of common resources made for a much more fluid social dynamic, difficult to fit into neat contrapositions.[38] The central government was aware of this and, in the second half of the 1810s, had noted the impossibility of

---

35 Meriggi 1983, pp. 169–91.

36 Following the issuing of the 1819 law, which limited the assembly model to municipalities with less than 300 taxpayers, in Cadore there were 10 municipalities with a council (Pieve, Calalzo, Domegge, Valle, Vodo, Auronzo, Comelico Superiore, Comelico Inferiore, Lozzo, Vigo) and 10 with an assembly (Borca, Cibiana, Ospedale, Perarolo, San Vito, Selva, Zoppè, Lorenzago, San Nicolò, San Pietro). In that period Danta was part of the San Nicolò municipality and Sappada was in the Udine province, cf. *Compartimento territoriale delle provincie venete*, Venezia 1821.

37 For examples, see the dispute that pitted the Poli and Bettina families against the deputies Benedetto Pellizzaroli and Giovanni Battista Comis: BSC, *Fondo De Pol*, b. 15, f. 435; or the dispute between the political deputy of Comelico Superiore Benedetto Zandonella dall'Aquila and the faction led by the Zambelli family: ACCS, *Corrispondenza*, 1820. On the role of factional dynamics in the rural conflicts of that period, see Caffiero 1999, pp. 322–24.

38 Cf. Zannini 2012a, p. 181.

finding reliable local contacts during disputes on the payment of the tenth and on how to proceed with felling works.

In that situation, opposition to government intervention had been eclectic and had held together the different interests under the banner of a 'traditional' management model of common resources. On the one hand, there were the interests of the majority of the population, who received basic income through forestry work – and therefore were opposed to the idea that this activity should be contracted by public tender – and who obtained food subsidies thanks to the systematic falsification of municipal budgets. And then another strongly asymmetric interest group was superimposed on this one, deriving from the profits from the sale of timber. This mainly benefited merchants, but also local middlemen (of interest here was the share of the secret municipal budgets intended for the expenses of council leaders).

However, as we have already seen, these margins of autonomy (or illegality) had been progressively reduced by the intervention of the state, even with the granting of some circumscribed exemptions. This should be understood not only in terms of the constraints, regulations and controls that reduced the freedom with which, at the local level, common resources and the income deriving from them could be managed. Much more concretely, the weight of this process of state centralisation and administrative modernisation redefined the role of these resources and the criteria for their use.[39] And this situation was also affected by other contemporary economic and social changes (for example the rapid growth in population).

Although it never touched the levels reached during the Napoleonic period, the tax burden on the Venetian territories was much greater than at the time of the collapse of the Serenissima and grew steadily during the Austrian domination.[40] However, the new bureaucratic constraints and the growing tax burden did not weigh on the entire population in the same way. In fact, some of the elites were in favour of these changes since they saw the attendant advantages

---

39   Similar dynamics are described in Caffiero 1992, p. 762.

40   For the Venetian and Napoleonic period, see Gullino 1982. For the Austrian rule, see Meriggi 1987, pp. 271–88.

in terms of infrastructure (roads, schools, cemeteries) and services (basic education, medical and veterinary services); in other words, the benefits of modernisation.

The reaction of the rest of the population was very different. The poorer classes complained about the end of those forms of reciprocity and assistance that had previously guaranteed a certain level of social protection and the recognition of a 'right to subsistence'.[41] In addition, there was the discontent of those elders who felt excluded, entirely or in part, from the advantages emerging from the new political-social order.

Giuseppe Bettina, a lawyer and deputy from Comelico Inferiore, described these dynamics and the discontent felt by his fellow citizens in this way:

> A treasure was accumulated in the municipal coffers because it was no longer known how to spend it, and then it was transported with pomp from the municipal to the provincial coffers, while here subsidies were refused for the destitute families who, disappointed in their hopes for a normal harvest, were fighting hunger and the typhus fever caused by it, which decimated them. A subsidy to the living was illegal; but the law was more lenient with the dead. New cemeteries, larger and better built, were constructed to reward the fallen victims with a more comfortable rest in the graveyard.[42]

However, although it may be more effective to comment on the cemeteries from the rhetorical point of view, it was the road improvements that absorbed the largest share of the profits from common resources.

The new Comelico road and the original inhabitants

At the end of the 1810s, partly to remedy the poor legacy inherited from the Serenissima in this strategic sector, the Lombardo-Venetian government began a series of projects that, within two decades, completely changed the viability of the Venetian provinces. Central government funding was directed towards the building of some roads that were strategic from the economic and military points of view (postal and commercial roads). However, around these main

41   Scott 1976.
42   Bettina 1869, p. 12.

routes there grew a substantial network of other roads, the building of which bore mainly on the municipal budgets.[43]

Giorgio Scarpa has estimated that at the height of activity in this sector (1825–1849), 18,236,660 Austrian lire were invested by the Veneto municipalities; and he has also proposed an average investment per hectare and per inhabitant.[44] The province of Belluno was the province that invested the least, both in overall terms (710,572 lire) and in relation to the surface area (2.76 lire per hectare) and population (4.42 lire per inhabitant); while the Veneto average was respectively 9.05 lire per hectare and 8.49 lire per inhabitant. This is not unexpected, considering that the province was among the least advanced economically in Lombardy-Venetia, and that the level of intervention was directly proportional to the financial resources of the municipalities.

However, if we look at the data at the district level, the province of Belluno presents a strongly disproportionate situation. The municipalities of the Auronzo district carried out works to the sum of 543,591 lire, equal to 76.5 per cent of those of the entire province. This resulted in an average investment of 11.42 lire per hectare (slightly above the overall average for the Veneto provinces), and an average investment of 31.48 lire per inhabitant (not even the richest provinces of the plain approached this figure). This expenditure was borne almost exclusively thanks to the income deriving from common resources, since both personal tax and the surtax on the land valuations were kept to a minimum in the municipalities of the district.[45]

The issue of effective communications was important above all for the Comelico municipalities, whose main link with the rest of the Auronzo district was the Sant'Antonio pass (1,476 metres above sea level). It was important that they should not be excluded from the new highway provided by the Alemagna road, approved in 1819 and finally completed in the 1830s.

At first, the municipalities of the area agreed with those of the Carnic district of Rigolato to ask the government to improve an old

43   Saurer 1989.

44   Scarpa 1988–1989.

45   ASVe, *Governo*, 1840–1844, XXVII, b. 6236, f. 50/1.

route that – via Sappada, the Comelico valley and the Monte Croce pass – would have joined Carnia to the imperial territories and the Alemagna road near to Dobbiaco. The initiative was supported by the main officials and notables of both Comelico and the district of Rigolato, but the project was never brought to fruition, despite the constant requests sent to central government during the 1820s.[46]

An alternative route was then chosen, which from Cima Gogna, in the municipality of Auronzo, reached Comelico Inferiore following the course of the Piave river. It was a journey of about ten kilometres, mostly excavated in the rock, not easy for travellers with vertigo. This initiative was also supported mainly by the political deputies of the various municipalities, members of prominent local families: the Monti, Bettina, Vettori, Zandonella and Zandonella dall'Aquila families.[47] The work was carried out between 1838 and 1840 by the builder of the Alemagna road, Antonio Tallachini, and was financed, as the Carnic doctor Giovanni Battista Lupieri wrote with a certain envy, using the 'inexhaustible resources' coming from the woodlands of the area.[48]

The steady growth in the proportion of municipal budgets devoted to the building of big infrastructural works and, at the same time, the constraints placed on initiatives to promote the common welfare, sharpened social tensions, especially among the poorest sections of the population.[49] The situation is summarised in some lines by Giuseppe Bettina:

> Let us compare the *Regole* administrations with those of today, and two opposite extremes emerge. Then we never thought of the future, but always of the present; nothing was done for the public utility, but everything for the belly ... Now on the contrary everything is directed towards the public good, nothing towards the private citizen; everything is to promote a general civilisation, and nothing benefits the individual body.[50]

---

46   Agarinis Magrini 2000, pp. 207–53.

47   On the construction of the road, cf. BSC, *Ex-Ciani*, b. 641, f. 6; BSC, *Fondo De Pol*, b. 15, ff. 432, 439. The families supporting the project are listed in Fontana 1980, pp. 167–70.

48   Agarinis Magrini 2000, p. 250

49   BSC, *Fondo De Pol*, b. 15, f. 455.

50   Bettina 1869, p. 19.

Chapter 4

Figure 9.

The new road between Cima Gogna and Comelico Inferiore in a painting by Osvaldo Monti, second half of the nineteenth century. Source: Museo Civico di Belluno.

In this climate of growing discontent, petitions began to appear to reintroduce a system of management of the common patrimony that was considered to be customary and inspired by the *regoliere* traditions. Such a system did find apparent legitimacy in the cadastral registers; but in practice its everyday use was denied or limited by bureaucratic constraints, by the costly responsibilities that the local administration had to face and by the constant attempts by the government and its local offshoots to monitor and direct municipal budgets.

One of these appeals was sent to Venice on 4 December 1829, signed by some of the deputies of the district.[51] It recalled the titles and privileges that had allowed the people of Cadore to draw their living from the wealth of their woodlands since the days of the patriarchs of Aquileia. The woodlands, according to these prerogatives, belonged

---

51   BSC, *Fondo De Pol*, b. 15, f. 445.

neither to the royal treasury nor to 'the municipalities in the sense of the present day administrative arrangements', but rather to the original population of those valleys: 'what else is the municipality if not the aggregate of the citizens ...? If there is an abundance of riches within the municipality, who should have the right to profit? We believe, with all due respect, that the good fortune of the municipality is the good fortune of its citizens.' Moreover, the supplicants remembered that only in recent years had the practice of distributing grain to the population thanks to the earnings from felling in the common woodlands been limited; and they asked for the practice to be restored.[52]

Among the signatories of the appeal was the then municipal deputy of Comelico Superiore, Valentino Zannantoni, who was to be a central figure during the protests that shook Cadore in the months following the issuing of the 1839 law. Zannantoni wrote an unpublished account of these events, which presents an alternative version of the protests – and the grievances from which they arose – to that proposed by the administrative and police authorities. It is necessary to consider the background of Zannantoni and to evaluate his account, which is a partisan piece of writing, but useful to understand where the demands regarding the common land originated from and how they were formulated.[53]

Valentino Zannantoni was born in 1785 in Dosoledo (Comelico Superiore) and was a middling landowner and shopkeeper. He was several times a municipal deputy (1823–25; 1828–30) and the representative of his village.[54] Having grown up during the final years of the *regole*, Zannantoni was part of that middle class that did not feel a part of the new model of municipal administration and rather

---

52 This is a widespread dispute in Italian jurisprudence of the nineteenth century. The distinction was between common resources as *universitas civium* – and then property of original members and their heirs only – and common resources as belonging to the communities conceived as administrative units – and so, in this interpretation, common resources belonging to *regole* and, after their abolition, to municipalities. Cf. Caffiero 1988; Bonan 2016.

53 The document is dated 1847 and it is conserved in BSC, *Fondo De Pol*, b. 15, f. 455. See Sacco 1988.

54 He owned 6.43 hectares (priced at 32.64 Austrian lire) in the villages of Dosoledo and Casamazzagno: ASBl, *Censo stabile*, partitari 173–4. On the administrative appointments see ACCS, *Nuova Segnatura*, b. 67, f. 1.

favoured the restoration of a system inspired by the *regoliere* tradition that was considered more suited to the Cadore territory.

This 'nostalgia', probably idealised, was widespread in these years, both among the poorest sections of the population and among the middling sort. It emerges in numerous claims regarding common land, always accompanied by documents aimed at showing the ancient and exclusive title to those lands belonging to the 'ancient original' inhabitants of the area. The constraints placed by the new administrative model, on the other hand, were perceived as an abuse that had reduced 'the owner [of the woodlands] to a simple paid worker'.[55]

As will be seen, the passing of the 1839 law was perceived as an opportunity finally to reassign the common lands and their profits for the exclusive benefit of the 'ancient originals', who were the native families of the various villages in which the *regole* assemblies had once met.

In his account of the events, especially with regard to the uprising of May 1840, Zannantoni tried to present himself as a moderate, unconnected with the organisation of the riots and forced to become the spokesman of popular discontent just to broker a compromise between the demands of the insurgents and those of the government. His account was written 'to serve the class of the wretched, who are need of the public patrimony; and if there is only one thing that I have deserved, it is to be remembered as their benefactor'.[56]

This profile does not accord with that given by the opposing side. In government dispatches, his activism and the influence that he exercised in the district are considered proof that he was one of the main 'demagogues' who deluded the population with false promises. Giovanni Bettina, in his pamphlet written in opposition to popular protests, also directed his polemic against a few troublemakers: 'but it is necessary to distinguish, as I said, those original inhabitants acting out of desperation from those acting from speculative motives: I intend to excuse the former, to speak in favour of them; and I shall always condemn the latter'.[57]

---

55   ACCS, *Corrispondenza*, 1840, 31 Dec. 1839.

56   BSC, *Fondo De Pol*, b. 15, f. 455.

57   Bettina 1869, p. 14. The abbot Giuseppe Monti proposed a similar assessment: BSC, *Fondo Manoscritti*, ms. 499.

Regardless of the foreseeable difference in opinion concerning the involvement of Zannantoni in all this, the events, people and dates in his account agree with the version that emerges from government documents. As for the requests that were made in those months, even assuming that they had been formulated by a few troublemakers, as the authorities claimed, there was a basic awareness on the part of the government that these demands had active support from almost the entire Cadore population.

A troubled winter

The first signs of the protests appeared about two months after the issuing of the law. On 19 September, the citizens of Auronzo presented two petitions calling for 'the sharing out of the common pastures and woodlands'. These demands were to be discussed at the municipal council meeting set for 28 September and were signed by all the councillors, 'some out of fear, others out of real conviction'. In communicating the news to the provincial delegation, the district commissioner, Giovanni Battista Monego, wanted that 'if this were to take place, the municipality would certainly be ruined'.[58]

The news did not raise particular concerns on the part of the provincial delegate, the Tyrolean count Giovanni Battista Marzani. He supported the idea of allowing the petitions presented by the citizens to be discussed since, whatever the municipal council decided on the matter, it was bound by the decision of the guardian authorities. The latter were obliged to conserve the common land of the district, which Marzani considered of fundamental importance from all points of view: important for the public good, since the alpine woodlands were the main bulwark ensuring the stability of the territory; for the local population, which derived income from these lands and products essential to their livelihood; and finally for the municipalities, which with the income from the lands were able to meet their own expenses without burdening the inhabitants with extra taxes.[59]

58   ASVe, *Governo*, 1835–1839, XLIV, b. 5303, f. 68/94.

59   ASVe, *Governo*, 1835–1839, XLIV, b. 5303, f. 68/94.

Meanwhile, the population of the Auronzo district had appointed prosecutors, elected by each village and charged with acting to obtain the division of all the common land amongst the original inhabitants of the respective villages. Among the prosecutors, Valentino Zannantoni assumed a prominent role, representing the village of Dosoledo; and so did Giovanni Battista Martini Faitel, representing the village of Padola. These two, according to Zannantoni, were in possession of documents that could demonstrate full and absolute ownership of the common land by the original inhabitants of Cadore.

On 19 September, the day when the first demands were presented, all the prosecutors met in Auronzo and decided how to proceed. A common fund was set up, entrusted to Martini Faitel, to meet any expenses, and it was decided to contact a lawyer, Fortunato Serrafini of Serravalle, to draft a formal appeal to be sent to the government.[60]

The appeal was drawn up over several meetings between the end of September and the beginning of October and was structured in two parts. On the one hand, on the basis of the documents in the possession of Zannantoni and Martini Faitel, it was reiterated that the lands in question were the exclusive property of the inhabitants of Cadore, despite the interference of the government in their management in recent years (for example the imposition of the tenth on cuts in the woodlands and the use of profits for the construction of infrastructure). And if some magistrates insisted on considering that property to be owned by the municipality as an administrative body, then it must be remembered that 'the august monarch ... by a stroke of incomparable magnanimity' had decided to renounce all rights to the common lands and had granted that they could be divided between the relevant citizens, recalling the Italian decree of 25 November 1806. In line with these two considerations, the prosecutors of the villagers called for the immediate division of the common lands between the villages of the municipality, and then their distribution among the original inhabitants of the respective villages.[61]

60   BSC, *Fondo De Pol*, b. 15, f. 455; these details are confirmed by the governmental reports: ASVe, *Governo*, 1840–1844, XXVII, b. 6236, f. 50/1; ASVe, *Governo*, 1840–1844, XV, b. 5997, f. 27/2.

61   ACCS, *Corrispondenza*, 1840, 31 Dec. 1839.

At the same time as the village prosecutors and the lawyer Serrafini were drafting the appeal, the municipal assemblies and councils of the district of Auronzo were being held. At these meetings, commissioner Monego, following the directives of the delegation, ordered the assemblies to declare the absence in the municipal districts of uncultivated property, i.e. those lands regarding which privatisation was obligatory and had to be done quickly.

Contrary to what the delegate Marzani had hoped, the rejection of these first demands, instead of restoring peace to the district, sharpened popular discontent, which had also spread to the neighbouring district of Pieve di Cadore. The situation was also worsened, noted the provincial delegate, because certain demagogues had begun 'to spread mistrust among the common people of all those who represented authority in their respective regions, so that they were persuaded, out of fear and against their consciences, to press their strange demand that all the property now forming the patrimony of the municipalities should be divided up freely amongst them'.[62] In particular, there was a widespread conviction (according to government sources) that the king had resolved to grant the common land to the people, but that the administrations had blocked this resolution.

The results were soon apparent: 'anonymous letters, nocturnal gatherings, death threats and assaults are the means ... adopted by the unruly protesters, to intimidate the municipal deputies and other sensible people who are not willing to pander to the demagogues' every move'. This same district commissioner had been attacked in Valle di Cadore while attempting to go and preside over the municipal council meeting. The situation was becoming critical and the municipal deputies realised that it was time to step back: 'at which point everyone, under one pretext or another, asked to be released from their office; someone wanted also to request a permit to be able to pass into Tyrol, and thus to put himself, as he said, beyond the snares of the current popular agitations'.[63]

---

62 ASVe, *Governo*, 1840–1844, XXVII, b. 6236, f. 50/1.

63 ASVe, *Governo*, 1840–1844, XXVII, b. 6236, f. 50/1. These requests were denied by the provincial delegate: ACA, *Amministrazione*, 1839–1840, I, b. 80, 28 Dec. 1839. On the role of nocturnal mock ceremony – similar to the *charivari* – in the social conflicts in Veneto, see Fincardi 2009, pp. 103–08.

The lack of backing from the municipal administrations pushed the village prosecutors to forward the appeal to the government through the provincial delegation. In Belluno, however, Count Marzani was monitoring the evolution of events in Cadore with increasing concern and was far from willing to meet the demands of the population.

The delegate considered both components of the appeal to be inadmissible. Firstly, this was because the documents on which the claims were based 'prove nothing except that the woodlands, which already constitute the principal patrimony of Cadore, indeed appertained to those populations, but as a moral entity'. It followed that the property in question 'was never under private sway, but was administered by formal bodies, firstly the said *regole*, then the municipalities, and now the deputations; and they always did it under a public supervision'. And even if, in years gone by, 'in some parts of Cadore, motivated by the continuing feeling of freedom widespread in that region, they continued to sell timber and to dispose of the related products without any legal basis', we are speaking of 'wilful actions that, as soon as they were discovered, were stopped and avenged, and which as such cannot give rights to anyone'.[64]

As for the second part of the appeal, the delegate pointed out that Article 6 of the new law did not state that the Italian decree of 25 November 1806 was brought back into force, as the prosecutors erroneously wished to argue, but remained in force. Therefore, the timeframe provided on that occasion within which to assert the rights of the 'ancient originals' (six months) had expired decades ago.[65]

Mindful of recent developments, the provincial delegate was aware that rejection of the appeal would further exacerbate the tension in Cadore. Therefore, he put in place some initiatives to stem the popular discontent as much as possible.

The first of these was to involve the clergy and to exploit the ascendency that it had over the poorest people in order to instruct them on the correct approach to the 1839 law. Moreover, according

---

64   ASVe, *Governo*, 1840–1844, XXVII, b. 6237, f. 50/10.

65   ASVe, *Governo*, 1840–1844, XXVII, b. 6237, f. 50/10; more details in: ACCS, *Corrispondenza*, 1840, 27 Jan. 1840.

to Count Marzani, there was an obvious way to start dealing with the false beliefs widespread among Cadore inhabitants. Among the requests made during the protests that had preceded the calling of the municipal assemblies, one demanded that all the funds allocated to the payment of the municipal forest guards should be removed from the draft budgets of 1840, 'since, in their view, the woodlands being regarded as a pertinence of the people, the guards were superfluous'. The delegate decided to respond to these claims by ordering an increase in the numbers of forest guards. This provision not only acted to protect the common woodlands from possible abuses, but could also prove useful to suppress 'every disturbance of the public peace'.[66]

Faced with the violation of public order, Count Marzani reacted in the usual conventional way: the use of propaganda (through the clergy), increased coercive force (the forest guards) and selective arrests, made both to punish the offenders and to act as an example to the rest.

At the start of 1840, Lorenzo Callegaro, Floriano dal Favero and Gioacchino Dal Favero (a former municipal agent), all born and living in Lozzo di Cadore, were arrested. Floriano Dal Favero was accused of having been the first to spread among the population of the municipality the idea that the common lands should be freely divided among the villagers. He had organised clandestine meetings, had asked his fellow villagers to sign powers of attorney and had collected money together. The other two arrested were accused of having supported him with every means at their disposal.[67] At the same time, a similar operation was attempted in the neighbouring municipality of Comelico Superiore. This time, however, things did not go as the authorities had planned.

On 9 January, the district commissioner sent some guards to the house of Giovanni Battista Martini Faitel in order to arrest him and to take possession of documents that he claimed to have concerning the Cadore woodlands and pasture. The villagers of Padola noticed what was happening – in government reports they were always marked out as particular troublemakers – and they gathered to defend Martini

66   ASVe, *Governo*, 1840–1844, XXVII, b. 6236, f. 50/1.
67   ASVe, *Governo*, 1840–1844, XV, b. 5997, f. 27/2.

Faitel, and escorted him to the nearby village of Candide, the municipal seat, where he was expected by the district commissioner. At that point, the commissioner realised that the only way to get back to Auronzo unharmed was to do so without Martini Faitel.[68]

At the end of the month, the provincial delegate blamed the failure of the initiative on his deputy, whom he said had acted with insufficient discretion in the attempted arrest of Martini Faitel, and he said that soon the government would respond to the demands presented by the villagers.[69] In fact, over several sessions held between late February and early March, the government discussed the fate of the common lands of Cadore and ratified the line already taken by the provincial delegation, refusing in full the requests to divide them up.[70]

At this point, according to the account of Valentino Zannantoni, the prosecutors decided to go directly to Venice to present a new appeal. Zannantoni, Martini Faitel and Francesco Osta (who was a member of the municipality of Comelico Superiore) travelled down at the beginning of April, accompanied by the lawyer Serrafini. It was on the return leg of this trip that Valentino Zannantoni claimed to have repeatedly heard his fellow villagers say 'we are close to May, and we shall see all sorts of things'. Asking for an explanation of this, his companions replied 'if they want to brand the logs, they shall ask us'.[71] Indeed, in that period the fair was due to take place, in which the *taglie* (standard size logs) extracted from the common woodlands were sold to the timber merchants, who branded them with the marks of the respective companies; they were then put in the river to be transported downstream along the Padola and then the Piave river. Contemporaries called this event 'the heart of the trade of Piave'.[72]

On this occasion, in line with the rest of his account, in which he always presents himself as a moderate, Zannantoni denied any involve-

68   BSC, *Fondo De Pol*, b. 15, f. 455.

69   ASVe, *Governo*, 1840–1844, XXVII, b. 6236, f. 50/1.

70   ASVe, *Governo*, 1840–1844, XXVII, b. 6237, ff. 50/4, 50/6, 50/7, 50/8, 50/9, 50/10, 50/11, 50/15.

71   BSC, *Fondo De Pol*, b. 15, f. 455.

72   Quoted in Caniato 2000, p. 313.

ment in the events that led to the May riots. In his favour, it must be said that the epicentre of the riots was the village of Padola, where the prosecutors were Giovanni Battista Martini Faitel and the deputy Francesco Osta. However, in police despatches Zannantoni is considered one of the main people responsible for the popular discontent and one of the ringleaders of the May protests. Irrespective of his real responsibility in organising the protests, the prediction he said he had heard during his return journey to Cadore did not take long to come true.

A noisy spring

On the evening of 5 May, the political deputy Giovanni Battista Zandonella dall'Aquila informed the district commissioner that the villagers of Dosoledo had refused to proceed with the branding of the logs set for that morning. When questioned why, the villagers had replied that they wanted to wait and see what they did in the nearby village of Padola, where the same work had been scheduled for the following day and where, the deputy warned, 'the main dissent is focused, and from there the opinions and insinuations branch out into the other villages and municipalities'.[73]

The next day, the district commissioner went to Padola and, unsurprisingly, found everything halted there too. When he asked for an explanation, those present – many more than expected – replied that they would start the work only if the buyers paid them directly for the goods; this rather than paying the municipality which, by the latest estimate, had already allocated the proceeds from the sale of the forest products to pay off debts contracted with the Tallachini company for the upgrading of the roads. And this was precisely the attitude of the Dosoledo villagers too.[74]

Informed of the situation on 7 May, while completing military exercises with the conscripts, the provincial delegate ordered the inspector of the public security guards to leave immediately for Cadore

---

73   ASVe, *Governo*, 1840–1844, XV, b. 5997, f. 27/2.

74   ASVe, *Governo*, 1840–1844, XV, b. 5997, f. 27/2.

with the largest possible force.[75] The urgency was also driven by the petitions of the timber merchants involved, who had already threatened to retaliate as a result of the delays in the delivery of the goods, since the unrest risked losing the period when the rivers were high, the most suitable period for transporting the timber.

On 9 May, the deputies Giovanni Battista Zandonella dall'Aquila and Liberale Monti, practically the only municipal representatives on whom the authorities could still count, declared that, given the extreme pressures, they could not be responsible for any further developments, and they handed in their resignations.[76] Two days later, the villagers of Candide also refused to begin work for the sale of logs to the Gera company.

After the arrival of forces from Belluno, to reinforce the forest guards and the other local officers (in total about forty men), the district commissioner decided that it was time to put an end to the protests. He read out a statement in which he enjoined the inhabitants of Comelico Superiore to carry out the operations necessary to begin the rafting of the timber by 14 May. Furthermore, it was forbidden for anyone to enter the places used for these activities, under pain of arrest, unless they had been regularly recruited for such work. However, it was clear the following day that the commissioner's threats had not had the desired effect:

> the people pressed on with their demands, not listening to the voices of reason, and indeed always reacting against the advice of the authorities, yesterday 13 [May], about 130 workers from each village, in total 520, moved en masse into their respective woodlands. In contempt of the forest laws, without any licence and in locations other than those that had been marked out for cutting operations by the relevant officials, they proceeded to fell about 2,500 trees.[77]

The forestry inspector and representatives of the Gera, Masi and Fabbro companies made their way there to try to restore calm, but the rioters, armed with axes, 'unanimously replied that the woodlands and

75   ASVe, *Governo*, 1840–1844, XVI, b. 6020, f. 14/5.

76   ACCS, *Corrispondenza*, 1840, 15 May 1840.

77   ASVe, *Governo*, 1840–1844, XXVII, b. 6236, f. 50/1.

the logs that are taken out of them, and those that are lying on the forest floors, according to the latest sovereign resolutions, are their exclusive property, and they want to have and dispose of their property themselves'.[78] Indeed, the district commissioner warned his superiors that the only hope of avoiding anarchy was to bring in the army.

When this news reached Belluno, the provincial delegate decided to abandon military manoeuvres with the conscripts and to depart for the site of the riots on the morning of 14 May. However, he first sent a courier to Venice to advise that, in order to contain the uprising, which was spreading to other villages in the district, regiments of troops should be despatched. The following day, the provincial delegate went to the village of Padola, the epicentre of the riots, and announced that if the protests were not brought to an end that very day the army would be intervening. Initially he received chaotic and confused replies:

> someone said that the deputation had consumed and was still consuming their woodlands in the construction of roads, another one said that the deputation was not willing to permit the sharing out of the uncultivated land as ordered by his majesty; another said that the deputation had refused to give them grain subsidies; the women brought out their children in front of the royal delegate, showing how they had been reduced to the extremes of poverty and hunger ...[79]

Finally, Valentino Zannantoni acted as spokesman for the popular discontent, and he laid out to Count Marzani the demands of the villagers regarding the common land; statements that were welcomed with shouts of approval by the crowd present, as confirmed by the same delegate:

> Valentino Zannantoni of Dosoledo, bankrupt meddler and bold talker, even ventured in my presence to explain, with the people also present, the well-known notions regarding the so-called original inhabitants. He recalled their alleged rights, which were according to him incontrovertible and recognised by his majesty in the notification of 10 July 1839; and this exposition was accompanied by the acclamations of the people.[80]

At that point, the provincial delegate realised that the threat of the army

---

78   ASVe, *Governo*, 1840–1844, XXVII, b. 6236, f. 50/1.

79   BSC, *Fondo De Pol*, b. 15, f. 455.

80   ASVe, *Governo*, 1840–1844, XV, b. 5997, f. 27/2.

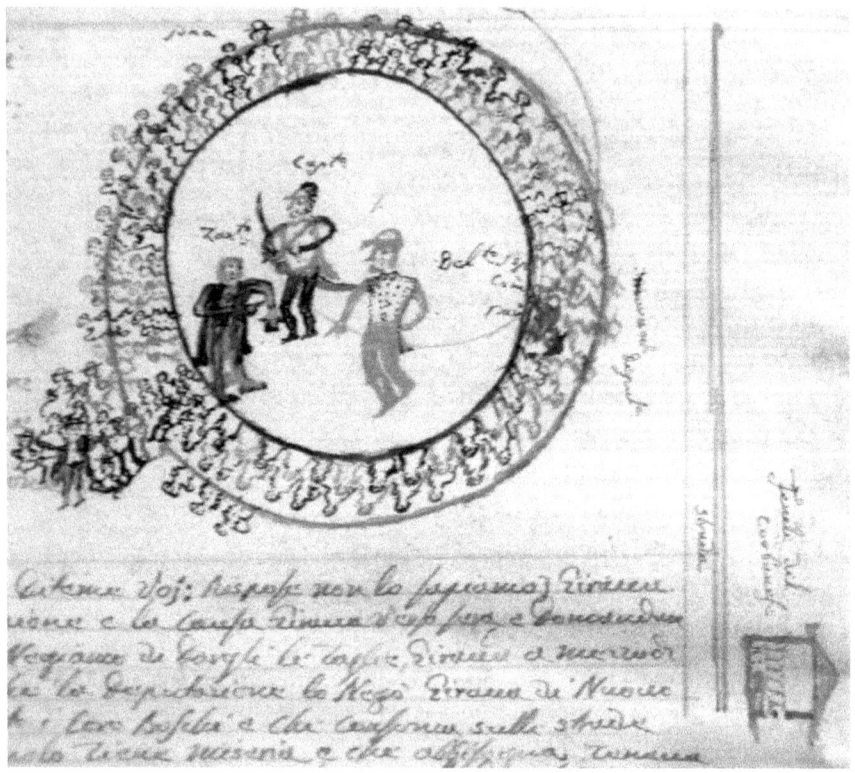

Figure 10.

The provincial delegate, Count Marzani, meets the rioters. Source: BSC, *Fondo* De Pol, b. 15, f. 455.

would not be sufficient to make them start the work, not least because there was a rumour that the government was about to assent to the long awaited division of land that the people had demanded.[81] Therefore, Count Marzani allowed the various villages to arrange meetings according to the ancient formula of the village assembly, in order to appoint representatives with the power to negotiate an agreement that would guarantee the carrying out of work for the sale of the timber.

The following day, three requests emerged from these meetings: the immediate grant of a food subsidy for all the families of the municipal-

81   ASVe, *Governo*, 1840–1844, XXVII, b. 6236, f. 50/1.

ity; permission to continue the actions taken for the claiming of the common land; and an amnesty for the illegal cuts made on 13 May. The provincial delegate replied that he could authorise the first two requests, and he undertook, together with the forestry inspector, to intercede for an amnesty with the relevant authorities. The agreement was made and the delegate was able to inform the government of the end of the riots and the imminent start of the work on 17 May.[82]

The carrot and the stick

These events highlighted the problems faced by the central government in applying the law of 16 April 1839, especially in mountain areas. Already at the beginning of March, two months before the explosion of popular discontent, Francesco Coletti, Pieve's forestry inspector, had sent a note to the head office of the inspectorate 'warning of the possible effects of granting unrestricted permission to the municipalities to sell or share out their woodlands'. The inspector claimed that in private hands the woodlands would be quickly destroyed through excessive cutting, causing serious future damage without producing any immediate advantage, since the surplus of timber put on the market would cause an inevitable 'lowering of prices, to the detriment not only of the more ill-advised sellers, but also of those who traded their merchandise in a more judicious manner'.[83]

In a long report sent to the government two days after the end of the revolt in Comelico, the provincial delegate took up these concerns. Count Marzani's opinion was that sharing out the common lands (both woodland and pasture) would lead to the ruin of the valleys within a few years. The protection of the forests deserved particular attention, because 'the spoiling of those woodlands will ruin not only Cadore, but also those districts with sawmills that form the industry in the Longarone and Belluno districts; also the families of the watermen who live all along the Piave up to the sea; and finally

---

82   BSC, *Fondo De Pol*, b. 15, f. 455; ASVe, *Governo*, 1840–1844, XV, b. 5997, f. 27/2; ACCS, *Corrispondenza*, 1840, 16 May 1840.

83   ASVe, *Ispettorato generale ai boschi*, 1840–1844, b. 250, f. 3.

the dominance of Venice will suffer, since our timber feeds its most important export trade'. Since this situation was common to other districts of the province, Count Marzani asked the government for an appendix to the 1839 law, in order to protect common woodlands and pastures in the territories that he was responsible for. He also suggested sharpening up the penalties for forestry offences and increasing the pay rates for forestry work carried out by the population. These latter measures would aim to discourage the abuses of private individuals and make municipal management more popular.[84]

The points raised by the provincial delegate were discussed in the government session of 27 May. On the question of tightening up the penalties for forestry offences, the government chose to postpone the decision to a future session. As for increasing the rates for forestry work, the delegate was asked to revise them. Finally, given the importance of the issue, it was deemed appropriate to hear the opinion of the Viennese chancellery on the question of whether to exempt the province of Belluno from the application of the 1839 law.[85]

Vienna responded on 11 June with a harsh reprimand to the Belluno delegation. As for the concessions made to end the revolt, 'it is not the place of the administrative authority to offer impunity to persons indicted for actions that fall under the criminal law, nor to guarantee them exemption from investigation and possible punishment'. With regard to the idea of granting an exemption from the 1839 law: 'if certain agitators take it upon themselves to twist the meaning of a royal resolution for the sake of their own particular interests, then this must certainly not induce the sovereign to produce a clarification, but rather it is the responsibility of the authorities to correct the ill-conceived ideas'.[86]

The provincial delegate replied to the accusations made against him with a letter sent directly to the count of Spaur, governor of the Venetian provinces. Firstly, he denied having promised impunity to persons suspected of having broken the law, but had confined him-

---

84   ASVe, *Governo*, 1840–1844, XXVII, b. 6236, f. 50/1.

85   ASVe, *Governo*, 1840–1844, XXVII, b. 6236, f. 50/1.

86   ASVe, *Governo*, 1840–1844, XV, b. 5997, f. 27/2.

self to presenting the reasons of the population to the competent authorities, provided that the illegally felled trees were delivered. He also pointed out that if they wanted to prosecute those offenders, they would have to bring to justice the entire population of the municipality. As for the leaders of the uprising, he had suggested not arresting them at *that* particular time.

Regarding the 1839 law, Marzani did not object to the response from Vienna, but he insisted on at least asking for instructions on how the regulation should be applied correctly, especially with respect to the common woodlands and pastures and the claims of the so-called original inhabitants. Indeed, behind these requests lay a worrying situation:

> We are facing a population of two districts, 30,000 inhabitants, most of whom cling onto their albeit absurd claims in good faith and with the tenacity of the mountain idiot, because they find apparent support for them in the stories of their old people, in their reminiscences, and in the council of the lawyers who flatter and support them ... On anything to do with the municipal patrimony, the population of Cadore has always been brooding and troublesome rather than docile and quiet. For thirty years or more, that is since 1806, the authorities have acted energetically and persistently to suppress inveterate abuses and popular notions about being able freely to dispose of municipal property.[87]

The delegate's response raised two issues for the attention of the central government. The first concerned the management of public order in Cadore. It was necessary to prevent claims being made on the common land, since these had not stopped with the end of the May protests, leading to new riots. The second issue was broader and the Cadore questions were in part subsumed within it. The methods of applying the 1839 law had to be clarified so that they did not give rise to new protests. Any instructions had to take into account the particular context of common land within mountain terrain; for the most part, at least according to Count Marzani, privatisation was not advisable in this context, and could even prove very dangerous.

Meanwhile, in Cadore the agitation for the sharing out of common land had resumed. On 8 June, the district commissioner gath-

---

87   ASVe, *Governo*, 1840–1844, XV, b. 5997, f. 27/2.

ered the prosecutors of the villages in his office and ordered them to desist from taking new action, under penalty of arrest. However, once again the threats did not have the desired results.[88]

In the autumn, the district commissioner informed the delegation that popular ferment was growing and becoming dangerous in the Auronzo district, since plans to divide up the common property had begun to appear, each underwritten by many signatures.[89] In Valentino Zannantoni's account, two plans are discussed in detail; one written by Zannantoni himself for the municipality of Comelico Inferiore, the other drawn up by Giovanni Battista Martini Faitel for the municipality of Comelico Superiore. The latter was not particularly detailed: it provided for the definitive division of all the property of the municipality, first between the villages composing it and then between the family units residing in the respective villages. Zannantoni had also prepared his plan for the municipality of Comelico Superiore, but after discovering that Martini Faitel's plan had already been delivered to the council, signed by many of the inhabitants, he decided to avoid division and gave his to the villagers of Comelico Inferiore, since they had asked him for it.[90]

Zannantoni's plan shared some aspects of the *regoliera* management, but also reflected the experience that the author had built up regarding the new administrative system during his time as a municipal deputy. Furthermore, legal and social considerations were brought together. According to Zannantoni, in support of the division of land there were not only titles that proved the rights of the original inhabitants, but also the conviction that the sharing out of the lands was the best way of coping with the rapid increase in population.

Apart from the Alpine pastures, which could only be managed collectively, all the other common lands would need to be divided between the villages and therefore among the original inhabitants. The beneficiaries of the division would not be individuals but family

88   BSC, *Fondo De Pol*, b. 15, f. 455.

89   ASVe, *Governo*, 1840–1844, XV, b. 5997, f. 27/2.

90   BSC, *Fondo De Pol*, b. 15, f. 455. The plans are described also by the provincial delegate in a report conserved in ASVe, *Ispettorato generale ai boschi*, 1839–1846, Presidio, b. 666, 16 Dec. 1840.

units, according to the criteria of assignment and succession provided for in the *regole*. The most appropriate method of division would be based on the emphyteutic lease, both because the municipality was still burdened by debt (and therefore free division was not compatible with the 1839 law), and because the land appertained to the Cadore population, to the future population as well as to the current inhabitants. For this reason, the leaseholders would also be subject to tight constraints aimed at preventing the land from being sold, mortgaged or not managed in accordance with the provisions of the village assemblies. Finally, the fee would have to be minimal, aimed only at covering the predial tax to be paid to the municipality.

The presentation of these proposals was met with increasing concern in Belluno, with the Cadore example spreading to other parts of the province as well. For example, in Mis, a former *regoliera* community that had become part of the municipality of Sospirolo, the inhabitants had begun to claim some mountain pastures that the municipality was renting out to finance (here too) the construction of a road. After the issuing of the 1839 law, some of the inhabitants 'had made journeys, and had taken legal advice in various places, and had returned all fired up with the Cadore maxims to spread their ideas among the people'. As in Cadore, the outcome of the protest was the invasion of the disputed lands and a brief riot that required the intervention of the public security guards.[91]

In order to contain the outbreak of new protests in the province as quickly as possible, the government decided to deploy a company of military in Belluno. This was in accordance with the request of Count Marzani, who in the days following the May revolt had pointed out that his province was the only one without an adequate military garrison.[92]

In autumn, feeling more secure in the event of a riot as a result of the army presence, the provincial delegate drew up a plan of action to prevent the situation in Cadore degenerating again with the approach of the period favoured for the sale of timber. Marzani's strategy was to have the work done ten days in advance in the village of Padola, 'the

---

91   ASVe, *Governo*, 1840–1844, XV, b. 5997, f. 27/7.

92   ASVe, *Presidio di governo*, 1840–1844, I, b. 972, f. 8/4.

root of evil, where the most resolute and bold men are to be found'. In this way, it would be easier to circumscribe any insubordination. As a further precautionary measure, to appease the population of the district, new forestry rates were drawn up, with an expected increase in salaries for the cutting, preparation and logging out of the timber.[93]

However, these parts of Marzani's plan risked being ineffective if first of all the main fermenters of the popular discontent were not silenced. Therefore, the preventive arrests were arranged of those who were considered to have been behind the disorders: Giovanni Battista Martini Faitel and Valentino Zannantoni.[94] Giovanni Battista Martini Faitel was the first to be arrested by the police on 27 December. It was the turn of Valentino Zannantoni on 1 January, arrested after Mass outside the church of San Rocco in Dolosedo and then taken to the Belluno prison.[95]

In early April the district commissioner summoned the municipal council of Comelico Superiore to discuss the correct application of the 1839 law. At the opening of the session, the commissioner informed them 'that the vote is free, and that each member of the council can make any observations that he wishes; but it should be noted that if the deliberations accord with the provisions of the authorities, they shall be well received and approved, and that if they do not thus accord they shall be rejected'. On that occasion the council proposed keeping almost all the common lands within the present management system.[96]

On 19 April, work in the village of Padola began without incident. Over the following weeks, the scheduled works also took place as planned in the other villages of the district. As a result, the detention of the two prosecutors was no longer necessary. Valentino Zannantoni and Giovanni Battista Martini Faitel were released at the end of May after five months in prison, without any charge being brought against them.[97]

---

93   ASVe, *Ispettorato generale ai boschi*, 1839–1846, Presidio, b. 666, 16 Dec. 1840.

94   ASVe, *Governo*, 1840–1844, XV, b. 5997, f. 27/2.

95   BSC, *Fondo De Pol*, b. 15, f. 455.

96   ACCS, *Corrispondenza*, 1841, 13 Apr. 1841; ASVe, *Governo*, 1840–1844, XXVII, b. 6241, f. 50/207.

97   ASVe, *Governo*, 1840–1844, XV, b. 6005, f. 35/234; ASVeG, *Tribunale di appello generale (1815–1871)*, 1843, L, b. 1463, f. 620.

The impossible privatisations

In the meantime, the government did not remain indifferent to the concerns voiced by the Belluno delegate and the forestry inspector on the advisability of protecting the common lands of the mountain areas, since for the majority of these there was no better form of cultivation.

On 30 July 1840, after representations made by Venice, the Viennese state chancellery softened its position and issued a dispatch in which it declared common woodlands to be cultivated land; so that 'the alienation of the same by the municipalities could only be allowed if the obligations regarding their cultivation were maintained, and the forest regulations were observed'.[98] One month later, a circular highlighted the objectives of the legislation:

> That the entire history of culture is nothing but the narration of the stages and methods by which common property dissolves into private, freehold property; that with the progression of civilisation, the dividing out of the common lands proceeds hand in hand; that the possession and cultivation by the municipalities of their lands is injurious to them and to agriculture in general; injurious to the development of the same, to the increase of the population, and thus to the national economy in all its aspects.[99]

In the same circular pastureland was declared to be uncultivated property, and it was announced that to be considered an inhabitant of a municipality, just one of the criteria provided for by the 1839 law was sufficient. However, in the following March, this 'progression of civilisation' was placed under a new constraint. Another circular, which made explicit reference to the situation in Cadore, laid out that mountain pastures, despite being grazing land, should be considered cultivated land.[100] Complaints, and requests for clarification on the methods by which the 1839 law was to be applied, began to pour in from other provinces. More worryingly for the authorities, the popular reactions that had stirred up Cadore and other parts of Belluno province also began to spread. Particularly dramatic were the

98   ASVe, *Governo*, 1840–1844, XXVII, b. 6236, f. 50/2.

99   *Legislazione in materia di Regole e di usi civici* 1998, pp. 30–31.

100   *Legislazione in materia di Regole e di usi civici* 1998, p. 34.

events unfolding in the Friulian plain where, in 1840–41, the army had to be sent in to some districts to restore order.[101]

Given the continuing disputes and tensions, the government intervened again in June 1841, with the publication of instructions addressed to all territorial bodies (provincial, district and municipal) 'to properly execute the venerable sovereign resolution of 16 April 1839'. The fact that this instruction contained 36 articles, whereas the 1839 law had only eight, is indicative of the complications that had arisen.[102]

The first nine articles clarified the dichotomy between cultivated and uncultivated land. All mountain pastures that, because of the poor soil, were not suited to anything except 'alpine grasses', were considered cultivated. As for forest lands, including areas containing just bushes or a few trees, it was necessary to hear the opinion of the general inspectorate of the woodlands. The only explicit reference to the category of uncultivated land was those lands devoted to loose grazing throughout the year.

The tenth article specified that the renunciation made by the king two years earlier was not for the benefit of municipalities, but of villages. The thirteenth article laid out that local administrations should deal with the alienation of uncultivated lands only. As for the methods of alienation, the emphyteusis was preferable (§28), 'while a portioning out between the community members is by far the worst [method] and not to be allowed without much reservation' (§ 29), and was strictly forbidden if the area to be divided was either too small or too large (§30).

How did these new provisions affect the implementation of the 1839 law? To understand the various effects of privatisation on the Veneto provinces, the significant data are those drawn up by the central accounting authorities using the reports on the progress of the alienations regularly sent by the delegations. Among the available statistical tables, the most complete is that drawn up in September 1847, on the eve of the revolutionary movements.[103]

Eight years after the issuing of the law, 34,839 hectares of land

---

101   Brunello 2011, pp. 3–85.

102   *Legislazione in materia di Regole e di usi civici* 1998, pp. 35–42.

103   Table 7.

Contested forests

Table 7.

State of alienations in the Venetian provinces following the issuing of the 1839 law; summary presented on 27 September 1847.

Province	Belluno	Padua	Rovigo	Treviso	Udine	Venice	Verona	Vicenza	Total
Surface area of common land	126,015.30	2,901.70	319.70	21,528.50	256,118.00	11,149.40	9,342.60	6,0487.20	487,862.40
Common land sold	211.99	0	0	581.91	9,988.02	7.25	103.11	122.07	11,014.35
Common land rented	1,000.63	51.91	0	452.1	21,945.34	1.04	31.51	342.16	23,824.69
Total	1,212.62	51.91	0	1,034.01	31,933.36	8.29	134.62	464.23	34,839.04
% of alienated common land/surface area of common land	0.96	1.79	0.00	4.80	12.47	0.07	1.44	0.77	7.14
Income derived from sales	13,701.30	0	0	92,209.84	1,210,921.51	6,384.35	5,817.57	787.65	1,329,822.22
Income derived from rents	87,986.75	1,406.30	0	80,063.00	2,775,404.42	13.77	15,158.05	48,314.93	3,008,347.22
Total	101,688.05	1,406.30	0	172,272.84	3,986,325.93	6,398.12	20,975.62	49,102.58	4,338,169.44
Common land still to be sold	53.06	0.00	0	1,509.08	4,384.11	8,300.53	1,852.03	3,807.02	19,905.83
Common land still to be rented	8,725.41	10.90	0	4,618.24	53,735.96	0	561.80	14,309.23	81,962,00
Total	8,778.47	10.90	0.00	6,127.32	58,120.07	8,300.53	2,413.82	18,116.25	101,867.37
% of common land to be alienated/surface area of commond land	6.97	0.38	0.00	28.46	22.69	74.45	25.84	29.95	20.88

Source: ASVe, *Presidio di governo*, 1845–1848, XII, b. 1348, f. 6/5. Surface area unit hectares; monetary unit Austrian lire.

had been ceded (sold or rented), and 101,867 hectares were still to be ceded. Overall it was about 28 per cent of the entire Veneto common patrimony identified in the report of Pietro Maniago. However, these figures were not equally distributed in the Veneto provinces. Almost all the land ceded (31,933 hectares) was located in the province of Udine. Of the land still to be ceded, the largest part was situated in Friuli: 58,120 hectares. In both cases, it was located mainly in the flatlands and foothills of the province, used by the inhabitants of the respective municipalities for the loose grazing of their animals.[104] Indeed, in that area was concentrated the majority of the common land where the work of agricultural conversion proposed by Maniago and other landowners could actually be attempted.

To understand the impact of the law on the mountain areas, the province of Belluno provides the most useful comparison. This province contained the highest proportion of common land after Friuli. However, these lands were concentrated in an orographically less

104   ASVe, *Presidio di governo*, 1845–1848, XII, b. 1348, f. 6/5.

Chapter 4

Table 8.

State of alienations in the province of Belluno following the issuing of the 1839 law;
summary presented on 27 September 1847.

District	Agordo	Auronzo	Belluno	Feltre	Fonzaso	Longarone	Mel	Pieve di Cadore	Total
Surface area of common land	8,745.30	30,850.40	14,615.90	20,281.30	7,967.20	16,943.70	7,685.00	18,926.50	126,015.30
Common land alienated	0	0	4.27	0	0	13.69	1,000.65	194	1,212.61
% of alienated common land/surface area of common land	0.00	0.00	0.03	0.00	0.00	0.08	13.02	1.03	0.96
Total income	0	0	1,630.00	0	0	607.90	87,986.75	11,452.40	101,677.05

Source: ASVe, *Presidio di governo*, 1845–1848, XII, b. 1348, f. 6/5. Surface area unit hectares; monetary
unit Austrian lire.

varied area than that of Friuli. These were lands of varied nature and
value, but falling within the category, coined in the Venetian period,
of mountain common land. It appears that in 1847 only 1,212 hectares had been ceded, of which more than 1,000 were in the pre-
alpine district of Mel, while 8,778 hectares remained to be sold
or rented. These are very small figures, considering that there were
126,016 hectares of common land in the province overall.[105]

Several factors contributed to limiting privatisation in the mountain areas. There were 'technical' difficulties due to the absence of
experts able to assess the land, and also the fact that many areas were
fairly inaccessible, especially in the winter months.[106] Moreover, forestry inspectors, who had to advise on any moves to privatise woodland, scrubland or even land sparsely populated with trees, always
took a very conservative approach, so that not infrequently the administrative authorities became exasperated by denials and delays.[107]

However, the main brake on the implementation of the 1839 law
came from the government itself. The decision to limit privatisation to
uncultivated land, the definition of which had been limited to areas of

---

105   Table 8.

106   ASVe, *Governo*, 1840–1844, XXVII, b. 6242, f. 50/263; ASVe, *Governo*, 1845–1849,
XXXIII, b. 7212, f. 50/13.

107   ASVe, *Magistrato camerale*, 1840–1844, XIX, b. 1030, f. 15/9.

loose pasture, almost completely excluded the mountain regions from the application of the law. Indeed, already in the autumn of 1839, the Belluno delegate had communicated to the central congregation that in his area the uncultivated lands were limited to 'landslides, to the bare slopes, to areas of gravel ... and to the scrubby rocks'.[108]

The privatisation of other land, especially woodland and alpine pastures, presented too many uncertainties and risks for central government to favour it. The concerns of the government were twofold. On the one hand, the sale of these types of land was complicated and would have triggered popular discontent again. On the other hand, the authorities were convinced that sharing out the land amongst the inhabitants would have caused, within a short time, the degradation of the land, with disastrous consequences both from the environmental and the socio-economic points of view. This therefore seems to support the argument that the 1839 law was 'decisive' only for Friuli, in its foothills and flatlands.[109]

Contemporaries also confirm the limited impact of the legislation in the mountain areas. As early as 1847, the Lamonese doctor, Jacopo Facen, admitted that the effects of the law in the province of Belluno were limited to claims on common lands usurped by private individuals, that in almost all cases had been assigned, after an administrative transaction, to the occupant, who had regularised his prior possession of the land.[110]

A similar assessment was made by the landowner and mayor of Belluno, Antonio Maresio Bazolle, who dealt extensively with the theme both in his memoirs and in a manuscript essay.[111] Bazolle was a great supporter of the privatisation of the common land, to the extent that he wished to see the privatisation not only of uncultivated

108   ASVe, *Governo*, 1835–1839, XLIV, b. 5303, f. 68/94.

109   Marino Berengo considered the 1839 law decisive, see Berengo 1963, p. 13. On this, see Pitteri 2005, p. 127.

110   Facen 1847; such a practice was already widespread before the issuing of the 1839 law, see Zannini, Gazzi 2003, I, pp. 94–96.

111   Cf. Maresio Bazolle 1986–1987, I, pp. 246–48 and *Memoria sullo stato attuale della pendenza relativa all'utilizzazione dei Beni Comunali della Comune di Belluno* conserved in ASCB.

lands but of all common land. He complained about how ineffective the legislation was, and he ascribed this to the long list of categories, special provisions and exemptions that were introduced regarding the different types of common lands.

Twenty years later, this assessment was reiterated by Cesare Paladini, the first prefect of Belluno after Italian unification. While confirming the validity of the 1839 law in the new political context, Paladini wrote that the legislation was poorly applied in the province, since nearly always only sterile land was identified as being suitable for privatisation.[112]

A rebellious and traditional culture

Studying the rural unrest of the Veneto region pre-unification, Piero Brunello found 'a rebellious traditional culture', as E.P. Thompson described English society in the latter half of the eighteenth century.[113] Some years later, Thompson himself identified in these two apparently contradictory terms one of the distinctive characteristics of subaltern subjects within a paternalistic society.[114]

This combination of 'rebellious and traditional' made it possible to resolve another apparent dichotomy, that between 'tradition and modernisation'. Considering these two terms as complementary, the popular unrest of these decades no longer appears as reaction (usually understood in a conservative sense) to change imposed from outside, but as part of a relationship of continuous political mediation – more or less conflictual – between the different actors involved.[115]

From the analysis of the protests that followed the issuing of the 1839 law, in Cadore as in other places, there constantly emerges a layered picture of subversive behaviour motivated by customary el-

---

112   Paladini 1867.

113   Cf. Brunello 2011, p. 191; Thompson 1978, p. 154. Ranajit Guha identified two tendencies (i.e. conservative and radical), which are only apparently similar, since in this case the two terms are in a 'mutually contradictory' relation, see Guha 1983, p. 11.

114   Thompson 1993, p. 9.

115   Cf. Rosemberg 1988; Sahlins 1994. In both cases the critical reference is to Weber 1976.

ements.[116] For example, the ultimate interceder for the popular demands was identified in the emperor, the 'good sovereign' whose intervention was invoked to support the people and who was often opposed to the stances of those local administrators who tried to block the division of the common land. Another recurring aspect of the claims was the presence of ancient documents capable of proving the people's legitimate ownership of the lands administered by the municipalities, mainly copies of donations and privileges granted by previous rulers. The leaders of the protests (e.g. Valentino Zannantoni and Giovanni Battista Martini Faitel) gained particular prestige and influence from having possession of these papers.

Alongside these specific appeals to titles that documented the rights of the inhabitants, there was one that was more generic to local customs. Once again, popular protest had assumed the symbolic form of an invasion of the woodlands, already seen in previous decades and acted out in order to reaffirm the rights that the inhabitants boasted they held over those lands.[117] When it was then decided to mediate an agreement with the provincial delegate, the villages that made up the municipality of Comelico Superiore met according to the ancient form of the *regoliere* assembly. The request to share out the lands was not made at the municipal, but at the village level, according to a geography of the *ancien régime* that corresponded to that of the *regoliere* institutions. Moreover, only those inhabitants considered 'original' would be able to benefit from the division of lands, while 'foreigners' would be excluded.

Yet these claims, all inspired by references to a traditional world, were taken forward by exploiting the contingencies of the new political-administrative context, and in particular the possibilities offered by the most recent legislative developments.[118] The application of the 1839 law was urged in order to restore a system of local management of the resources that had already been invoked in previous years. The appeals drawn up by the lawyer Serrafini and the popular petitions were, at least until the pub-

116 For a comparison with other protests following the issuing of the 1839 law, see Brunello 2011, pp. 7–42.

117 Hobsbawm 1974.

118 Cf. Water 2001.

lication of the circulars in 1840–1841, compatible with the legislation and, indeed, called for its application according to the criterion of division between the inhabitants of the municipality. The same appeals to the cadastral documentation and to the ambiguous wording with which the common lands had been described legitimised these claims.[119]

Furthermore, the constant references to customs or traditional rights functioned to support demands that, on the contrary, proposed an innovative land structure. In fact, the legitimate tenure of the original inhabitants of Cadore regarding the common lands, supported by documents from the feudal era, did not provide for the restoration of the *regole* or of the methods of territorial management associated with the *regole*. The traditional regulations could prove useful to identify the beneficiaries of these resources (the original inhabitants), the assignment criterion (to the household) and those that would have regulated its use, but the sharing out of the lands between the inhabitants of the respective villages was something different from the ancient communal management.

According to Valentino Zannantoni's account, the most detailed source available on the protests and demands associated with them, there were two issues that required a radical transformation of the existing system. The first was of an administrative character, namely the attempt to free the local management of community resources from the growing burden arising from the process of institutional modernisation – modernisation that the majority of the Cadore population felt extraneous to their own interests. The second was of a social nature and concerned the constant demographic growth that was compromising the balance between population and resources. For Zannantoni, in the situation that was taking shape, most of the inhabitants, constrained by poverty, would no longer see the common woodlands as something to be taken care of and would be forced to undertake more and more illegal cuts, leading to the ruin of the forest areas and the filling up of the Auronzo prison.[120]

In Cadore, the conflict that followed the enactment of the 1839 law

---

119 See the 'paradigm of manipulation' approach in Ago 2006, p. 246.
120 BSC, *Fondo De Pol*, b. 15, f. 455.

was more severe than in other areas of Lombardy-Venetia. After all, the lands in question, for the most part woodlands, represented a patrimony of immense value, both for those that wanted its division and for the state apparatus that opposed it. However, the demands put forward by the rural population following the enactment of the law were the same in the other Veneto provinces, including those in which common property, due to the location and nature of the land, was coveted by the local landowners, and its disposal was supported by government directives.

In this sense, developments in San Daniele are indicative. Here there broke out the most significant protest of the Friuli plain after the issuing of the 1839 law. On this occasion, also, the initial reaction of the population was to clamour for the division of common property among the inhabitants. Only when they feared that the land would be assigned by auction, with the participation of foreigners too, did the crowd forcefully prevent the sales operation from going ahead. The reasons for the revolt are well illustrated by the slogan shouted by the inhabitants who were crowded around the town hall: '*non vogliamo l'asta, ma bensì la divisione* [we do not want the auction, but rather the division]'.[121]

This type of demand prevailed amongst the poorest social groups, while the attitude of the middle and upper classes was more varied and, often, more difficult to decipher clearly. In the first place, this is because quarrels over the management of common resources must be placed within the context of more complex political power struggles at the local level.[122]

The situation was complicated by the diversity of the territorial contexts. On the Friulian plain, the project of economic modernisation proposed by count Pietro Maniago and those earlier landowners who had seen themselves as agronomic experts, met with support both from the landed elites and central government. However, the situation in the Alpine regions was very different. Here these lands consisted of woodland and pasture of high value. In these areas, in fact, privatisation was op-

---

121   Brunello 2011, p. 48. For other examples, cf. Fabris 2011; Munno 2015.

122   See the disputes opposing Martini Faitel and Francesco Osta against the Zandonella Dall'Aquila family in BSC, *Fondo De Pol*, b. 15, f. 455; BSC, *Fondo Manoscritti*, ms. 499; ACCS, *Corrispondenza*, 1840, 27 Mar. 1840, 8 June 1840.

posed by the state, which was concerned to protect the forest resources and the territorial balance, and also by the elites, who wanted to cover the costs of modernisation through proceeds from these lands. These costs would otherwise weigh on personal taxes and the land surcharge.

Yet the prospect of sharing out the lands, which was defeated by circumstances, was not only supported by the mountain smallholders and by the more traditionalist elites.[123] These proposals, although they sprang from very different assumptions, had similarities with those put forward a few years later by individuals who were certainly not sympathetic to feudal institutions or opposed to agrarian modernisation. For example, the Carnic doctor Giovanni Battista Lupieri saw in the division of the woodlands among the inhabitants of the area 'the only means of giving a strong and general drive to domestic agriculture and silviculture'.[124] A similar opinion was expressed regarding the Lombard Alps by the future organiser of the first agrarian survey of the Kingdom of Italy, Stefano Jacini.[125]

Finally, it is important to consider the relationship between the riots that followed the issuing of the law and the Risorgimento movement, especially during the revolts of 1848. According to the classic historiographical interpretation, the 1839 law has been seen as one of the main causes of the rupture between the Austrian administration and the rural population, above all in mountain areas. The severity of the unrest that followed the law's publication supports this interpretation. However, I would argue that the reasons for this discontent need to be reviewed; as does the suggestion that it translated into strong support by the rural population, especially in the Alpine areas, for the political project of Daniele Manin. I propose to undertake this task in the next chapter.

---

123   Simona Cerutti understood E.P. Thompson's notion of 'history from below' as a call to focus research on those cultures which had been delegitimised during the historical process: see Cerutti 2015.

124   Lupieri 1852, p. 41.

125   Jacini 1854, pp. 116–17. On Jacini, see Betri 1998.

5.

FROM REVOLUTION TO UNIFICATION. THE SUNSET OF THE CIVILISATION OF WOOD

Land and freedom

They hung the tricolor kerchief from the campanile, sounded the alarm with the bells, and began to shout in the square: 'Hail to freedom!' Like the sea in the thick of a storm. The crowd foamed and swayed before the rich men's club, in front of the City Hall, on the steps of the church – a sea of white caps. Axes and sickles glistened in the sun. Then they burst into an alley. 'You first, Baron! Who had people whipped and lashed by your field watchmen.' At the head of the group there was a witch, her old hair standing on end, armed with nothing but her nails. 'You, priest of the devil, who sucked our souls out of us! You, wealthy pig, who can't even run away, so fat you are with the blood of the poor. You, cop, who brought to justice only the poor because they didn't own anything. You, woods-keeper, who sold your own flesh and your neighbour's flesh for two *tanari* [twenty cents] a day!'[1]

When I read the novel *Libertà* for the first time, what struck me most was to find the woods-keeper among the first victims of popular rancour. Of course, this figure belonged to the security apparatus (a group that usually does not sit easily in the presence of an armed crowd); but with subtle differences, in that his main task was not the maintenance of social order, but of the environment. The reason for this resentment is explained a few pages later, where Giovanni Verga describes the fermenters of the riots, on the evening of the first day of 'freedom', intent on planning the partition of the woodlands above the village.

Verga's contemporaries were aware that, although the name of the village where these events occurred is not given, the novel was inspired by the tragic and well-known events that took place in Bronte in the

---

1   The novel *Libertà* ['Freedom'] was published for the first time in the journal *Domenica Letteraria* on 12 March 1882. Here I quote from Verga 1973, pp. 206–07.

summer of 1860, during Garibaldi's campaign in Sicily. Recently, Lucy Riall has shown how the popular discontent that triggered the violence of those days was linked both to the political circumstances of the time and to long-standing disputes that affected the local community and, at the same time, set it against the external forces. Indeed, it was precisely the combination of these two elements that unleashed the tensions, since the population considered the arrival of Garibaldi's forces as the opportunity finally to obtain the division of the common land, something that had been consistently sought over the previous decades and always blocked by the local elites.[2]

This analysis also allows us to reconsider the role of the Bronte peasants, who in Verga's novel appear unable to understand the significance of the political upheavals in progress, forced into a sort of unconscious participation in the events of the Risorgimento. And the educated classes certainly depicted the actions and demands of the rural world at the onset of revolutionary events in this way for a long time.

Ippolito Nievo, an author with very different sensibilities and ideals from those of Verga, painted a similar picture. In Chapter 10 of his *Confessioni di un italiano*, the news of the arrival of the French troops is greeted by the inhabitants of Portogruaro with chaotic cries and disparate demands: 'Bread! Bread! ... Freedom! ... Polenta! ... String up the merchants! Open up the granaries!'[3]

These are just two of many possible examples that illustrate the authors' implicit denial of any political awareness or autonomy on the part of the rural population. This judgement has had a long life in the historiographical debate, also following the opinions of the main exponents of the democratic strand of the Risorgimento movement after the failure of the 1848 revolts.[4]

However, in recent decades, and paying particular attention to the great revolutionary wave of 1848, historians have attached more importance to the rural dimension of the political conflict, and also to the mutual interactions between local and supra-local events, analys-

---

2   Riall 2013.

3   Nievo 1964, p. 457.

4   Cf. Della Peruta 1965; Betri 2002.

ing how the different players within society reinterpreted the revolutionary events according to specific contextual objectives.[5]

In Italy, this line of research has been less advanced than in other European countries, since the most recent historiographical developments have mainly dealt with cultural issues, such as representations, perceptions and myths related to the national discourse.[6] However, a return to the study of the rural world and its role in the 1848 revolts and in the wider Risorgimento movement has often been urged.[7] A project of this type requires a preliminary analysis of the different local contexts, since then it is possible to understand more precisely the connections 'between economic situations, social relations and cultural and political orientations, and the intersection between short-term phenomena and long-term realities'.[8]

With this in mind, it seems worth making some observations on the development of revolutionary movements in Cadore, in the hope that this can help us to understand the widespread and varied involvement of rural populations in the broader events of the 1848 revolts and the Risorgimento. These dynamics have several peculiarities due to the particular Cadore context. For example, they differ from the Mantovano case analysed by Maurizio Bertolotti, which was characterised by a modern capitalistic agricultural system and the political initiative of some tenant farmers.[9] Instead, the Cadore events accord with Jonathan Sperber's assessment:

> As we have seen, peasant resentment about use of the forest was the greatest source of social tension in rural society before the revolution; it was also the single most common and most prevalent source of violence in the countryside during the spring of 1848. Everywhere that there were forests, there were forest riots.[10]

---

5   Sperber 2005, pp. 2–3. On Italy, see Francia 2012 (pp. 270–83 on the rural areas).

6   Banti, Ginsborg 2007.

7   Francia 2013. See also Alberto Mario Banti's assessment in Soldani 2008, pp. 31–32.

8   Bertolotti 2008, p. 531. See also Francia 2007. On the French historiography, see Balzani 1999.

9   Bertolotti 1998.

10   Sperber 2005, p. 124.

Chapter 5

It is generally agreed that by the second half of the 1840s the support initially enjoyed by the Austrian authorities in the rural areas of Lombardy-Venetia had largely disappeared. Even if the military governor of Milan, Marshal Radetzky, in a memorandum written at the beginning of 1848, proposed to exploit the devotion that the sovereign enjoyed in the countryside by establishing militias, potentially useful to prevent possible revolts in urban areas, his optimism was not shared by the contemporary reports of the local Austrian police officers.[11]

Several factors contributed to making the situation unfavourable to the Austrians. There were aspects of their rule that had never been accepted in rural areas, such as military service (lasting eight years) and some characteristics of the tax burden (especially the taxes on stamped paper and salt). These were compounded by the consequences of the economic crisis of 1846–1847, the effects of which were particularly severe in mountain areas, since self-sufficiency was limited by poor yields in cereal production and by potato blight, the potato having by now become of central importance in the population's diet.[12]

The discontent caused by the 1839 law for the privatisation of common land deserves a separate mention. As already mentioned in the previous chapter, the main studies on the Kingdom of Lombardy-Venetia have identified the issuing of the 1839 law and the consequent privatisation of the common land as causing a decisive breakdown in relations between the Austrian administration and the rural population. According to Marco Meriggi, in the mountain areas

> the government attempts to proceed with the sale of common property, given the recalcitrant resistance of the assemblies dominated by the members of the community, were plagued by riots, rebellions and bloodshed that discouraged the authorities from persevering in their course of action.[13]

For Paul Ginsborg, after the outbreak of the Venetian revolution in March 1848, 'in the mountain areas the actions of the peasantry

---

11   On Radetzky's memorandum, see Lucchini 1930. On the less optimistic evaluation of the local police officers, see *Carte segrete e atti ufficiali della polizia austriaca in Italia 1851–1852*.

12   On the period preceding the revolution in Veneto, see Ginsborg 1979, pp. 47–83.

13   Meriggi 1987, p. 191.

centred on the restitution of the communal rights and lands of which they had been deprived by the Austrian law of 1839'.[14] According to this interpretation, one of the factors that most influenced the strenuous resistance of the Cadore people to the Austrian reconquest was the resentment of the local population over the results of the 1839 law.[15]

There is no doubt that in those places where the lands had been sold to large landowners or speculators, the 1848 revolution aroused in the rural classes the hope of regaining what had been lost a few years before. For example, in Valtellina

> the Central Committee of Public Security was forced to issue a notice on 2 May 1848 to remind that 'the sale contracts regarding common property made by the respective Provincial Councils or other offices with approval from above' remained in full force, and that all those who had disturbed the peaceful enjoyment of such property 'that is the right of the buyer' should be held enemies of the public order and handed over to the competent courts to be punished according to the current laws.[16]

Similar situations occurred on the Friulian plain.[17] However, in these cases, it is important to understand what the demands of the population had been nine years earlier, when the law had been adopted. In fact, as I have sought to show, popular discontent did not arise from the issuing of the law, but from its non-implementation in the specific sense of the division of land among the local population. Only when it became clear that the land was to be sold by auction, and with the participation of foreigners, was the protest redirected against this eventuality.

This was not the case in Cadore, or in most of the mountain areas. In Cadore, in fact, less than 200 hectares of land were sold, all in the district of Pieve, consisting of some 'lower mountain slopes next to groups of houses'.[18] Any plans relating to the municipalities of the Auronzo district were stopped at the headquarters of the general

---

14   Ginsborg 1979, p. 173. On this line see also Ginsborg 1974; Davis 1988, pp. 60–65.
15   Ginsborg 1979, pp. 210–13.
16   Della Peruta 1965, pp. 90–91.
17   Brunello 2011, pp. 18–21.
18   ASVe, *Governo*, 1840–1844, XXVII, b. 6236, 50/2.

inspectorate for the woodlands in Treviso, where concerns about the protection of forest cover blocked any ideas of privatisation.[19] In fact, looking now at the entire province of Belluno, the privatisations were minimal, and almost entirely concentrated in the district of Mel (in the capital and in the town of Cesana), with no protests occurring in these municipalities.[20]

Therefore, in mountain areas popular discontent did not arise from any government attempts to privatise common property. On the contrary, one of the main sources of resentment towards the government was the failure to share out the lands. Moreover, this was noted by the surveillance police, as can be seen from a report sent to Venice by the Senior Police Commissioner of Belluno, Alessandro Benvenuti, on 18 January 1848, a few weeks before the start of the revolution. The population of the province was considered 'troubled by concerns and by poverty, as for example the Cadorini, the Comelicani and the Fonzatini, who want to divide up the woodlands, and therefore are easy to subdue by those who can make them hope for the division of the common lands, although this is not wanted by the government'.[21]

The question arose again in the spring of 1848, following the proclamation of the republic by Daniele Manin and the resulting collapse of the Austrian regime in the Venetian provinces. However, the question posed itself differently, depending on how the 1839 law was applied in the pre-revolutionary years.

In those areas where the land had actually been privatised by auction (mainly in the Friulian plain), the population requested that the sales be annulled and the lands shared out. In these cases, the incompatibility between 'political revolution and national revolution' was more evident.[22] In fact, in Friuli the main proponents of privatisation of the common lands (and often the beneficiaries of it) were the principal exponents of the revolution at the local level. Suffice it to mention Count Gherardo Freschi, a supporter and personal friend of

---

19   ASVe, *Ispettorato generale ai boschi*, 1845–1849, b. 319, f. 3.

20   ASVe, *Governo*, 1845–1849, XXXIII, b. 7212, f. 50/13.

21   *Carte segrete e atti ufficiali della polizia austriaca in Italia*, 1852, III, pp. 297–98, n. 674.

22   The reference is to Nievo 1988.

Daniele Manin, who for years had been campaigning for the sale of common property from the pages of his newspaper, *L'Amico del Contadino*.[23] The situation in Cadore was different, since in this case the dispute arose directly between the population and the revolutionary government.

Between revolution and reaction

As is well known, Cadore was one of the very few places in which the revolutionary forces were able to mount an effective resistance to the reconquest of the Veneto carried out by the Austrians in the spring of 1848. This resistance, despite the inferiority of men and equipment, lasted for more than a month, from the end of April to the beginning of June, and was shaped by several factors. The first of these was the strategic location of the resistance, since the few communication routes at the bottom of the valley could be easily controlled, even though the besiegers had superior forces. Moreover, unlike on other occasions, the provisional government in Venice managed to provide some military support to the local militias and, above all, sent one of its best officers, Pier Fortunato Calvi, who was later celebrated as one of the martyrs of the Risorgimento. One last factor that is often held to have motivated the commitment of the Cadore people to the republican cause was the emotional bond that still tied them to the government of the Serenissima.[24]

However, the reappearance of the Lion of St. Mark (the emblem of Venice) in Cadore was not just viewed in terms of old allegiances but also in terms of perceived rights. The news of the proclamation of the republic in Venice was received in Cadore with the cry: 'Hooray! Now we are masters of our woods!'[25] Moreover, the same symbolism

---

23   Brunello 1979a, p. 95.

24   On the 1848 revolt in Cadore, cf. Comitato Cadore 1848–1998 1999; Larese, Vendramini, Zavarise 2000; Franchi 2011, pp. 171–83: Ronzon 1894 is a typical example of Risorgimento hagiography, but with much information on local events and the main figures of the revolt.

25   ACA, *Amministrazione*, 1840–1896, I, b. 271, 7 July 1848.

used in the Venetian revolution provided legitimacy to the claims that had already characterised the Cadore protests in the preceding years.[26]

An appeal sent by Manin to the Cadore people in early April, in which loyalty to the new republic was invoked recalling the 'ancient privileges' of the Venetian era, provoked yet another mass invasion of the woodlands by the inhabitants of the Auronzo district. Once again, the popular demand was to proceed with the immediate division of the common land between the original families; and this claim was based on the privileges granted in the Venetian period and never recognised by the more recent French and Austrian regimes.[27] In fact, the population of Auronzo, gathered in the town square, in the presence of the municipal deputies and the civic guard, linked the request for weapons to defend the borders with the Tyrol – and therefore its support of the republican cause – to their request for the reinstatement of the rights enjoyed under the Serenissima, 'among which, that of the free management and full enjoyment of their common lands'.[28]

The provisional committee of Belluno, in informing the government of the state of 'anarchy' that prevailed in the area, urged the intervention 'of at least 500 armed men' to quell the riots.[29] Manin merely sent a decree urging 'respect for the laws in force, otherwise we shall fall into anarchy, an enemy more formidable than all the Austrian armies'.[30] The call for order did not have the desired effect since, just five days later, Manin was forced to retrace his steps and invited the Cadore municipalities to propose changes to the current forest law in order to better reconcile public and private interests.[31]

Meanwhile, the proclamation that asked the population to respect the forest law in force, issued by Venice in the hope of re-establishing

---

26 On the reappearance of the Lion of St. Mark in Venice, see Brunello 1999, pp. 131–35; Brunello 2018.

27 BSC, *Fondo Manoscritti*, b. 645, f. 3. On the Auronzo uprising cf. Ginsborg 1979, p. 174; Bernardello 1970.

28 ACA, *Amministrazione*, 1840–1896, I, b. 271, 10 Apr. 1848.

29 AMC, *Carte Manin*, n. 3619; Ventura 1957, p. 115.

30 BSC, *Fondo Manoscritti*, b. 645, f. 3.

31 AMC, *Carte Manin*, n. 3625.

order, did not obtain the desired result, although it was posted in every village and read out by all the parish priests of the area. The district commissioner warned that the protest had spread from Auronzo to the other municipalities of the district. In Villagrande, in the municipality of Auronzo, 2,000 trees were cut down in a municipal woodland.[32] In Dosoledo, in the municipality of Comelico Superiore, the *regola* 'according to the model of the pre-existing republic' had been reconstituted, and the respective *regoliere* representatives were elected. Comelico Inferiore, San Pietro and Lozzo decided not to submit to any higher authority on the question of the common property.

> Almost everywhere it is proclaimed that now there is no longer any law, those who try to go against the tide of events are threatened with abuse, and they protest that they no longer want any officials, teachers or doctors, nor any charges for the maintenance of the roads, in order to increase the dividend at the end of the year for the benefit of individual families.[33]

Unable to quell these protests, given the war commitments which at that time also involved the Cadore region, a conciliatory solution was proposed in Venice. This was opposed to the division of the lands but willing to hand full autonomy to the municipalities regarding the management of the surplus deriving from forestry work. The provisional government's intention was, however, to stall, and the development of military operations removed the problem from its authority, since the Austrians reoccupied Cadore at the beginning of June.[34]

However, the return of the Austrians did not lead to the end of popular claims on the common woodlands. As it had been during the revolutionary phase, the municipality of Auronzo was the epicentre of the protests. In an attempt to implement a plan conceived during the turbulent weeks of the provisional government, the heads of the families of Villagrande and Villapiccola met on 19, 20 and 24 June and decided to share out the common woodlands. This initiative

---

32   AMC, *Carte Manin*, n. 3627.

33   ASVe, *Governo provvisorio*, 1848–1849, b. 12, 20 Apr. 1848.

34   ASVe, *Governo provvisorio*, 1848–1849, b. 12, 5 May 1848 and 18 May 1848. Cf. Brunello 2011, p. 78.

was not legitimised by the re-established provincial delegation.[35]

However, despite this the protests intensified during the summer and spread also to the neighbouring municipalities of Comelico Inferiore and Vigo.[36] The commissioner Domenico Scaglia warned his superiors that order was far from being restored in the district, since the majority of the population were refusing to return the rifles they had acquired during the brief revolutionary period. There were reports of ambushes of those who opposed the division of the woodlands, while the population prevented municipal councillors from attending council meetings, since only assemblies of the heads of families were considered legitimate for the purpose of managing the common land.

On 27 August, the district commissioner attended an assembly of the villagers of Villapiccola, at which the organiser (*abboccatore*) of the forestry work was to be nominated. The villagers also decided to fell 300 trees without authorisation. When Commissioner Scaglia objected they replied 'that they no longer wanted to hear about licences, brandings or forest inspections'. On Tuesday 8 September, after the Mass at Villagrande, outside the church of Santa Giustina, a ceremony was organised at which each head of the family was assigned by lot a portion of the patrimony that had previously belonged to the *regola*. One hundred and ninety eight families benefited from the division of the land.

Commissioner Scaglia warned that the only way to restore order would be a military occupation of the district, possibly to be carried out at night, in order to arrest the main supporters of the division of the woodlands and to disarm the population while everyone was sleeping. Thus, on the night of 23/24 September, 150 soldiers entered Auronzo and occupied the centres of the main villages (Villagrande and Villapiccola). They arrested eight of those who had been most involved in the protests and began to destroy the boundary markers of the woodland plots that had been assigned to the villagers by lot.

On the morning of Sunday 25 September, a decree was posted up

---

35   ACA, *Amministrazione*, 1848–1850, I, b. 99, 22 Aug. 1848.

36   The following information is from ACA, *Amministrazione*, 1840–1896, I, b. 271.

in the square and read out during the Mass, announcing the extension of the *statario* judgement.[37] This was a procedure of summary justice that provided for a wide use of the death penalty. Giovanni Battista Zandegiacomo Zampogna, father of five children and described by the district commissioner as 'a good man', was caught with a shotgun at home and shot on the spot.

The situation remained tense over the following months, since the families who had been assigned the woodland plots repeatedly tried to restore the boundary markers destroyed by the military and to make cuts in those parts of the forest that they considered their property.[38]

At the end of the military occupation, the chosen target of popular hatred was the forestry inspector Francesco Erasmo Coletti, 'regarded by the troublemakers of the two districts of Cadore as the opponent of the division of the common property and especially of the woodlands'. He was even unable to set foot in the district of Auronzo, where 'there took hold the false idea that he had been behind the arrival of the imperial troops in those parts'.[39] On 1 November, Coletti was transferred to the forestry department of Padua, since it was impossible to guarantee his safety in Cadore, and the Asolo forestry inspector Adolfo di Bérenger was appointed in his place.[40]

Forestry violations, customary practices, prophecies

In addition to the collective outbursts of protest, such as those that occurred following the 1839 law or in conjunction with the 1848 revolts, the conflict around the use of the forest resources was evidenced also by less striking forms of opposition, but ones just as rooted among the population. These took the shape of systematic violations of the forestry codes. This phenomenon was widespread almost everywhere in Europe during those decades, part of the more

---

37   Ginsborg 2002; Rossetto 2018.
38   ACA, *Amministrazione*, 1848–1850, I, b. 99; ACA, *Amministrazione*, 1850–1853, I, b. 103.
39   ASVe, *Ispettorato generale ai boschi*, atti riservati, b. 667, 9 Oct. 1848.
40   ASVe, *Ispettorato generale ai boschi*, 1845–1849, b. 330, f. 59.

general process whereby customary practices became criminalised, within the dynamic of social and economic transformation that affected most of the continent.[41]

There is no doubt that it was a widespread phenomenon. Since the early years of Austrian rule in the Veneto region, the political and financial magistracies of the various provinces had repeatedly sent requests to the government to curb the spread of forest crimes.[42] Moreover, the problem was perceived to be getting worse, so much so that, at the start of the 1850s, it was proposed to concentrate the efforts to protect only certain woods that were considered strategic from an economic or environmental point of view. Overall the report implies that it was not possible to implement an effective policy to limit transgressions for the entire forest patrimony.[43]

I refer to the perception of the problem since violations of the forestry laws formed a type of crime difficult to measure. The most obvious reason for this, and a reason often reiterated by the Austrian authorities, is that the available data, made up of complaints and convictions, represented a too small part of the actual abuses to construct reliable assessments. This was especially so given that the most densely wooded areas were those in which environmental constraints made social control more difficult.

Furthermore, violations of forest laws varied in several ways. A first differentiation was made in the Austrian legislation. Crimes committed in a forest area could fall into two distinct categories: 'forest infringements' and 'serious offences against the security of property'. The first category covered the most minor crimes committed in public woodlands: the felling of a few trees for personal use, unauthorised entry into a woodland with felling tools or animals

---

41   For an analysis of forest crimes as clues of a broader social tension, cf. Thompson 1975; Bushaway 1982; Ceschi 1996; Sansa 2003, pp. 92–116; Grewe 2004; Bobba 2015, pp. 146–59. The classical model, in this respect, is an article published by a young German journalist, destined to great intellectual influence, in the *Rheinische Zeitung* (1842): Marx 1975.

42   ASVe, *Governo veneto*, 1819, XXIX, b. 1483, f. 3.

43   ASVe, *Luogotenenza provincie venete*, 1852–1856, LXX, b. 623, 1/5.

etc. The second in theory covered the more serious crimes.[44] However, it was a very nuanced distinction, evidenced by the fact that the abusive felling of a tree in a common wood was considered a 'forest infringement' only if the accused came from the village that owned the woodland, while if he came from another village within the same municipality, the theft was considered a 'serious offence against the security of property'.[45]

According to research carried out using the records of some of the local courts (in Friuli) for the 1850s and 1860s, it seems that forest crimes made up the majority of offences committed in rural areas.[46] Obviously the crimes varied greatly in terms of the extent of the spoils, the type of people involved and the way in which they operated. For example, in serial or larger thefts, alongside timber merchants, the very people in charge of enforcing the laws were frequently involved, and these figures could extract the greatest spoils.

With regard to the forestry inspectors, it must be said in their defence that their working conditions and salaries were far worse than those of other employees of equal rank in the Austrian administration.[47] It is not surprising that they looked for other ways of supplementing their income. At the lowest level of forest management, the municipal foresters experienced even greater problems. In their case, intransigence was inconceivable, since they were appointed from among the inhabitants of the municipalities they were supposed to oversee, with all the risks that this proximity entailed. Indeed, such was the case for the other municipal officers.

As already explained, unlawful acts were carried out by the municipal officers of the Auronzo district (with the suspected complicity of the forestry inspector and the chancellor) during the 1810s; and neither were such practices uncommon in the following decades. In the autumn of 1852, in Comelico Superiore, the municipal deputy Francesco Osta,

---

44   Guazzo 1853, II, pp. 484–541.

45   ASVe, *Governo*, 1840–1844, LXXIX, b. 6912, f. 11/9; ASVe, *Governo*, 1840–1844, LXXIX, b. 6910, f. 9/350.

46   Cf. Brunello 2011, p. 68; Bianco 2002b, pp. 142–43.

47   Lazzarini 2009, pp. 139–40.

the assistant commissioner Giovanni Talamini and the forestry actuary Antonio Kramer were investigated for having falsified the sizes of the logs that the village of Dosoledo had sold in the spring to the merchant Francesco Fabbro.[48] A year earlier, the municipal deputies had been accused of a similar offence to benefit the merchant Girolamo Gera.[49]

These were minor allegations compared with those levied at the gang led by Antonio Moretti, municipal deputy of Taibon Agordino who, with the complicity of a colleague, the municipal agent, a municipal forester and three relatives, was in the habit of simulating anonymous infringements in the common woodlands in order then to sell the timber at a preferential price, systematically forging the administrative documentation.[50]

According to the district commissioner of Auronzo, the municipal foresters Santo Frigo and Osvaldo Zandegiacomo, who were appointed in 1849 by the municipality of Auronzo, had a reputation for being specialists in forestry infringements, 'and indeed undeserving of all trust, since the overseers are worse than those being watched'.[51] And, as we have seen, those being watched were hardly blameless in those years.

These are just a few of the many possible examples. If the records of forestry officials in service during the years of Austrian domination are examined, it is clear that the majority of officials were suspected and repeatedly accused of embezzlement. In some cases, it is likely that these were unfounded allegations, deliberately made against an inspector who had proved too intransigent with the merchants or over those small violations carried out by the population in the district under his jurisdiction. Most of the time, however, their behaviour was far from irreproachable.[52]

Alongside these more elaborate and systematic offences – to which should be added all those not carried out directly in forest areas, but relating to forest products, such as the theft of logs in sorting areas

48   ASVe, *Presidenza della Luogotenenza*, 1852–1856, IV, b. 227, f. 6/3.

49   ASVe, *Presidenza della Luogotenenza*, 1852–1856, IV, b. 227, f. 6/1.

50   ASVe, *Governo*, 1840–1844, LXXIX, b. 6911, f. 9/408.

51   ACA, *Amministrazione*, 1844–1852, III, b. 134, 9 Mar. 1849.

52   Lazzarini 2009, pp. 163–85.

or during transport[53] – there was a huge amount of petty crime that comprised mainly small infringements in the common woodlands.

Legislative bans had no effect on this kind of behaviour, since the people arrested were acting according to 'the conviction of good or bad faith in the exercise of a personal right'.[54] The tolerant attitude of the local clergy was also influential in this respect, at least according to the testimony of the Belluno landowner Antonio Maresio Bazolle. In his memoirs, Bazolle recalls that an archpriest of his acquaintance told him 'that he always gave absolution to those who confessed to having stolen wood to make polenta. Yes, to make polenta, he said, because it is necessary to make it, but not in order to sell it.' This is because 'morally they [the villagers] are convinced that they are not doing wrong because, they say, the wood comes by itself, the master has not laboured for it'.[55]

This is very similar to the attitude noticed by Senator Emilio Morpurgo in the 1880s who, in his report on the Veneto region in the context of the Jacini agrarian survey, stressed 'the tendency of peasant farmers to believe that those fruits of the earth that are not produced by man are made available by providence to man'.[56]

Despite the progressive tightening of sanctions, the forestry infringements reported in Veneto steadily increased during the Austrian domination. For example, between the six-year period of 1821–26 and that of 1841–46, they went from 5,817 to 19,643. During both these periods, the province of Belluno was the worst offender of the entire Austrian Veneto region, with 2,712 infringements reported in the period 1821–26 and 6,069 in that of 1841–46. The number of complaints also exceeded those for the province of Udine, which had a larger area of forest.[57]

Faced with these steadily deteriorating statistics, the government

53   ACA, *Amministrazione*, 1835–1843, III, b. 133, 23 July 1836; ASVe, *Ispettorato generale ai boschi*, 1835–1839, b. 199, f. 15.

54   ASVe, *Governo*, 1845–1849, XLVI, b. 7375, f. 13/10.

55   Maresio Bazolle 1986–1987, II, p. 238.

56   Foa 1977, p. 9.

57   The data on the first period are in ASVe, *Governo*, Allegati, 1839, b. 278. The data on the second period are in ASVe, *Governo*, 1840–1844, LXXIX, b. 6912, f. 11/9; ASVE, *Governo*, 1845–1849, XLVI, b. 7375, f. 13/10.

and the forestry authorities took a rather wavering attitude. At first, 'given the very high number of forest infringements, and since most of them are committed by people unable to pay the corresponding fines', it was proposed to allow magistrates to apply a prison sentence directly, since in any case this was provided for in case of non-payment of the fine.[58] However, a bit later a contrary measure was promulgated, limiting punishment to the pecuniary sanction. This was because 'the supplementary punishment of detention for forest infringements, affecting mostly individuals of no education, belonging to the peasantry, does not act as a deterrent, since the general opinion is that detention for these reasons does not at all affect the good name of the convict'.[59] The phenomenon was endemic, therefore, and the sentence was not associated with any moral sanction. In most cases, the accused belonged to the poorest sections of the population, and they were often 'women and children'.[60]

The social nature of the crimes also emerges from the size of the thefts. The complaints mainly concerned the theft of one or two logs, bundles of firewood, or material needed to prepare litter for animals. As already noted, the pecuniary sanctions provided for were rarely paid, and those convicted usually served their sentence in prison.[61] Two further offences, which appear almost ancillary to the forest infringements, emphasise the sense of legitimacy with which those who contravened the prohibitions acted. These dealt with insults and threats to forestry officials who tried to prevent the unlawful actions.[62] Finally, there is a case that went beyond the terms of the forestry legislation and entered the sphere of canon law.

---

58   ASVe, *Magistrato Camerale*, 1830–1834, XXIV, b. 286, f. 1/3.

59   ASMi, *Agricoltura, parte moderna*, b. 6, 18 Sept. 1851.

60   ASVe, *Governo*, 1835–1839, LXXII, b. 5720, f. 14/17.

61   On the sanctions see *Regolatore amministrativo teorico-pratico, ad uso degli impiegati amministrative in genere* 1846, VIII, pp. 332–33.

62   Unfortunately, the sources on forest crimes are limited for the Austrian rule. There are no sources in the Belluno state archive, while the Venice state archive conserved only the appeals and the documentation is incomplete. I carried out a sample survey for the period 1840–1844, the one in which the documentation is more complete: ASVe, *Governo*, 1840–1844, LXXIX, b. 6909–6911, ff. 9/1–9/538

> Sappada is the furthest and highest of the municipalities in this alpine province, situated in the mountains that divide Belluno province from Friuli, and which join up with the Carnic Alps; its borders lap the Tyrol and Carinthia. Sappada has a population of about 1300 souls; once part of the province of Udine, it now forms part of the district of Auronzo, the inhabitants of which speak a rough Alemannic and are neither fully Germanic nor fully Italian in character. They are rough people, but good, frugal and industrious. Nowadays, from its position of obscurity, Sappada is attracting attention due to a curious event, as it has become the cradle and seat of a new Prophet, a self-styled reformer of the Christian religion.

With these words, the provincial delegate of Belluno introduced to the governor of Venice the events that had occurred at Sappada over the preceding months. The prophet was called Celestino Colle: he was eighteen years old, the son of a local timber merchant and nephew of the parish priest.[63]

On 26 July 1859, Celestino Colle informed the municipal delegation of Sappada that he had discovered a plaque on Mount Ostans. The find was dated 1215 and contained the express wishes of Ferdinando 'son of a Roman emperor'. He gave to the first 25 inhabitants of Sappada and to their heirs the woodland around the village; furthermore, the discoverer of the plaque was considered to be a bearer of imperial blood and was awarded the title of Prince of Archenstein (the stone of the ark).

The story emerged during a period of acute tensions between various factions in Sappada who were at loggerheads over the common woodlands, in particular the Digola woodland, over which there was also an unresolved dispute with the municipality of Lorenzago. Therefore, the municipal delegation reported to the district commissioner of Auronzo, who in turn warned the provincial delegate. The latter, however, did not take it further, dismissing 'the fact for an absolute fairy tale'. The delegate was also sceptical because, as he later

---

63   The following information is from ASVe, *Presidenza della Luogotenenza*, 1857–1861, IV, b. 328, f. 2. Claudio Lorenzini provided me this archival reference and a conference paper on Celestino Colle: see 'Stones, Woods and Blood. The Messiah of Sappada (Venetian Alps) revisited (1859–1860)', paper presented at the conference *Revisiting Early Modern Prophecies (c1500–c1815)*, University of London, 26–28 June 2014; I would like to thank him for this. See also Brunello 2011, pp. 87–92.

warned, the father of Celestino, Pietro Colle, was among those most active in the disputes over the common woodlands, and he was considered the director of the whole affair.

However, the miracles were not finished. Over the following weeks, Celestino Colle claimed to have fallen into a state of mystical ecstasy during which he had been to Purgatory and had saved a soul who had been suffering there for 600 years. The exorcism performed by the local parish priest, Father Mattia Kratter (brother of the mother), on 23 November was to no avail, since the following day Celestino returned to the parish priest and asked him to follow him to Mount Ostans, where a supernatural force led him to search for a new stone.

The two men, together with Celestino's father, an uncle and one of his friends, went onto the mountain in the evening and there, thanks to Celestino's new ecstatic vision, they found a stone in the shape of a rhombus. It bore an inscription designating the discoverer a prince, 'appointed by God and of Roman blood'. Furthermore, the inscription commanded that the find should be celebrated in honour of the 25 inhabitants who had founded Sappada, already mentioned on the previous stone. So, the following day, the event was celebrated: the church bells were rung and the parish priest, who had now become a witness to the miraculous events, officiated at a solemn Mass.

On 27 November, in the presence of the parish priest, Celestino Colle preached his first sermon in his house, in which he explained the meaning of the stones and declared himself destined by God to proclaim a new religion. On 11 December a second sermon was preached, liturgically more elaborate. Celestino entered the room where the 'faithful' had gathered, preceded by a crucifix and flanked by two followers, each carrying a lighted candle. Having blessed those present, he picked up three pebbles from the ground and threw them, calling them the nails of the crucifix. One of the pebbles struck a woman, 'a Magdalene, and the new Christ Celestino told her that she was saved'. Then he declared that no one, 'neither Priests, nor Bishops, nor the Pope; neither gendarmes, nor the entire army, nor His Majesty', could prevent his preaching, and he called the local parish priests 'priests of the devil'.

At that point, the parish priest Mattia Kratter, who until then, probably influenced by his kinship with the prophet, had supported the cause, understood that events were becoming dangerous and decided to report the matter to the district commissioner of Auronzo, who ordered the arrest of Celestino Colle.

The arrest took place on 16 December, while he was preaching yet another sermon. However, Celestino was not at all perturbed and gave an appointment to the faithful for a new sermon on 27 December, the day of St. John the Evangelist. On this occasion, the magistrate of Auronzo contributed to Celestino's fame because, probably unaware of the promise made by the prophet to his followers, he immediately released him, much to the amazement of the provincial delegate.

The fulfilment of the prophecy represented the culmination of the messianic career of Celestino Colle. On St. John's Day, in the presence of about 200 people, he declared himself a 'prophet sent by God' and appointed twelve apostles and four evangelists in order to begin to proselytise.

The same evening, the municipal deputy Giacomo Krotter tried to interrupt a meeting that Celestino Colle was holding with some followers in his house, but was threatened and forced to leave. This latest incident prompted the provincial delegate to take action to end the unrest. A new warrant was issued for Celestino Colle and for his father, two brothers and brother-in-law, who were all arrested on 1 January and transferred to the Auronzo prison. Ten days later, two other supporters of the prophet were arrested after they insisted on publicly supporting his doctrines[64].

At the same time, the civil authorities began a correspondence with the archdiocese of Udine for the removal of the parish priest Mattia Kratter, who was considered too implicated in the events of the previous months and also unreliable 'for the abuse of wine and liqueurs, as well as for suspicion of an immoral relationship ... with his own servant'. The issue remained unresolved for some months, given the need to find a replacement able to speak fluent German but, with the threat of a canonical trial, Kratter was forced to resign

---

64   ASVeG, *Tribunale di appello generale (1815–1871)*, 1860, IV, b. 2855, f. 12.

his parochial benefice and to leave Sappada in the summer.[65]

The other suspects were detained for some months in the prisons at Auronzo and then released, once public order had clearly been restored in Sappada, without any trial being brought against them. According to the commissioner Pietro Rodolfi, who had led the investigation, the only motive for the Colle family to stage this complicated hoax had been the idea 'to have in absolute private ownership the common woodlands in general, and in particular that woodland called Digola'.[66]

The era of this new messiah in Sappada was short-lived. Although his sermons saw a growing popular participation, undoubtedly high for such a small community, the second arrest of Celestino Colle and his main followers put an end to the spread of the new cult.[67] Over the following decades, the story was recalled by local writers, but it did not produce the folk memory that developed elsewhere around coeval heretical experiences. The best-known of these was that started a few years afterwards by Davide Lazzaretti on Mount Amiata.[68]

However, as noted by Claudio Lorenzini, the phenomenon of the messiah of Sappada can also be placed within the context of the malaise in rural areas caused by the great economic and social changes of those decades, of which the widespread appearance of millennial religious movements was a side effect.[69]

In this respect, the role of the parish priest Mattia Kratter in the story seems to me indicative. It would be a mistake to think that Celestino Colle's attack on the parish priest in one of his sermons was motivated by his immoral conduct and by any discredit that such conduct might cause in the district, rendering him an awkward ally for the new sect. Kratter's passions for wine and women (his housekeeper in particular) were well known. Yet the community of Sap-

---

65   Peratoner 2005, pp. 244–59

66   ASVe, *Luogotenenza*, 1857–1861, LIX, b. 1061, f. 34/311.

67   According to a testimony collected by the journalist Angelo Arboit in 1871, Pietro Colle committed suicide shortly after his release: see Arboit 1871, p. 164.

68   Hobsbawm 1971, pp. 57–73.

69   Claudio Lorenzini, see paper referenced in n.63. On the widespread heretical movements as a consequence of social and economic transformations in the Italian mountains, cf. Armiero 2011, pp. 54–62.

pada had the right to elect its own parish priest and to re-confirm his appointment annually. The well-known vices of Kratter had not prevented him from being elected and reconfirmed as parish priest of the community, even when the archdiocese had tried to oppose him with its own candidate.

The fact that the sect created by the Colle family had rejected the parish priest's support and did not hesitate to publicly accuse him perhaps shows that among the many changes taking place in those decades there was also a progressive erosion of the local clergy's capacity to mediate, and a marginalisation of its position within the reference hierarchy of the rural population.[70]

After unification

The tensions over the management of forest resources boiled over again in the form of collective protests in the period immediately after the annexation of Veneto to the Kingdom of Italy in 1866.[71] The three main reasons for the confrontations were: the use of water for the transport of timber, new demands for the sharing out of common woodlands and the so-called system of '*lavoranzie*' (forestry work).

The first of these concerned a dispute that had arisen during the final years of Austrian rule between some timber merchants and the municipalities of Cadore due to the free floating of the logs down the Boite and Piave rivers.[72] The main merchants active in the Cadore area had set up a company that was to take care of the management and maintenance of the *cidoli*, the main one of which was situated in the municipality of Perarolo, at the confluence of the two rivers. Article 14 of the company ordinances established a transit tax for the goods of non-members at double that of members. Given that the floating of the logs was at that time the most used and convenient method of transport, the measure was in fact attempting to introduce a monopoly on the trade of Cadore timber. For this reason, the Vene-

---

70   Cf. Fincardi 2001.

71   On the administrative transformation of this period, see Vendramini 2004.

72   The following information is from Follador 1988.

Chapter 5

Figure 11.

The cidolo of Perarolo in a early twentieth century photo. Source: Museo degli Zattieri del Piave, Codissago.

tian governor blocked the concession in March 1864.

Four years later, the merchants tried to obtain a new grant from the newly-installed Italian government. Once again, the municipalities of the area opposed the claims of the merchants. In the various appeals sent by the municipal officials to the prefecture of Belluno, the consortium's request was denounced as lacking any historical or legal legitimacy, as it was detrimental to the rights of free use of the waters that the Cadore people had always enjoyed. In confirmation of these prerogatives, all the attestations were listed which, from the Germanic emperors through to the Serenissima and then the recent Austrian rulers, confirmed the arguments of the officials.[73]

The consortium of merchants, described by the mayor of Selva as 'a handful of millionaires who, not content to be immensely rich from our goods', engage in new speculative actions, was accused of

---

73   On the traditional rights of the Cadore communities over the Piave waters, see Caniato 2006, p. 138.

not only wanting to harm the rights of the local communities on their own rivers, but also to oppose the principle of free trade.

On this last point, the municipal officials could count on the support of some timber merchants who were hostile to the monopolistic initiatives of the consortium; in particular, Bortolo Francesco Gera, a member of one of the most illustrious families of Comelico, which had been active in the Cadore timber trade for centuries. Bortolo Gera sent a memorandum to the prefecture that opposed these operations, behind which, according to the author, lay attempts at commercial expansion of the Wiel company.[74]

The documents sent by the local officials had the desired effect, since in September 1868 the prefecture of Belluno, in response to the request made by the consortium of timber merchants, declared 'that by virtue of ancient documents on which is based the ownership of those waters in the municipalities of Cadore, it could not grant them that claimed privilege'.[75]

A second element of the tensions was the renewed protests for the sharing out of common property that broke out in the months immediately following the annexation of Veneto to the Kingdom of Italy. As had already happened during the brief revolutionary period of 1848, the disintegration of the Austrian regime and the changed institutional context were exploited by a part of the population in the district of Auronzo to re-submit their long-standing claims regarding the common lands.

Major protests took place in the municipalities of Auronzo, Comelico Superiore and Lozzo, where some agitators

> interpreting in their own way the imperial resolution of 16 April 1839, do everything possible to share out these precious common forests among the individuals, to be enjoyed as they please; and even more so now, as they say, in that by entering under a new, totally free regime, it is no longer necessary to submit to the forest authorities.[76]

The hope placed in the new government by advocates of the division of land did not last long. While reaffirming the validity of the

---

74 On the Gera and Wiel (or Viel) families, cf. Vianello 1993; Vendramini 2010.

75 Quoted in Volpe 1873, p. 55.

76 ASBl, *Gabinetto di prefettura*, III, b. 12, f. 2, 24 Sept. 1866.

1839 law within the new institutional context, the prefect of Belluno forbade the possibility of dividing the woodlands and sent the royal carabinieri into the Auronzo district to quell the protests.[77] There were scuffles in the village of Candide, where eight people were injured. To restore order, 58 people were arrested, most of whom were sentenced in July 1867 to prison terms of between eight months and three years.[78]

Finally, a further cause of friction stemmed from the introduction in Cadore of the municipal legislation already issued for the Kingdom of Italy on 20 March 1865, and extended to the Veneto the following year. Article 128 of the new law provided that any sale, lease or contract for goods or works valued at more than 500 lire in a municipality should take place by public auction.[79]

Traditionally, in the district of Auronzo, the forestry works carried out in the common woodlands (cutting, first processing and logging) were not contracted by tender, but were managed by the local population under the supervision of leaders (called *abboccatori*) appointed by the same people. This system, known as '*lavoranzie*', guaranteed an essential supplementary income for a large part of the population, since each family had the right to have at least one member participate in the work.

As we have seen, the introduction of the forest law of 1811, which prescribed that public auctions should be held for logging concessions in public woodlands with 'living trees', had already caused serious problems in the Auronzo district, since the population demanded the maintenance of the existing labour system. On that occasion, the French authorities had agreed to grant an exemption on the matter, given the particular situation in the region and the importance of the forest resources for the subsistence of its inhabitants. This exemption was later confirmed by the Austrians.

Despite the clear opposition to the introduction of the auction by all the district's municipal administrations, Italian legislation proved less

---

77   Cf. *La voce delle Alpi*, 5, 7 Feb. 1867, p. 3. See also the reports in *La voce delle Alpi*, 3, 24 Jan. 1867, p. 3. Cf. Fabbiani 1990, p. 251. On the validity of the 1839 law after 1866, see Palatini 1867, p. 20.

78   *La voce delle Alpi*, 7, 21 Feb. 1867, p. 3; *La Gazzetta di Venezia*, 195, 22 July 1867, p. 776.

79   De Sterclich Napoli 1865, p. 729. On this law, see Aimo 2015.

flexible than that of the Kingdom of Lombardy-Venetia when it came to granting exemptions.[80] So, in 1870, to prevent new riots with regard to the common woodlands and the cutting and logging methods, the prefect sent a corps of riflemen to Comelico to oversee the forestry work.[81]

In many respects, the protests of these years replayed elements already experienced in previous decades: the symbolic invasion of common land, the demands made at a village rather than municipal level, the constant reference to ancient customs or privileges to legitimise perceived rights. However, one can see that the claims regarding these issues were gradually assuming a different form from that which had characterised previous unrest. Alongside the traditional elements, the institutional aspect of the dispute was becoming more important.

The juxtaposition of local specificities and state constraints became more a confrontation between the various levels – local and central – of public administration. There was also an increasing response to these events in provincial and regional publications, in which alternative arguments were put forward to those 'classical' ones presented by the liberal landowners.[82]

Thus, the president of the Belluno Chamber of Commerce, Riccardo Volpe, accused the supporters of the system of *lavoranzie* of being the same as those who had invoked the division of the woodlands in previous decades:

> slackers, hoping to live by scrounging, with little or no effort; debtors demanded it, hoping to free themselves from their importunate creditors; the poor, hoping suddenly to enrich themselves; some wealthy men and usurers, sure that the property would fall to them, enabling them to become still wealthier, to the detriment of the less affluent; then a great many demanded it, disgusted with the poor administrations over many years, very badly managed by both local and royal authorities, authorities that all agreed to draw their own individual profits from the common lands, and to mutually foster and protect themselves in defiance of the law.[83]

---

80   BSC, *Fondo De Pol*, b. 16, f. 491, 17 Mar. 1871.

81   Talamini 1871a, p. 1.

82   For a wide bibliography on the Cadore area, cf. Fabbiani 1938, sub voce 'Boschi' and 'beni comunali'.

83   Volpe 1871, pp. 85–86; Volpe 1873, pp. 47–48.

The first Cadore deputy in the Italian parliament, the priest Natale Talamini, while condemning the attempts to share out the woodlands, sided in favour of the system of *lavoranzie*. This was the only system, in his opinion, to simultaneously guarantee the economic development of the area and the protection of environmental resources.[84]

A few years later, *L'Esopo Bellunese*, a journal with democratic sympathies, supported the rivermen who were working in the timber trade on the Piave, in a dispute that pitted them against the timber merchants (described by the newspaper as the 'Lords of Cadore') in order to obtain better wages. In pleading the cause of the rivermen, the newspaper asserted its role in the confrontation between social classes:

> The struggle against individuals who, entrenched behind knightly crosses and senatorial togas, tyrannise that part of the population that is constrained to ask them for work, is not always without danger; nor is the inauguration of a just and holy crusade for the emancipation of slave labourers who have no means (because they have no education) to shake off their chains on their own.[85]

This is an example of how such conflicts were now placed within the wider social question that agitated the Italian countryside in that period. The issue was first signalled clearly at the end of the previous decade with the outbreak of the *macinato* riots, and was photographed over the following years with the publication of the findings of the Jacini agrarian survey.[86]

Furthermore, in the specific case of forest resources, these issues were intertwined with the contemporary debate in the local and national press, as well as in parliament, on the formulation of a forestry law that would allow the new state to supersede all pre-existing legislation, some of which dated back to the beginning of the century (for example the Napoleonic law of 1811). The debate was heated, and lasted

---

84   The pamphlet against the sharing out of the woodlands is Talamini 1867a. This publication opened a debate among the educated elite of the area, cf. Venzo 1867; Talamini 1867b. On the *lavoranzie* cf. the different opinions in Talamini 1871a; *Osservazioni sull'opuscolo di un anonimo. Le lavoranzie boschive nel circondario di Auronzo* 1871; Talamini 1871b. On Talamini, see Fabbiani 1977, pp. 178–79.

85   *L'Esopo bellunese*, 11, 16 June 1877. Quoted in Vendramini 2005, p. 78.

86   On the *macinato* riots in Veneto, see Casellato 2012. On the Jacini agrarian survey, see Lazzarini 1983. On the transformation of the rural world in that period, cf. Fincardi 2000.

Figures 12 and 13.

Timber transport on the Piave river in two early twentieth-century photos. Source: Museo degli Zattieri del Piave, Codissago.

from 1862, when the first proposal was made by Minister Pepoli, until the effective enactment of the 1877 law, during the Majorana-Calatabiano ministry.[87] The latter was strongly liberal in inspiration, and it immediately proved inadequate to safeguard and augment the forest patrimony as a central element in the protection of the territory. As a result, from the time of its enactment, the law was subject to proposals for substantial modification and even complete replacement.[88]

Epilogue

I chose to start this research at an institutional watershed – that is, the introduction of a new administrative system and new methods for the management of forest resources that occurred during the French rule of the early nineteenth century. I hope that I have shown that this choice is only meaningful within the context of the long-term changing relationship between the population, institutions and resources in the region examined and in the different political and economic systems in which it was embedded.

The logical choice would have been to adopt the same criterion for the endpoint of the research. In this respect there were two possible end-dates, the first of which was the annexation of these territories to the Kingdom of Italy in 1866. On the one hand, this date would not have taken into account certain continuities, such as the validity of French forestry law until 1877; indeed, the continuity was even more striking regarding the legislation on common resources, since there was no national legislation in this area until Royal Decree n. 751 was issued in 1924 (limited to civic uses only), then converted into Law n. 1766 in 1927 (which is still the reference standard). On the other hand, 1866 represented a moment of clear institutional discontinuity, also as regards the sources used in the research.

The second possible institutional endpoint was 1877, the date of enactment of the forest law that replaced the legislation introduced

---

87   Cf. Vecchio 1994; Sansa 2000; Celetti 2008, pp. 86–114.

88   Gaspari 1992; Agnoletti 2002.

by the French at the beginning of the century. However, this choice seemed at odds with the course I had followed in my research. Even taking into account only the judicial and administrative transformations, other changes had a more significant impact on the management of forest resources – for example, the conjunction between administrative reform and the related transformation of the predial tax through the introduction of the new cadastre.

In fact, the most suitable end-date to signal the discontinuity in the events examined so far – although it is not exempt from the critical issues inherent in setting a time limit – seemed to me to be 24 August 1867. This was the opening day of the railway line that connected Verona to Innsbruck through the Brenner Pass, creating a much faster connection between north-eastern Italy and central Europe than the existing Alemagna road.[89]

The Brenner route was just one section of the 50,000 miles of new railway line built in Europe between 1850 and 1870 (compared with 15,000 miles built before 1850). According to some interpretations, this development must be considered the main factor in understanding the transformation of the European continent in those decades.[90]

This transformation is known as the Industrial Revolution; a term that has been much debated and has assumed many meanings and interpretations. One of these is that proposed by Anthony Wrigley, who describes it as the transition from an organic economy, based on the ability to intercept the flows of solar energy made available by the process of photosynthesis, to an economy based on the use of fossil fuels.[91]

In this model, organic economies were first and foremost wood economies, since wood was both the most widespread raw material and the main source of energy. Thus, Wrigley's periodisation does not differ much from that already mentioned as having been proposed by Fernand Braudel: 'Civilizations before the eighteenth century were

---

89 Schram 1997, pp. 105–08; Cafaro 2000.

90 Landes 1969, p. 201. On the cultural and social impact of this transformation, see Schivelbusch 1986.

91 That is the stock accumulated over the millennia by an analogous process: see Wrigley 1988; Wrigley 2016.

civilizations of wood and charcoal, as those of the nineteenth were civilizations of coal. Everything in the European scene points to it'.[92] Indeed, half a century earlier, Werner Sombart had proposed a similar model; in *Der moderne Kapitalismus*, he defined the period that preceded 'the capitalism of coal' as the 'wooden age'.[93]

For the Italian Alpine region, as well as for most of continental Europe, the nineteenth century can be considered both the apex and the period of rapid decline of this so-called 'wooden age'. The century had opened with the debate, begun in the second half of the eighteenth century, on the disappearance of woodlands and the wood crisis. Such a debate was driven in the first place by the continuous increase in timber prices, part of a trend that, for the region covered by this study, continued until the second half of the nineteenth century.[94]

However, from this point on, the situation quickly changed. Certainly this was not due to a decline in the consumption of timber; indeed, consumption even increased as a result of the process of industrialisation. Suffice it to say that in 1897, for the Italian railway network, it was estimated that 2,031,000 cubic metres of timber was used in the construction of sleepers, and the maintenance of the lines absorbed 170,000 cubic metres of timber annually.[95] However, wood progressively lost its central importance in many economic sectors and also, in some ways, its symbolic value. In other words, there was a growth of consumption in absolute terms, but a decline in relative terms. From an energy perspective, there was an increasing use of other sources of energy, above all those of the 'subterranean forest' consisting of fossil fuels.[96] These new energy reserves guaranteed economic growth which, combined with technological developments, led to the use of alternative materials to wood (in particular metals)

---

92   Braudel, 1981, p. 362.

93   Sombart 1916–1927.

94   According to Pietro Bajo, the price of timber doubled between the 1820s and the 1850s: Bajo 1858, p. 12. For Natale Talamini the price of timber tripled in that period: Talamini 1871a, p. 36.

95   Vecchio, Piussi, Armiero 2002, p. 181. On the growth of timber consumption during the industrial transition, cf. Iriarte-Goñi, Ayuda 2012; Iriarte-Goñi 2013.

96   Sieferle 2001.

in various construction, industrial and manufacturing processes.[97]

Yet these changes, which in the longer term marked an evident discontinuity, occurred in Italy in a slower and more gradual way than elsewhere. With regard to energy consumption, the available data show that fossil fuels surpassed wood only at the end of the first decade of the twentieth century.[98] It is difficult to evaluate to what extent individuals and social groups were aware of this transformation, especially in a rural area such as Cadore.

However, there is one element of this process of modernisation whose impact, at least in the Veneto mountains, was also evident to contemporaries, who describe it clearly. The rapid development of the railway network in the third quarter of the nineteenth century completely redefined the geography of the timber trade and marked the end of the competitive advantages of Cadore and the other valleys of the Italian Alps, which were based on the presence of the watercourses that had kept transport costs low, rather than on greater availability of raw materials.[99] This process was similar to that analysed for the Baltic area and defined as 'the expansion of the timber frontier'.[100]

The situation is clearly described in an article that appeared in the *Gazzetta di Belluno* in December 1881. The opening of the Brenner railway line, and the subsequent connection of Trieste to the Fortezza-Villach line in 1871, are identified as the main causes of the collapse in the price of timber in the province over the previous decade since, by lowering transport costs, they had made timber from the forests of central and eastern Europe more competitive:

> [timber prices] remained sufficiently high in the years 1871 to 1874, but then in the following period from 1875 to 1878, depending on the quality of the goods, more or less perfect, they dropped by 7 to 9 [per cent], in 1879 by 13 to 17 percent, and finally, in the last two years, 25 to 30 per cent.[101]

In this context, the flooding of the following year, which caused

---

97 Kander, Malanima, Warde 2013, pp. 159–208.

98 Toninelli 2010.

99 Agnoletti 1998.

100 Cf. Daheur 2016; Lotz 2016.

101 *Gazzetta di Belluno*, 34, 21 Dec. 1881, p. 1.

huge damage to the district where the sawmills were concentrated, between Perarolo and Longarone, dealt a blow from which the timber supply chain did not recover. From then on, the 'forest question' was less and less seen in terms of timber supply, given the opening of new markets and the drop in prices, and increasingly in terms of territorial instability.[102]

In Cadore, as in the rest of Italy, the crisis in the timber supply chain did not signify a relaxation of the anthropic pressure on forest resources. Rather, the character of the pressure changed, as it became driven less and less by the timber trade and increasingly by population growth, by the intensification of activities linked to cattle breeding and by the consumption of wood in rural areas, which declined more slowly than in urban areas.[103]

However, the centrality of these resources in the lives of the inhabitants and communities quickly waned. Thereafter, the main employment opportunities involved temporary migration (especially linked to the construction sector), which peaked precisely in those areas where previously the economy linked to the exploitation of forest resources had been most relevant.[104]

The fact that this migration was directed mainly towards the construction sites of central and eastern Europe, in order to build the infrastructure that was to transform the social and economic order at the local level, can be seen as the other side of the process of modernisation. The analysis of the new possibilities opened up by this process, as well as its costs, which appear more obvious from the perspective of our protagonists – Francesco Perucchi, Valentino Zannantoni and Celestino Colle amongst others – is another story.

---

102   Lazzarini 1991; Vendramini 2000.

103   Agnoletti, 2005; Celetti 2008. On the cattle population in Belluno province, see the data in Zannini, Gazzi 2003, II, p. 467.

104   Lazzarini 1990, p. 191.

BIBLIOGRAPHY

Printed Primary Sources

Annali dell'Agricoltura del Regno d'Italia compilati dal Cav. Filippo Re **12** (1811): 193–207.

Annali dell'Agricoltura del Regno d'Italia compilati dal Cav. Filippo Re **17** (1813): 133–57.

Gazzetta di Belluno **34**, 21 Dec. 1881.

Giornale d'Italia **5** (1769): 401–06.

Giornale d'Italia **10** (1774): 389–90.

Agarinis Magrini, B. (ed.) 2000. *Caro amico pregiatissimo. Un epistolario dell'Ottocento fra Carnia, Cadore, Comelico.* Udine: Forum.

Antonini, G. 1789. *Opuscolo sopra i comunali di monte*, in *Raccolta delle memorie delle pubbliche accademie d'agricoltura, arti e commercio dello Stato Veneto.* Venice: presso Gio Antonio Perlini, I. pp. 109–90.

Arboit, A. 1871. *Memorie della Carnia.* Udine: Tip. Carlo Blasig.

Bajo, P. 1858. *Studi intorno al sistema forestale del Regno Lombardo-Veneto.* Venice: Tipografia del Commercio.

Bajo, P. 1882. *Sulla decadenza economica della provincia di Belluno: cause e provvedimenti.* Venice: Tipografia del Tempo.

Barpi, A. 1876. *La pastorizia del Cadore. Studi statistici, zootecnici, igienici ed agricolo-veterinari.* Pieve di Cadore: Tip. Tiziano.

Berengo, M. (ed.) 1962. *Giornali veneziani del Settecento.* Milan: Feltrinelli.

Bettina, G. 1869. *I boschi comunali nel distretto di Auronzo.* Belluno: Tip. Deliberali.

Buja, B. 1847. *Quali misure sarebbero da adottarsi onde conseguire lo scopo della rimboscazione dei monti nelle venete provincie.* Belluno: Tissi.

Carte segrete e atti ufficiali della polizia austriaca in Italia dal 4 giugno 1814 al 22 marzo 1848. 1851–1852. Capolago: Tipografia Elvetica.

Cattaneo, C. 1844. *Notizie naturali e civili sulla Lombardia*, I. Milan: Tip. G. Bernardoni.

Cattaneo, C. 1972. *Opere*, IV. Turin: Einaudi.

Cattaneo, C. 1956. 'Sulla bonificazione del Piano di Magadino a nome della Società promotrice. Primo rapporto', in A. Bertolino (ed.), *Scritti economici*, III. Florence: Le Monnier. pp. 174–237.

Codice di Napoleone il Grande pel Regno d'Italia. 1806. Florence.

Compartimento territoriale delle provincie venete. 1821. Venice: Per Francesco Andreola.

Da Ronco, P. 1903. *La famiglia Zandonella dall'Aquila di Dosoledo in Cadore. Memorie.* Lodi: Tipo Lit. C. Dell'Avo.

Da Ronco, P. 1905. *La villa di Gera in Cadore e le famiglie Vettori, Gera e Gera-Doriga.* Udine: Premiata Tipografia del Patronato.

Da Ronco, P. 1906. *Le famiglie Poli, Fabris e Pellizzaroli. Notizie genealogiche e biografiche.* Treviso: Tip. Turazza.

De Sterclich, A. 1865. *Annotazioni alla legge sull'amministrazione comunale e provinciale del 20 marzo 1865*. Naples: Tip. A. Trani.

Di Bérenger, A. 1863. *Saggio storico della legislazione veneta forestale dal sec. VII al XIX*. Venice: Ebhardt.

Di Bérenger, A. 1871. *Nuovo metodo di tassare i boschi ed assestarne l'economia*. Forlì: Febo Gherardi.

Di Bérenger, A. 1965. *Studii di archeologia forestale*. Florence: Accademia italiana di scienze forestali.

Doglioni, L. 1816. *Notizie istoriche e geografiche della città di Belluno e della sua provincia*. Belluno: Fissi.

Duhamel du Monceau, H. 1772. *Del governo dei boschi ovvero mezzi di ritrar vantaggio dalle macchie e da ogni genere di pianta da taglio e di dar loro una giusta stima*. Venice: per Giambatista Pasquali.

Duhamel du Monceau, H. 1774. *La fisica degli alberi in cui si tratta dell'anatomia delle piante e dell'economia vegetale*. Venice: nella stamperia di Carlo Palese.

Fabbiani, G. 1938. *Saggio di bibliografia cadorina*. Feltre: Castaldi.

Facen, J. 1847. 'Dei beni comunali incolti nella provincia di Belluno'. *Il Tornaconto* 2: 387–88.

Gautieri, G. 1812. *Notizie elementari sui boschi ad uso degli impiegati de' boschi del Regno d'Italia*. Milan: Stamperia Reale.

Gautieri, G. 1816. *Dei vantaggi e dei danni derivanti dalle capre in confronto alle pecore*. Milan: Gio Giuseppe Destefanis.

Gautieri, G. 1817. *Dell'influsso dei boschi sullo stato fisico dei paesi*. Milan: G. Pirotta.

Gené, G. 1833. *Necrologia di Giuseppe Gautieri*. Milan: dall'I.R. Stamperia.

Gervasis, G. 1790. *Dissertazione sopra i beni comunali della provincia Bellunese*, Verona: per gli eredi di Marco Moroni.

Gloria, A. 1855. *Dell'agricoltura nel Padovano*, II. Padua: Angelo Sicca.

Guarnieri, A. 1862. *Cubazione dei legnami squadrati e rotondi*. Trieste: Colombo Coen.

Guazzo, V. 1853. *Enciclopedia degli affari*. Padua: Crescini.

Jacini, S. 1854. *La proprietà fondiaria e le popolazioni agricole in Lombardia. Studi economici*. Milan: Borroni e Scotti.

Legislazione in materia di Regole e di usi civici. 1998. Seren del Grappa: Regione Veneto-Istituto Culturale di Zoldo.

Lupieri, G.B. 1852. *Osservazioni sui boschi della Carnia*. Udine: Vendrame (originally published in *L'Alchimista friulano*).

Maresio Bazolle, A. 1986–1987. *Il possidente bellunese*, I-II. Feltre: Comunità montana feltrina-Comune di Belluno.

Miari F. 1819. *Epistola del signor conte Francesco Miari al signor Vittore Gera*. Vienna: P.P. Mechitaristi.

Negrelli, A.M. 2010. *Memorie*. Seren del Grappa: Agorà Libreria Editrice.

Nievo, I. 1988. *Due scritti politici*. Padua: Liviana.

Nievo, I. 2010. *Il conte pecoraio. Storia del nostro secolo. Testo critico secondo l'edizione a stampa del 1857*, Simone Casini (ed.). Venice: Marsilio.

Bibliography

Nievo, I. 1964. *Le confessioni di un italiano*. Turin: Einaudi.

Osservazioni sull'opuscolo di un anonimo. Le lavoranzie boschive nel circondario di Auronzo. 1871. Padua: Prosperini.

Paladini, C. 1867. *Risposte ad alcune delle più frequenti questioni sull'amministrazione dei beni comunali*. Belluno: Tipo-litografia A. Guernieri.

Peratoner, A. (ed.). 2005. *Documenti per la storia di Sappada/Plodn. 1295–1907*. Pieve di Cadore: Associazione Plodar.

Raccolta degli atti di governo e delle disposizioni generali, Imperial Regio Governo di Milano. 1820. I/2., *Patenti e notificazioni pubblicate dall'I. R. governo di Lombardia dal 1 luglio al 31 dicembre 1820*. Milan: dall'Imp. regia stamperia.

Regolatore amministrativo teorico-pratico, ad uso degli impiegati amministrativi in genere. 1846. VIII. Milan: Stabile Civelli Giuseppe e Comp.

Ronzon, A. 1894. *Luigi Coletti. Memorie della sua vita, della sua famiglia, dei suoi tempi*. Milan: E. Rechiedei & C.

Ronzon, A. 1990. 'Dal bosco alla laguna', in G. Secco (ed.), *La Piave*. Cornuda: Belumat Editrice. pp. 72–77.

Sette, A. 1843. *L'agricoltura veneta*. Padua: Tipi del Seminario.

Soravia, P. 1988. *Descrizione delle risine e palorci della provincia di Belluno*. Belluno: Sommavilla.

Statuti della Communità di Cadore (Venezia MDCXCIII), ristampa anastatica. 1987. Bolgna: Forni.

Talamini, N. 1867a. *I boschi del Cadore*. Belluno: Tipografia Deliberali.

Talamini, N. 1867b. *Appendice alla memoria sui boschi del Cadore di N. Talamini in risposta alle osservazioni di Sebastiano Venzo*. Belluno: Tipografia Deliberali.

Talamini, N. 1871a. *Le lavoranzie boschive nel circondario d'Auronzo*. Venice: Tipografia Sociale della Gioventù.

Talamini, N. 1871b. *Risposta alle osservazioni pubblicate in Padova sulla memoria delle lavoranzie boschive*. Belluno: Tipo-litografia A. Guernieri.

Tariffa dei legnami in magazzino coll'aggiunta della misura del metro col piede veneto ed altri ragguagli. 1865. Venice: Brizeghel.

Ventura, A. (ed.). 1957. *Verbali del consiglio dei ministri della repubblica veneta. 27 marzo – 30 giugno 1848*, Venice: Deputazioni di storia patria per le Venezie.

Venzo, S. 1867. *Sui boschi del Cadore di Natale Talamini. Osservazioni*. Belluno: Tipografia Deliberali.

Verga, G. 1973. *The She-Wolf and Other Stories*. Berkeley–Los Angeles: University of California Press.

Volpe, R. 1871. *La provincia di Belluno. Notizie economico-statistiche*. Belluno: Tipografia Deliberali.

Volpe, R. 1873. *Sui boschi e sul commercio del legname nella provincia di Belluno*. Belluno: Tipografia Deliberali.

Volpe, R. 1880. *Terra e agricoltori nella provincia di Belluno*. Belluno: Tipografia Deliberali.

Wessely, J. 1993. 'Le segherie veneziane delle valli della Piave', in G. Caniato (ed.), *La via del fiume. Dalle Dolomiti a Venezia*. Verona: Cierre. pp. 325–68.

Secondary Sources

a Marca, A. 2001. *Acque che portarono: Il commercio del legname dal Moesano al lago Maggiore fra 1700 e 1850.* Prosito-Lodrino: Edizioni Jam.

Agnoletti, M. 1993. 'Gestione del bosco e segagione del legname nell'alta valle del Piave', in G. Caniato (ed.), *La via del fiume. Dalle Dolomiti a Venezia.* Verona: Cierre. pp. 73–126.

Agnoletti, M. 1996. 'Aspetti tecnici ed economici del commercio del legname in Cadore (XV-XVI secolo)', in S. Cavaciocchi (ed.), *L'uomo e la foresta.* Florence: Le Monnier. pp. 1025–40.

Agnoletti, M. 1998. 'Commercio e industria del legname fra XIX e XX secolo nell'Italia nord-orientale: aspetti tecnici e scelte imprenditoriali', in G.L. Fontana, A. Leonardi and L. Trezzi (eds), *Mobilità imprenditoriale e del lavoro nelle Alpi in età moderna e contemporanea.* Milan: Cluep. pp. 31–45.

Agnoletti, M. 2001. 'Fra storia e tecnica: sviluppi e tendenze della storia forestale', in Id. (ed.), *Storia e risorse forestali.* Florence: Accademia Italiana di Scienze Forestali. pp. 1–36.

Agnoletti, M. 2002. 'Le sistemazioni idraulico-forestali dei bacini montani dall'unità d'Italia alla metà del XX secolo', in A. Lazzarini (ed.), *Disboscamento montano e politiche territoriali. Alpi e Appennini dal Settecento al Duemila.* Milan: Franco Angeli. pp. 389–416.

Agnoletti, M. 2004. 'Legnami, foreste e costruzioni navali fra XV e XVIII secolo', in P. Galetti (ed.), *Civiltà del legno. Per una storia del legno come materia per costruire dall'antichità ad oggi.* Bologna: Clueb. pp. 143–70.

Agnoletti, M. 2005. 'Osservazioni sulle dinamiche dei boschi e del paesaggio forestale italiano fra il 1862 e la fine del XX secolo'. *Società e storia* **108**: 377–96.

Agnoletti, M. 2018. *Storia del bosco: il paesaggio forestale italiano.* Bari–Rome: Laterza.

Ago, R. 2006. 'Cambio di prospettiva: dagli attori alle azioni e viceversa', in J. Revel (ed.), *Giochi di scala. La microstoria alla prova dell'esperienza.* Rome: Viella. pp. 239–50.

Aimo, P. 2005. *Il centro e la circonferenza. Profili di storia dell'amministrazione locale.* Milan: Franco Angeli.

Aimo, P. 2015. 'Comuni e Province, funzioni e controlli (all. A)'. *Amministrare* 1/bis: 7–54.

Antonielli, L. 1983. *I prefetti dell'Italia napoleonica. Repubblica e Regno d'Italia.* Bologna: il Mulino.

Appuhn, K. 2000. 'Inventing Nature: Forests, Forestry, and State Power in Renaissance Venice'. *The Journal of Modern History* **72**: 861–89.

Appuhn, K. 2009. *A Forest on the Sea. Environmental Expertise in Renaissance Venice.* Baltimore: Johns Hopkins University Press.

Armano, L. 2015. 'Solero: la casata ai vertici di Sappada nel Bellunese', in L. Giarelli (ed.), *I signori delle Alpi. Famiglie e poteri tra le montagne d'Europa.* Tricase: Ista. pp. 369–80.

Armiero, M. 1999. *Il territorio come risorsa. Comunità, economie e istituzioni nei boschi abruzzesi (1806–1860).* Naples: Liguori.

Armiero, M. 2000. 'Una risorsa ambientale: il bosco tra Otto e Novecento', in M. Costantini and C. Felice (eds), *Storia d'Italia. Le regioni dall'Unità ad oggi. L'Abruzzo.* Turin: Einaudi. pp. 877–920.

Armiero, M. 2007. 'Misurare i boschi', in R. De Lorenzo (ed.), *Storia e misura. Indicatori sociali ed economici nel Mezzogiorno d'Italia (secoli XVIII-XX).* Milan: Franco Angeli. pp. 238–59.

Bibliography

Armiero, M. 2011. *A Rugged Nation. Mountains and the Making of Modern Italy*. Cambridge: The White Horse Press.

Balzani, R. 1999. 'Immagini del '48 francese'. *Contemporanea* **2**/I: 15–33.

Banti, A.M. and P. Ginsborg (eds). 2007. *Storia d'Italia*, XXII, *Il Risorgimento*. Turin: Einaudi.

Barbacetto, S. 2000. *'Tanto del ricco quanto del povero'. Proprietà collettive ed usi civici in Carnia tra Antico Regime ed età contemporanea*. Pasian di Prato: Circoli Culturali della Carnia.

Barbacetto, S. 2008. *'La più gelosa delle pubbliche regalie'. I 'beni comunali' della Repubblica Veneta tra dominio della Signoria e diritti delle comunità (secoli XV–XVIII)*. Venice: Istituto Veneto di Scienze Lettere ed Arti.

Barca, S. 2010. *Enclosing Water. Nature and Political Economy in a Mediterranean Valley, 1796–1916*. Cambridge: The White Horse Press.

Beloch, K. J. 1994. *Storia della popolazione d'Italia*. Florence: Le Lettere.

Beltrami, D. 1954. *Storia della popolazione di Venezia dalla fine del secolo XVI alla caduta della Repubblica*. Padua: Cedam.

Beltrami, D. 1961. *Forze di lavoro e proprietà fondiaria nelle campagne venete dei secoli XVII e XVIII. La penetrazione economica dei veneziani in Terraferma*. Venice: Istituto per la collaborazione culturale.

Berengo, M. 1963. *L'agricoltura veneta dalla caduta della Repubblica all'Unità*. Milan: Banca commerciale italiana.

Bernardello, A. 1970. 'La paura del comunismo e dei tumulti popolari a Venezia e nelle provincie venete nel 1848–49'. *Nuova rivista storica* **1–2**: 1–64.

Bertogliati, M. 2014. *Dai boschi protetti alle foreste di protezione. Comunità locali e risorse forestali nella Svizzera italiana (1700–1950)*. Bellinzona: Casagrande.

Bertolotti, M. 1998. *Le complicazioni della vita. Storie del Risorgimento*. Milan: Feltrinelli.

Bertolotti, M. 2008. 'Non solo nelle città. Sul Quarantotto nelle campagne', in E. Cecchinato and M. Isnenghi (eds), *Gli Italiani in guerra. Conflitti, identità, memorie dal Risorgimento ai giorni nostri*, I, *Fare l'Italia: unità e disunità nel Risorgimento*. Turin: UTET. pp. 526–39.

Betri, M.L. 1998. *La giovinezza di Stefano Jacini. La formazione, i viaggi, la 'proprietà fondiaria' (1826–1857)*. Milan: Franco Angeli.

Betri, M.L. 2002. 'Le campagne e i contadini lombardi nel 1848', in N. Del Corno and V. Scotti Douglas (eds), *Quando il popolo si desta... 1848: l'anno dei miracoli in Lombardia*. Milan: Franco Angeli. pp. 123–44.

Bettega, G. and U. Pistoia. 1994. *Un fiume di legno. La fluitazione del legname dal Vanoi e Primiero a Venezia*. Tonadico: Ente Parco Paneveggio-Pale di San Martino.

Bianco, F. 1997. *Nobili castellani, comunità, sottani. Il Friuli dalla caduta della Repubblica alla Restaurazione*. Monfalcone: Edizioni della Laguna.

Bianco, F. 2000a. *Carnia. XVII-XIX secolo. Organizzazione comunitaria e strutture economiche nel sistema alpino*. Pordenone: Biblioteca dell'immagine.

Bianco, F. 2000b. 'Tumulti, agitazioni sociali e istituzioni comunitarie nel Cadore di fine Settecento', in A. Bondesan, G. Caniato, F. Vallerani and M. Zanetti (eds), *Il Piave*. Verona: Cierre. pp. 228–44.

Bianco, F. 2001. *Nel bosco. Comunità alpine e risorse forestali nel Friuli in età moderna (secoli XV-XX)*. Udine: Forum.

Bianco, F. 2002a. 'Comunità e risorse forestali nella montagna friulana di antico regime', in A. Lazzarini (ed.), *Diboscamento montano e politiche territoriali. Alpi e Appennini dal Settecento al Duemila*. Milan: Franco Angeli. pp. 98–123.

Bianco, F. 2002b. 'Lo spaventevole flagello dell'agricoltura. Furti campestri e diritti consuetudinari nel Friuli di fine Ottocento', in Id., *Contadini e popolo tra conservazione e rivolta. Ai confini orientali della Repubblica di Venezia tra '400 e '800. Saggi di storia sociale*. Udine: Forum. pp. 123–48.

Bianco, F. 2003. *Riforme fiscali e sviluppo agricolo nel Friuli napoleonico. Francesco Rota pubblico perito e agrimensore 'con il coraggio della verità e nell'interesse della nazione'*. Udine: Forum.

Bianco, F. 2005. *Contadini, sbirri e contrabbandieri nel Friuli del Settecento. La comunità di villaggio tra conservazione e rivolta (Valcellina e Valcolvera)*. Verona: Cierre.

Bianco, F. 2008a. *L'immagine del territorio. Società e paesaggi del Friuli nei disegni e nella cartografia storica (secoli XVI–XIX)*. Udine: Forum.

Bianco, F. 2008b. 'La tragedia dei comunali. Le foreste comunali in Carnia e nel Friuli agli inizi dell'Ottocento', in Id., A. Burgos and G. Ferigo (eds), *Aplis. Una storia dell'economia alpina in Carnia*. Tolmezzo: Consorzio boschi carnici. pp. 83–158.

Bianco, F. and A. Lazzarini. 2003. *Forestali, mercanti di legname e boschi pubblici. Candido Morassi e i progetti di riforma boschiva nelle alpi carniche fra Settecento e Ottocento*. Udine: Forum.

Bloch, M. 1930. 'La lutte pour l'individualisme agraire dans la France du XVIII siécle'. *Annales d'histoire économique et sociale* 7/II: 329–83.

Bloch, M. 1930a. 'La lutte pour l'individualisme agraire dans la France du XVIII siécle. Première partie: l'œuvre des pouvoirs d'ancien régime'. *Annales d'histoire économique et sociale* 7/II: 329–83.

Bloch, M. 1930b. 'La lutte pour l'individualisme agraire dans la France du XVIII siécle. Deuxième partie: conflits et résultats. Troisième partie: la Révolution et le "Grand Œuvre de la propriété"'. *Annales d'histoire économique et sociale* 8/II: 511–56.

Blockmans, W., A. Holenstein and J. Mathieu (eds). 2009. *Empowering Interactions. Political Cultures and the Emergence of the State in Europe 1300–1900*. Farnham: Ashgate.

Blok, A. 1974. *The Mafia of a Sicilian Village, 1860–1890. A Study of Violent Peasant Entrepreneurs*. Oxford: Blackwell.

Bobba, D. 2015. *Boschi, comunità, stato. Piemonte 1798–1861*. Rome: Carocci.

Bonan, G. 2015. 'Beni comuni: alcuni percorsi storiografici'. *Passato e presente* 96: 97–115.

Bonan, G. 2016. 'The Communities and the *Comuni*: The Implementation of Administrative Reforms in the Fiemme Valley (Trentino, Italy) during the First Half of the 19th Century'. *International Journal of the Commons* 10/II: 589–616.

Bonan, G. 2017. '"Di tutti e di nessuno". I beni comunali nel Veneto preunitario'. *Quaderni storici* 155: 445–70.

Bonan, G. 2018. 'Confronting Hardin. Trends and Approaches to the Commons in Historiography'. *Theoretical Inquiries in Law* 19/II: 617–32.

Bonazza, M. 2009. 'Evoluzione istituzionale e maturazione archivistica in quattro comunità di valle dolomitiche (secoli XIV-XX)', in A. Bartoli Langeli, A. Giorgi and S. Moscadelli (eds), *Archivi e comunità tra medioevo ed età moderna*. Rome: Ministero per i beni e le attività culturali-Direzione generale per gli archivi. pp. 111–54.

Bordone, R., P. Guglielmotti, S. Lombardini and A. Torre (eds). 2007. *Lo spazio politico locale in età medievale, moderna e contemporanea*. Alessandria: Edizioni dell'Orso.

Bibliography

Bragaggia, R. 2012. *Confini litigiosi. I governi del territorio nella Terraferma veneta del Seicento*. Verona: Cierre.

Braudel, F. 1981. *The Structures of Everyday Life. The Limits of the Possible*. New York: Harper & Row.

Braunstein, Ph. 1988. 'De la montagne à Venise: les réseaux du bois au XVe siècle'. *Mélanges de l'École française de Rome. Moyen-Age, Temps modernes* **100**/II: 761–99.

Breschi, M., G. Gonano and C. Lorenzini. 1999. 'Il sistema demografico alpino. La popolazione della Carnia, 1775–1881', in M. Breschi (ed.), *Vivere in Friuli. Saggi di demografia storica (sec. XVI-XIX)*. Udine: Forum. pp. 153–92.

Brunello, P. 1979a. 'I contadini e la rivoluzione del 1848 nel Veneto', in Id., A. Bernardello and P. Ginsborg, *Venezia 1848–49. La rivoluzione e la difesa*. Venice: Comune di Venezia. pp. 77–106.

Brunello, P. 1979b. 'I mercanti di grano nella carestia del 1846–47 a Venezia'. *Studi storici* **20**: 129–56.

Brunello, P. 1999. *Voci per un dizionario del Quarantotto. Venezia e Mestre: marzo 1848 agosto 1849*. Venice: Comune di Venezia.

Brunello, P. 2008. *Note sul primo numero della rivista S-Nodi. Pubblici e privati nella storia contemporanea, 1, 'Rotte dell'io/rotte del noi', estate 2007*, in storiamestre.it, http://storiamestre. it/2008/02/notes-nodi/

Brunello, P. 2011. *Ribelli, questuanti e banditi. Proteste contadine in Veneto e in Friuli 1814–1866*. Verona: Cierre.

Brunello, P. 2018. *Colpi di scena. La rivoluzione del Quarantotto a Venezia*. Verona: Cierre.

Bushaway, R. 1982. 'From Custom to Crime: Wood-gathering in Eighteenth and Early Nineteenth-century England: a Focus for Conflict in Hampshire', in J. Rule (ed.), *Outside the Law: Studies in Crime and Order 1650–1850*. Exeter: Exeter University Press. pp. 65–101.

Cafaro, P. 2000. 'Trasporti e vie di comunicazione', in M. Garbari and A. Leonardi (eds), *Storia del Trentino. L'età contemporanea 1803–1918*. Bologna: il Mulino. pp. 745–77.

Caffiero, M. 1982. *L'erba dei poveri. Comunità rurale e soppressione degli usi collettivi nel Lazio (secoli XVIII–XIX)*. Rome: Edizioni dell'Ateneo.

Caffiero, M. 1988. 'Solidarietà e conflitti. Il sistema agrario consuetudinario tra comunità rurale e potere centrale (Lazio, XVIII–XIX secolo)'. *Mélanges de l'École française de Rome. Moyen-Age, Temps modernes* **100**/I: 373–99.

Caffiero, M. 1990. 'Usi e abusi. Comunità rurale e difesa dell'economia tradizionale nello Stato pontificio'. *Passato e presente* **24**: 73–93.

Caffiero, M. 1992. 'Terre comuni, fortune private. Pratiche e conflitti internotabilari per il controllo delle risorse collettive nel Lazio (XVIII-XIX secolo)', *Quaderni Storici* **81**: 759–81.

Caffiero, M. 1999. 'Perdono per i giacobini, severità per gli insorgenti: la prima restaurazione pontificia', in A. M. Rao (ed.), *Folle controrivoluzionarie. Le insorgenze popolari nell'Italia giacobina e napoleonica*. Rome: Carocci. pp. 291–324.

Caniato, G. 1997. 'Il controllo delle acque', in G. Benzoni and G. Cozzi (eds), *Storia di Venezia*, VII, *La Venezia barocca*. Rome: Istituto della Enciclopedia Italiana. pp. 479–508.

Caniato, G. 2000. 'Commerci e navigazione nel bacino plavense', in A. Bondesan, G. Caniato, F. Vallerani and M. Zanetti (eds), *Il Piave*. Verona: Cierre. pp. 307–31.

Caniato, G. 2006. 'I secoli della Serenissima', in R. Boschi, E. Turri and D. Zumiani (eds), *Viaggio alla montagna veneta*. Verona: Fondazione Cariverona. pp. 133–51.

Giacomo Bonan

Casellato, A. 2012. 'I moti del macinato in Veneto. Prima analisi di un caso regionale e spunti per una comparazione'. *Venetica* **25**: 47–78.

Celetti, D. 2008. *Il bosco nelle provincie venete dall'Unità ad oggi. Strutture e dinamiche economiche in età contemporanea*. Padua: Cleup.

Centre national de la recherche scientifique (CNRS). 1987. *Les eaux et forêts du 12e au 20e siècle*. Paris: Éditions du Centre national de la recherche scientifique.

Cerutti, S. 2015. 'Who is below? E. P. Thompson, historien des sociétés modernes: une relecture'. *Annales. Histoire, Sciences Sociales* **70**/IV: 931–55.

Ceschi, R. 1996. 'Delitti e conflitti forestali', in S. Cavaciocchi (ed.), *L'uomo e la foresta. Secc. XII–XVIII*. Florence: Le Monnier. pp. 567–78.

Ceschi, R. 1999. *Nel labirinto delle valli. Uomini e terre di una regione alpina: la Svizzera italiana*. Bellinzona: Casagrande.

Cittadella, A. 2012. 'Nel secolo dei Lumi. Il dibattito accademico sugli usi civici e sul possesso collettivo', in A. Tilatti (ed.), *L'abbazia di Santa Maria di Sesto nell'epoca moderna (secoli XV–XVIII)*. Udine: Lithostampa. pp. 273–307.

Colle, M. 2007. 'Boschi, regole e mercanti nel Cadore del XVII e XVIII secolo: il caso della Val Visdende e del Centenario di Comelico Inferiore', in M. Ambrosoli and F. Bianco (eds), *Comunità e questioni di confini in Italia settentrionale (XVI–XIX sec.)*. Milan: Franco Angeli. pp. 111–27.

Comitato Cadore 1848–1998. 1999. *1848. Una breve primavera di libertà*. Pieve di Cadore: Comitato Cadore 1848–1998.

Concina, E. 1982a. 'Alpi e Rinascimento. Questioni di storia del territorio e della cultura nel Cinquecento', in M. Muraro (ed.), *Titianus Cadorinus. Celebrazioni in onore di Tiziano, Pieve di Cadore, 1576–1976*. Verona: Cassa di Risparmio di Verona, Vicenza e Belluno. pp. 63–78.

Concina, E. 1982b. 'Il Cadore al tempo di Tiziano. Territorio e cultura', in M. Muraro (ed.), *Titianus Cadorinus. Celebrazioni in onore di Tiziano, Pieve di Cadore, 1576–1976*, Verona: Cassa di Risparmio di Verona, Vicenza e Belluno. pp. 49–59.

Congost, R., and J.M. Lana (eds). 2007. *Campos cerrados, debates abiertos. Análisis histórico y propiedad de la tierra en Europa (siglos XVI–XIX)*. Pamplona: Universidad Pública de Navarra.

Conte, P. 2001. 'Lamon: profilo storico di una Comunità di confine', in L. Corrà (ed.), *Il dialetto di Lamon. Cultura nelle parole*. Feltre: Comune di Lamon. pp. 9–65.

Coppola, G. 1989. 'La montagna alpina. Vocazioni originarie e trasformazioni funzionali', in P. Bevilacqua (ed.), *Storia dell'agricoltura italiana in età contemporanea. I. Spazi e paesaggi*. Venice: Marsilio. pp. 495–530.

Coppola, G. 1991. 'Equilibri economici e trasformazioni nell'area alpina in età moderna: scarsità di risorse ed economia integrata', in Id. and P. Schiera (eds), *Lo spazio alpino: area di civiltà, regione cerniera*. Naples: Liguori. pp. 203–22.

Coppola, G. 2000. 'Agricoltura di piano, agricoltura di valle', in M. Bellabarba and G. Olmi (eds), *Storia del Trentino. L'età moderna*, IV. Bologna: il Mulino. pp. 233–58.

Corazzol, G. 1997. *Cineografo di banditi su sfondo di monti. Feltre 1635–1642*. Milan: Unicopli.

Corazzol, G. 2016. *Piani Particolareggiati. Venezia 1580–Mel 1659*. Seren del Grappa: Edizioni Dbs-Libreria Pilotto Editrice.

Corbellini, R. 1992. 'Il dipartimento del passariano (1805–1813)', in *La provincia imperfetta. Il Friuli dal 1798 al 1848*. Udine: Accademia di Scienze Lettere e Arti di Udine. pp. 75–168.

Bibliography

Corona, G. 2010. 'The Decline of the Commons and the Environmental Balance in Early Modern Italy', in M. Armiero and M. Hall (eds), *Nature and History in Modern Italy*. Athens OH: Ohio University Press. pp. 89–107.

Corti, M. 2006. 'Risorse silvo-pastorali, conflitto sociale e sistema alimentare. Il ruolo della capra nelle comunità alpine della Lombardia e delle aree limitrofe in età moderna e contemporanea'. *Annali di San Michele* **19**: 234–340.

Corvol, A. 2000a. 'Une illusion française: la penurie des ressources ligneuses, 1814–1914', in M. Agnoletti and S. Anderson (eds), *Forest History: International Studies on Socioeconomic and Forest Ecosystem Change*. Wallingford-New York: CABI. pp. 127–42.

Corvol, A. (ed.). 2000b. *Duhamel du Monceau, 1700–2000. Un Européen du siècle des Lumières*. Orléans: Académie d'Orléans, Agriculture, Sciences, Belles lettres et Arts.

Da Deppo, I. 1999. *Le attività pastorali nell'area ladina del Centro Cadore. Osservazioni etnografiche e linguistiche*. Pieve di Cadore: Tipografia Tiziano.

Daheur, J. 2016. 'La Galicie autrichienne: "colonie du bois" de l'Empire allemand? (1890–1914)'. *Revue d'Allemagne et des pays de langue allemande* **48**/I: 25–42.

Dargavel, J. and E. Johann. 2013. *Science and Hope. A Forest History*. Cambridge: The White Horse Press.

Davis, J.A. 1988. *Conflict and Control. Law and Order in Nineteenth-Century Italy*. London: Palgrave.

De Felice, E. and C. Battisti. 1949. 'Vecchie voci amministrative delle comunità rurali alpine'. *Archivio per l'Alto Adige* **43**: 339–52.

De Moor, T. 2010. 'Participating is more important than winning: the impact of socio-economic change on commoners' participation in eighteenth and nineteenth-century Flanders'. *Continuity and Change* **25**/III: 405–33.

De Moor, T., L. Shaw-Taylor and P. Warde (eds). 2002. *The Management of Common Land in North West Europe, c. 1500–1850*. Turnhout: Brepols.

Della Peruta, F. 1965. 'I contadini nella rivoluzione lombarda del 1848', in Id., *Democrazia e socialismo nel Risorgimento. Saggi e ricerche*. Rome: Editori Riuniti. pp. 59–108.

Della, Peruta F. 1999. 'Il Veneto nel Risorgimento fino al 1848', in G. Benzoni and G. Cozzi (eds), *Venezia e l'Austria*. Venice: Marsilio. pp. 383–400.

Démelas, M.D., and N. Vivier (eds). 2003. *Les proprietés collectives face aux attaques liberals, 1750–1914*. Rennes: Presses Universitaires de Rennes.

Di Lucia Coletti, N. 1988. 'I boschi riservati della Marina da guerra austriaca (1814–1843)', in M. Dal Borgo and G. Caniato (eds), *Dai monti alla laguna. Produzione artigianale e artistica del Bellunese per la cantieristica veneziana*. Venice: La stamperia. pp. 121–28.

Donato, M.P., D. Armando, M. Cattaneo and J.F. Chauvard (eds). 2015. *Atlante storico dell'Italia rivoluzionaria e napoleonica*. Rome: École française de Rome.

Eicher Clere, P. and E. Riva de Bettin. 1994. *Una villa veneta nella Ladinia dolomitica. Girolamo Pellegrini e gli affreschi di Palazzo Poli-De Pol a San Pietro in Cadore*. Venice: Edizioni del Gazzettino.

Fabbiani, G. 1959. *Appunti per una storia del commercio del legname in Cadore*. Belluno: Tip. Benetta.

Fabbiani, G. 1970. *Stemmi e notizie di alcune famiglie del Cadore*. Belluno: Benetta.

Fabbiani, G. 1977. *Breve storia del Cadore*. Belluno: Magnifica Comunità di Cadore.

Fabbiani, G. 1985. *Il Cadore nell'età napoleonica*. Rome: Magnifica Comunità di Cadore.

Fabbiani, G. 1990. *Auronzo di Cadore. Pagine di storia*. Auronzo: Comune di Auronzo.

Fabris, A. 2011. 'La rivolta dei montanari di Castelvecchio a metà dell'Ottocento', in Id., M. Dal Lago, S. Fornasa and G. Trivelli (eds), *Risorgimento nella valle dell'Agno*. Valdagno: Gruppo storico Valle dell'Agno. pp. 67–93.

Ferigo, G. 2008. 'Boscadôrs, menàus, segàts, catârs. La filiera del legno nella Carnia del '700', in Id., F. Bianco and A. Burgos (eds), *Aplis. Una storia dell'economia alpina in Carnia*. Tolmezzo: Consorzio boschi carnici. pp. 15–80.

Fincardi, M. 2000. 'Culture comunitarie e moderni conflitti sociali nell'Italia rurale di fine XIX secolo', in *La politisation des campagnes au XIXe siècle: France, Italie, Espagne et Portugal*. Rome: École française de Rome. pp. 221–57.

Fincardi, M. 2001. *La terra disincantata. Trasformazioni dell'ambiente rurale e secolarizzazione nella bassa padana*. Milan: Unicopli.

Fincardi, M. 2009. *Il rito della derisione. La satira notturna delle battarelle in Veneto, Trentino, Friuli Venezia Giulia*. Verona: Cierre.

Foa, V. 1977. 'Introduzione', in F. Bozzini, *Il furto campestre. Una forma di lotta di massa*. Bari: Dedalo. pp. 5–14.

Follador, G. 1988. 'Il cidolo di Perarolo e la rivolta delle comunità cadorine contro la società dei commercianti di legname', in D. Perco (ed.), *Zattere, zattieri e menadàs. La fluitazione del legname lungo il Piave*. Feltre: Castaldi. pp. 131–46.

Fontana, G. 1980. *Notizie storiche del Comelico e di Sappada*. Feltre: Castaldi.

Fornasin, A. 2017. 'La demografia alpina in età preindustriale: Interpretazioni, problemi, prospettive', in M. Denzel, A. Bonoldi, A. Montenach and F. Vannotti (eds), *Oeconomia Alpium I: Wirtschaftsgeschichte Des Alpenraums in Vorindustrieller Zeit: Forschungsaufriss, -konzepte Und –perspektiven*. Berlin: De Gruyter. pp. 57–72.

Fornasin, A. and A. Zannini. 2002. 'Montagne aperte, popolazioni diverse. Temi e prospettive di demografia storica degli spazi montani', in Id. (eds), *Uomini e comunità delle montagne. Paradigmi e specificità del popolamento dello spazio montano (secoli XVI–XX)*. Udine: Forum. pp. 7–21.

Franchi, F.P. 2011. *La penna, la spada, le bandiere. Antologia ragionata della letteratura risorgimentale di Belluno, Feltre e Cadore*. Belluno: Isbrec.

Francia, E. 2007. 'Provincializzare la rivoluzione. Il Quarantotto "subalterno" in Toscana'. *Società e storia* **116**: 293–320.

Francia, E. 2012. *1848. La rivoluzione del Risorgimento*. Bologna: il Mulino.

Francia, E. 2013. 'Raccontare il Quarantotto italiano'. *Nuova informazione bibliografica* **10**/III: 593–612.

Frangsmyr, T., J.L. Heilbron and R.E. Rider (eds). 1990. *The Quantifying Spirit in the Eighteenth Century*. Berkeley: University of California Press.

Furter, R., A.L. Head-König and L. Lorenzetti (eds). 2014. 'Les ressources naturelles-Natürliche Ressourcen', Special Issue of *Histoire des Alpes – Storia delle Alpi – Geschichte der Alpen* **19**.

Gambi, L. 1972. 'I valori storici dei quadri ambientali', in *Storia d'Italia*, I. Turin: Einaudi. pp. 3–60.

Gaspari, O. 1992. *La montagna alle origini di un problema politico (1902–1919)*. Rome: Presidenza del Consiglio dei Ministri.

Bibliography

Gaspari, P. 1993. *Terra patrizia. Aristocrazie terriere e società rurale in Veneto e Friuli*. Udine: Istituto Editoriale Veneto Friulano.

Gellner, E. 1991. 'Il "rifabbrico": una nuova forma di organizzazione urbanistica del Cadore', in A. Lazzarini and F. Vendramini (eds), *La montagna veneta in età contemporanea. Storia e ambiente, uomini e risorse*. Rome: Edizioni di storia e letteratura. pp. 115–28.

Gianni, L. 2011. 'Maniago (di) Pietro Francesco, giurista e letterato', in C. Scalon, C. Griggio and G. Bergamini (eds), *Nuovo Liruti. Dizionario biografico dei friulani*, III, *L'età moderna*. Udine: Forum. pp. 2056–58

Ginsborg, P. 1974. 'Peasants and Revolutionaries in Venice and the Veneto, 1848'. *The Historical Journal* **17**: 503–50

Ginsborg, P. 1979. *Daniele Manin and the Venetian Revolution of 1848–49*. Cambridge: Cambridge University Press.

Ginsborg, P. 2002. 'After the Revolution: Bandits on the Plains of the Po, 1848–54', in Id. and J.A. Davis (eds), *Society and Politics in the Age of Risorgimento. Essays in Honour of Denis Mack Smith*. Cambridge: Cambridge University Press. pp. 128–51.

Grendi, E. 1977. 'Micro-analisi e storia sociale'. *Quaderni storici* **35**: 506–20.

Grewe, B.S. 2000. 'Shortage of Wood? Towards a New Approach in Forest History: the Palatinate in the 19th century', in M. Agnoletti and S. Anderson (eds), *Forest History: International Studies on Socioeconomic and Forest Ecosystem Change*. Wallingford-New York: CABI. pp. 143–52.

Grewe, B.S. 2004. *Der versperrte Wald. Ressourcenmangel in der bayerischen Pfalz (1814–1870)*. Vienna-Cologne-Weimar: Böhlau Verlag.

Grewe, B.S. 2010. 'Forest History', in F. Uekoetter (ed.), *The Turning Points of Environmental History*. Pittsburgh: University of Pittsburgh Press. pp. 44–54.

Grewe, B.S. and R. Hölzl. 2018. 'Forestry in Germany, c1550–2000', in J. Oosthoek and R. Hölzl (eds), *Managing Northern Europe's Forests. Histories from the Age of Improvement to the Age of Ecology*. New York-Oxford: Berghahn. pp. 15–65.

Grossi, P. 1977. '*Un altro modo di possedere*'. *L'emersione di forme alternative di proprietà alla coscienza giuridica postunitaria*. Milan: Giuffrè.

Guha, R. 1983. *Elementary Aspects of Peasant Insurgency in Colonial India*. Delhi: Oxford University Press.

Guha, R. 1990. *The Unquiet Woods. Ecological Change and Peasant Resistance in the Himalaya*. Berkeley: University of California Press.

Guha, R. 2016. *Ambientalismi. Una storia globale dei movimenti*. Turin: Linaria.

Guha, R. and M. Gadgil. 1989. 'State Forestry and Social Conflict in British India'. *Past & Present* **123**: 141–77.

Gullino, G. 1982. 'Considerazioni sull'evoluzione del sistema fiscale veneto tra XVI e XVIII secolo', in G. Borelli, P. Lanaro and F. Vecchiato (eds), *Il sistema fiscale veneto. Problemi e aspetti, XV-XVIII secolo*. Verona: Libreria Universitaria Editrice. pp. 61–91.

Hall, M. 1998. 'Restoring the Countryside: George Perkins Marsh and the Italian Land Ethic (1861–1882)'. *Environment and History* **4**: 91–103.

Harrison, R. 1992. *Forests: The Shadow of Civilization*. Chicago: The University of Chicago Press.

Hobsbawm, E. 1971. *Primitive Rebels: Studies in Archaic Forms of Social Movement in the 19th and 20th Centuries*. Manchester: Manchester University Press.

Hobsbawm, E. 1974. 'Peasant Land Occupations'. *Past & Present* **62**: 120–52.

Hollister-Short, G. 1994. 'The Other Side of the Coin: Wood Transport Systems in Pre-Industrial Europe'. *History of Technology* **16**: 72–97.

Hölzl, R. 2010. 'Historicizing Sustainability: German Scientific Forestry in the Eighteenth and Nineteenth Centuries'. *Science as Culture* **19**/IV: 431–60.

Hölzl, R. 2011. 'Forests in Conflict: Rural Populations and the Advent of Modern Forestry in Pre-industrial Germany, 1760–1860', in G. Massard-Guilbaud and S. Mosley (eds), *Common Ground: Integrating the Social and Environmental in History*. Newcastle upon Tyne: Cambridge Scholars Publishing. pp. 198–223.

Ingold, A. 2008. 'Les sociétés d'irrigation: bien commun et action collective'. *Entreprises et histoire* **50**: 19–35.

Ingold, A. 2009. 'To Historicize or Naturalize Nature: Hydraulic Communities and Administrative States in Nineteenth-Century Europe'. *French Historical Studies* **32**: 385–417.

Ingold, A. 2018. 'Commons and Environmental Regulation in History: The Water Commons beyond Property and Sovereignty'. *Theoretical Inquiries in Law* **19**/II: 425–56.

Iriarte-Goñi, I. 2013. 'Forests, Fuelwood, Pulpwood, and Lumber in Spain, 1860–2000: A non-Declensionist Story'. *Environmental History* **18**/II: 333–59.

Iriarte-Goñi, I. and M.I. Ayuda. 2012. 'Not only Subterranean Forests. Wood Consumption and Economic Development in Britain (1850–1938)'. *Ecological Economics* **77**: 176–84.

Jacoby, K. 2001. *Crimes against Nature. Squatters, Poachers, Thieves, and the Hidden History of American Conservation*. Berkeley: University of California Press.

Jones, P.M. 2016. *Agricultural Enlightenment. Knowledge, Technology, and Nature, 1750–1840*. Oxord: Oxford University Press.

Kander, A., P. Malanima and P. Warde. 2013. *Power to the People. Energy in Europe in the Last Five Centuries*. Princeton: Princeton University Press.

Lana J.M. 2008. 'From Equilibrium to Equity. The survival of the Commons in the Ebro Basin: Navarra from the 15th to the 20th Centuries'. *International Journal of the Commons* **2**: 162–91.

Landes, D.S. 1969. *The Unbound Prometheus. Technological Change and Industrial Development in Western Europe from 1750 to the Present*. Cambridge: Cambridge University Press.

Larese, G. 2005. 'La montagna bellunese negli scritti di Riccardo Volpe', in A. Lazzarini, A. Amantia (eds), *La 'questione montagna' in Veneto e Friuli tra Otto e Novecento. Percezioni, Analisi e Interventi*. Belluno: ISBREC. pp. 235–50.

Larese, G., F. Vendramini and M.L. Zavarise. 2000. *Jacopo Tasso e i moti del 1848 a Belluno*. Verona: Cierre.

Laven, D. 2002. *Venice and Venetia under the Habsburgs. 1815–1835*. Oxford: Oxford University Press.

Laven, D. and L. Riall (eds). 2000. *Napoleon's Legacy. Problems of Government in Restoration Europe*. Oxford-New York: Berg.

Lazzarini, A. 1981. *Campagne venete ed emigrazione di massa (1866–1900)*. Vicenza: Istituto per le ricerche di storia sociale e di storia religiosa.

Lazzarini, A. 1983. *Contadini e agricoltura. L'inchiesta Jacini nel Veneto*. Milan: Franco Angeli.

Lazzarini, A. 1990. 'Crisi della montagna bellunese e cause dell'emigrazione', in C. Grandi (ed.), *Emigrazione, memorie e realtà*. Trento: Provincia autonoma di Trento. pp. 189–215.

Bibliography

Lazzarini, A. 1991. 'Degrado ambientale e isolamento economico: elementi di crisi della montagna bellunese nell'Ottocento', in Id. and F. Vendramini (eds), *La montagna veneta in età contemporanea. Storia e ambiente, uomini e risorse*. Rome: Edizioni di storia e letteratura. pp. 47–68.

Lazzarini, A. 1998. 'Movimenti migratori dalle vallate bellunesi fra Settecento e Ottocento', in G.L. Fontana, A. Leonardi and L. Trezzi (eds), *Mobilità imprenditoriale e del lavoro nelle Alpi in età moderna e contemporanea*. Milan: Cuesp. pp. 193–208.

Lazzarini, A. 2001. 'I tecnici forestali nel Veneto dell'Ottocento. Formazione e identità'. *Archivio veneto* **192**: 77–144.

Lazzarini, A. 2002a. 'Il dibattito sul diboscamento montano nel Veneto fra Sette e Ottocento', in Id. (ed.), *Diboscamento montano e politiche territoriali. Alpi e Appennini dal Settecento al Duemila*. Milan: Franco Angeli. pp. 57–97.

Lazzarini, A. 2002b. *Patrizi, ussari, alboranti. Il bosco del Cansiglio fra Venezia, Napoleone e l'Austria*. Treviso: Dario De Bastiani Editore.

Lazzarini, A. 2004a. 'Boschi e malghe'. *Archivio storico di Belluno, Feltre e Cadore* **325**: 102–05.

Lazzarini, A. 2004b. *Fonti per la storia dell'economia bellunese. I primi rapporti della Camera di commercio*. Belluno: Isbrec.

Lazzarini, A. 2006a. 'Alla ricerca di risorse energetiche per le vetrerie di Murano. Due lettere dal Cansiglio (1793)', in F. Cavazzana Romanelli, M. Leonardi and S. Rossi Minutelli (eds), '*Cose nuove e cose antiche*'. *Scritti per monsignor Antonio Niero e don Bruno Bertoli*. Venice: Biblioteca nazionale marciana. pp. 225–62.

Lazzarini, A. 2006b. *La trasformazione di un bosco. Il Cansiglio, Venezia e i nuovi usi del legno (secoli XVIII–XIX)*. Belluno: Isbrec.

Lazzarini, A. 2007. 'I boschi nel Bellunese: cenni di storia', in G. Zampieri, A. Dalla Gasparina and A. Boranga (eds), *Alberi monumentali della provincia di Belluno*. Feltre: Agorà. pp. 35–46.

Lazzarini, A. 2008a. 'Boschi e territorio in area veneta', in L. Blanco (ed.), *Organizzazione del potere e territorio. Contributi per una lettura storica della spazialità*. Milan: Franco Angeli. pp. 159–71.

Lazzarini, A. 2008b. 'Carbone e legna da fuoco per le manifatture veneziane nella seconda metà del Settecento. Una crisi energetica?' *Natura. Rivista di scienze naturali* **98/I**: 159–68.

Lazzarini, A. 2009. *Boschi e politiche forestali. Venezia e Veneto fra Sette e Ottocento*. Milan: Franco Angeli.

Lazzarini, A. 2013. 'I boschi del Veneto prima dell'Unità'. *Archivio veneto* **5**: 7–18.

Lazzarini, A. 2014. 'Boschi, legnami, costruzioni navali. L'Arsenale di Venezia fra XVI e XVIII secolo (prima parte)'. *Archivio veneto* **145/VII**: 111–75.

Lazzarini, A. 2018. 'Boschi, legnami, costruzioni navali. L'Arsenale di Venezia fra XVI e XVIII secolo (seconda parte)'. *Archivio veneto* **149/XV**: 85–154.

Lorenzetti, L. and R. Merzario. 2005. *Il fuoco acceso. Famiglie e migrazioni alpine nell'Italia d'età moderna*. Rome: Donzelli.

Lorenzini, C. 2006. 'Spazi "comuni", comuni divisioni. Appunti sui confini delle comunità di villaggio (Carnia, secc. XVII–XVIII)'. *La ricerca folklorica* **53**: 41–53.

Lorenzini, C. 2011. 'Monte versus bosco, e viceversa. Gestione delle risorse collettive e mobilità in area alpina: il caso della Carnia fra Sei e Settecento', in G. Alfani and R. Rao (eds), *La gestione delle risorse collettive. Italia settentrionale, secoli XII–XVIII*. Milan: Franco Angeli. pp. 95–109.

Lorenzini, C. 2012. 'Di Paolo Biancone e degli altri. Mercanti, reti commerciali e risorse fra Valcanale e Canale del Ferro tra la fine del Cinquecento e il primo Seicento', in A. Bonoldi, A. Leonardi and K. Occhi (eds), *Interessi e regole. Operatori e istituzioni nel commercio transalpino in età moderna (secoli XVI–XIX)*. Bologna: il Mulino. pp. 231–58.

Lorenzini, C. 2018. 'Nei prezzi del bosco. Stime delle risorse forestali nella Repubblica di Venezia fra Sei e Settecento: il caso della Carnia', in M. Barbot, M. Cattini, M. Di Tullio and L. Mocarelli (eds), *Stimare il valore dei beni: una prospettiva europea. Secoli XIV–XX*. Udine: Forum.

Lorenzini, C. and G. Bernardin. 2013. 'Assenti più o meno illustri: "Comunità alpine" e il bosco. Il caso delle Alpi orientali'. *Histoire des Alpes – Storia delle Alpi – Geschichte der Alpen* **18**: 179–95.

Lotz, C. 2016. 'Opening Up Untouched Woodlands. Forestry Experts Reflecting on and Driving the Timber Frontier in Northern Europe (1880–1914)', in G. Winder and A. Dix (eds), *Trading Environments. Frontiers, Commercial Knowledge and Environmental Transformation, 1820–1990*. New York: Routledge. pp. 69–82.

Lowood, H. 1991. The Calculating Forester: Quantification, Cameral Science, and the Emergence of Scientific Forestry Management in Germany', in T. Frängsmyr, J.L. Heilbron and R.E. Rider (eds), *The Quantifying Spirit in the Eighteenth Century*. Berkeley: University of California Press. pp. 313–43.

Löwy, M. 2007. *Kafka sognatore ribelle*. Milan: Eleuthera.

Lucchini, A. 1930. 'Memoriale del maresciallo Radetzky sulle condizioni d'Italia al principio del 1848'. *Nuova rivista storica* **14**: 63–79.

Mancuso, F. and S. De Vecchi. 1991. 'Belluno. Città e territorio nell'ultimo secolo', in A. Lazzarini and F. Vendramini (eds), *La montagna veneta in età contemporanea. Storia e ambiente, uomini e risorse*. Rome: Edizioni di storia e letteratura. pp. 129–55.

Mannori, L. 2008. 'La nozione di territorio fra antico e nuovo regime. Qualche appunto per uno studio sui modelli tipologici', in L. Blanco (ed.), *Organizzazione del potere e territorio. Contributi per una lettura storica della spazialità*. Milan: Franco Angeli. pp. 23–44.

Marx, K. 1975. 'Proceedings of the Sixth Rhine Assembly. Debates on the Law on Thefts of Wood', in Id. and F. Engels, *Collected Works*, I. New York: International Publisher. pp. 224–63.

Massarotto, M. 1998. 'Sui beni comunali nelle provincie austro-venete (1798–1806)'. *Clio* **25**: 571–87.

Mathieu, J. 1998. 'La popolazione delle Alpi dal 1500 al 1900', in E. Cason Angelini (ed.), '*Mes Alpes à moi*'. *Civiltà storiche e comunità culturali nelle Alpi*. Verona: Fondazione G. Angelini. pp. 291–306.

Mathieu, J. 2001. 'Ovini, bovini, caprini. Cambiamenti nell'allevamento alpino dal XVI al XIX secolo'. *La ricerca folklorica* **43**: 17–25.

Mathieu, J. 2009. *History of the Alps, 1500–1900: Environment, Development, and Society*. Morgantown: West Virginia University Press.

Mathieu, J. 2019. *The Alps. An Environmental History*. Oxford: Polity Press.

Matteson, K. 2015. *Forests in Revolutionary France. Conservation, Community, and Conflict 1669–1848*. New York: Cambridge University Press.

McNeill, J. 1992. *The Mountains of the Mediterranean World. An Environmental History*. Cambridge: Cambridge University Press.

Bibliography

Meriggi, M. 1983. *Amministrazione e classi sociali nel Lombardo-Veneto (1814–1848)*. Bologna: il Mulino.

Meriggi, M. 1987. *Il Regno Lombardo-Veneto*. Turin: UTET.

Meriggi, M. 2000. 'Le istituzioni del Regno Lombardo-Veneto', in P. Preto (ed.), *Il Veneto austriaco 1814–1866*. Padua: Signum. pp. 29–40.

Meriggi, M. 2011. *Gli stati italiani prima dell'Unità. Una storia istituzionale*. Bologna: il Mulino.

Meriggi, M. 2016. *Racconti di confine. Nel Mezzogiorno del Settecento*. Bologna: il Mulino.

Migliardi O'Riordan, G. and D. Testa Benzoni (eds). 2003. *Archivi nella provincia di Belluno. Indagine conoscitiva per la ricerca storica*. Seren del Grappa: Provincia di Belluno.

Mocarelli, L. 2013. 'Spazi e diritti collettivi nelle aree montane: qualche riflessione su Alpi e Appennini in età moderna'. *Proposte e ricerche* **70**: 173–202.

Monteleone, G. 1969. 'La carestia del 1816–1817 nelle provincie venete'. *Archivio veneto* **121–122**: 23–86.

Moreno, D. 1990. *Dal documento al terreno. Storia e archeologia dei sistemi agro-silvo-pastorali*. Bologna: il Mulino.

Moreno, D. and G. Poggi. 1996. 'Storia delle risorse boschive nelle montagne mediterranee: modelli di interpretazione per le produzioni foraggere in regime consuetudinario', in S. Cavaciocchi (ed.), *L'uomo e la foresta. Secc. XII–XVIII*. Florence: Le Monnier. pp. 635–53.

Moreno, D. and O. Raggio. 1999. 'Dalla storia del paesaggio agrario alla storia rurale. L'irrinunciabile eredità scientifica di Emilio Sereni'. *Quaderni storici* **100**: 89–104.

Munno, C. 2015. 'Land at Risk: Distribution of Common Land between Networks and Elites in Nineteenth Century Veneto', in G. Fertig (ed.), *Social Networks. Political Institution and Rural Societies*. Turnhout: Brepols. pp. 125–52.

Navarra, E. 2002a. 'Comportamenti demografici e organizzazione socio economica in due comunità germanofone delle Alpi orientali: Sappada e Sauris (sec. XVIII e XIX)', in A. Fornasin and A. Zannini (eds), *Uomini e comunità delle montagne. Paradigmi e specificità del popolamento dello spazio montano (secoli XVI–XX)*. Udine: Forum. pp. 113–32.

Navarra, E. 2002b. 'La comunità di Sappada tra Settecento e Ottocento: aspetti economici e demografici', in E. Cason Angelini (ed.), *Comelico, Sappata, Gaital, Lesachtal: paesaggio, storia, cultura*. Belluno: Fondazione G. Angelini. pp. 187–224.

Netting, R. McC. 1981. *Balancing on an Alp. Ecological Change and Continuity in a Swiss Mountain Community*. New York: Cambridge University Press.

Netto, G. 1967. 'Le circoscrizioni amministrative del Veneto napoleonico'. *Rivista italiana di studi napoleonici* **6**: 129–44.

Novello, E. 1996. 'Una vexata quaestio: Giampaolo Tolomei e l'abolizione del pensionatico'. *Archivio veneto* **182**: 5–59.

Occhi, K. 2002. 'I dazi sulla legna. Qualche considerazione sulle vie di traffico (secoli XVI–XVII)'. *Società e storia* **98**: 681–90.

Occhi, K. 2006. *Boschi e mercanti. Traffici di legname tra la contea di Tirolo e la Repubblica di Venezia (secoli XVI–XVII)*. Bologna: il Mulino.

Occhi, K. 2015. 'Resources, Mercantile Networks, and Communities in the Southeastern Alps in the Early Modern Period', in M. Bellabarba, H. Obermair and H. Sato (eds), *Communities and Conflicts in the Alps from the Late Middle Ages to Early Modernity*. Bologna–Berlin: il Mulino–Dunker & Humblot. pp. 165–78.

Panjek, A., J. Larsson and L. Mocarelli (eds). 2017. *Integrated Peasant Economy in a Comparative Perspective. Alps, Scandinavia and Beyond.* Koper: University of Primorska Press.

Pavan, D. 2017. *Storia dell'industria del legno Bortolo Lazzaris.* Treviso: Antiga.

Perco, D. (ed.). 1988. *Zattere, zattieri e menadàs. La fluitazione del legname lungo il Piave.* Feltre: Castaldi.

Perco, D. (ed.). 1993. *Malgari e pascoli. L'alpeggio nella provincia di Belluno.* Feltre: Libreria Pilotto Editrice.

Pitteri, M. 2005. 'I boschi comunali e la sovrana risoluzione del 1839', in A. Lazzarini and A. Amantia (eds), *La questione 'montagna' in Veneto e Friuli tra otto e Novecento. Percezioni, analisi, interventi.* Belluno: Isbrec. pp. 117–36.

Pitteri, M. 2006. 'I pascoli di Tambre. Risorse locali e pratiche comunitarie tra antico e nuovo regime', in A. Amantia (ed.), *Tambre. Un comune della montagna bellunese tra Sette e Novecento.* Belluno: Isbrec. pp. 52–150.

Plack, N. 2009. *Common Land, Wine and the French Revolution. Rural Society and Economy in Southern France, c.1789–1820.* Farnham: Ashgate.

Pozzan, A. 2013. *Istituzioni, società, economia in un territorio di frontiera. Il caso del Cadore (seconda metà del XVI secolo).* Udine: Forum.

Preto, P. 1978. 'L'agricoltura bellunese nella seconda metà del settecento e l'Accademia degli Anistamici'. *Critica storica* **15**: 64–108.

Rackham, O. 1982. 'Boschi e storia dei sistemi silvo-pastorali in Inghilterra'. *Quaderni storici* **49**: 16–48.

Rackham, O. 1996. 'Forest History of Countries Without Much Forest: Question of Conservation and Savanna', in S. Cavaciocchi (ed.), *L'uomo e la foresta. Secc. XII–XVIII.* Florence: Le Monnier. pp. 297–326.

Radkau, J. 1990. 'Fine delle risorse rinnovabili? Economia del legno e foreste tra Sette e Ottocento', in A. Caracciolo and G. Bonacchi (eds), *Il declino degli elementi.* Bologna: il Mulino. pp. 187–202.

Radkau, J. 1996. 'Wood and Forestry in German History: In Quest of an Environmental Approach'. *Environment and History* **2**: 63–76.

Radkau, J. 2005. 'Germany as a Focus of European "Particularities" in Environmental History', in T. Lekan and T. Zeller (eds), *Germany's Nature: Cultural Landscapes and Environmental History.* New Brunswick: Rutgers. pp. 17–32.

Radkau, J. 2008. *Nature and Power. A Global History of the Environment.* Cambridge: Cambridge University Press.

Radkau, J. 2012. *Wood. A History.* Cambridge: Polity Press.

Ravi Rajan, S. 2006. *Modernizing Nature Forestry and Imperial Eco-Development 1800–1950.* New York: Oxford University Press.

Revel, J. 2006. 'Microanalisi e costruzione del sociale', in Id. (ed.), *Giochi di scala. La microstoria alla prova dell'esperienza.* Rome: Viella. pp. 19–44.

Riall, L. 2013. *Under the Volcano. Revolution in a Sicilian Town.* Oxford: Oxford University Press.

Rosemberg, H. 1988. *A Negotiated World. Three Centuries of Change in French Alpine Community.* Toronto: University of Toronto Press.

Rossetto, L. 2013. *Il commissario distrettuale nel Veneto asburgico. Un funzionario dell'Impero tra mediazione politica e controllo sociale (1819–1848).* Bologna: il Mulino.

Bibliography

Rossetto, L. 2018. 'Prospettive di ricerca sul Veneto asburgico del post '48: il caso della Commissione militare in Este'. *Le Carte e la storia* **24**/I: 101–12.

Rotelli, E. 1974. 'Gli ordinamenti locali della Lombardia preunitaria (1755–1859)'. *Archivio storico lombardo* **100**: 171–234.

Rothman, H. 1994. *'I'll Never Fight Fire with My Bare Hands Again'. Recollections of the First Forest Rangers of the Inland Northwest*. Lawrence: University Press of Kansas.

Sacco, A. 1988. 'Le Regole del Comelico tra fascismo e dopoguerra', in F. Vendramini (ed.), *Montagne e veneti nel secondo dopoguerra*. Verona: Bertani. pp. 553–69.

Sacco, A. 2002. '"Ultra Pennas", contatti, scontri, trasformazioni di un territorio e di una società, cenni storico-geografici su Comelico e Sappada', in E. Cason Angelini (ed.), *Comelico, Sappata, Gaital, Lesachtal: paesaggio, storia, cultura*. Belluno: Fondazione G. Angelini. pp. 133–85.

Sacco, A. 2007. *La vita in Cadore. Aspetti del dominio veneto nelle lettere di capitani e vicari 1500–1788*. Verona: Cierre.

Sahlins, P. 1994. *Forest Rites. The War of Demoiselles in Nineteenth-Century France*. Cambridge-London: Harvard University Press.

Sansa, R. 1997. 'La trattatistica selvicolturale del XIX secolo. Indicazioni e polemiche sull'uso ideale del bosco'. *Rivista di storia dell'agricoltura italiana* **37**/I: 97–144.

Sansa, R. 2000. 'Il mercato e la legge: la legislazione forestale italiana nei secoli XVIII e XIX', in P. Bevilacqua and G. Corona (eds), *Ambiente e risorse nel Mezzogiorno contemporaneo*. Rome: Donzelli. pp. 3–26.

Sansa, R. 2003. *L'oro verde. I boschi nello Stato pontificio tra XVIII e XIX secolo*. Bologna: Cleup.

Sansa, R. 2009. 'Agronomi o agrimensori? La percezione dei saperi contadini e delle pratiche locali nell'amministrazione pontificia tra Sette e Ottocento'. *Acta Histriae* **17**: 399–410.

Sansa, R. 2012. 'Una risorsa molti significati: l'uso del bosco nelle regioni italiane in età preindustriale', in G. Alfani, M. Di Tullio and L. Mocarelli (eds), *Storia economica e ambiente italiano (ca. 1400–1850)*. Milan: Franco Angeli. pp. 256–72.

Saurer, E. 1989. *Straße, Schmuggel, Lottospiel. Materielle Kultur und Staat in Niederösterreich, Böhmen und Lombardo-Venetien im frühen 19. Jahrhundert*. Göttingen: Vandenhoeck & Ruprecht.

Scarpa, G. 1963. *L'agricoltura del Veneto nella prima metà del XIX secolo*. Turin: Ilte.

Scarpa, G. 1988–1989. 'Strade e agricoltura nel Veneto della Restaurazione', *Atti e Memorie della Accademia di Agricoltura Scienze e Lettere di Verona* **165**: 219–302.

Scarpa, G. 1996. 'Il bosco e la proprietà comunale e collettiva nel Veneto e nel Friuli del primo Ottocento', in S. Cavaciocchi (ed.), *L'uomo e la foresta. Secc. XII–XVIII*. Florence: Le Monnier. pp. 155–88.

Schivelbusch, W. 1986. *The Railway Journey. The Industrialization of Time and Space in the Nineteenth Century*. Berkeley-Los Angeles: California University Press.

Schram, A. 1997. *Railways and the Formation of the Italian State in the Nineteenth Century*. Cambridge: Cambridge University Press.

Scott, J. 1976. *The Moral Economy of the Peasant. Rebellion and Subsistence in Southeast Asia*. New Haven: Yale University Press.

Scott, J. 1998. *Seeing Like a State. How Certain Schemes to Improve the Human Condition Have Failed*. New Haven-London: Yale University Press.

Segreto, L. 2011. *I Feltrinelli. Storia di una dinastia imprenditoriale (1854–1942)*. Milan: Feltrinelli.

Sereno, P. 1991. 'Il bosco: dello spazio sociale o della natura inventata', in D. Jalla (ed.), *Gli uomini e le Alpi. Les hommes et les Alpes*. Turin: Regione Piemonte. pp. 22–35.

Serrano, J. 2014. 'When the Enemy is the State: Common Lands Management in Northwest Spain (1850–1936)'. *International Journal of the Commons* **8**: 107–33.

Sieferle, P. 2001. *The Subterranean Forest. Energy Systems and the Industrial Revolution*. Cambridge: The White Horse Press.

Simon, L., V. Clément and P. Pech. 2007. 'Forestry Disputes in Provincial France During the Nineteenth Century: the Case of the Montagne de Lure'. *Journal of Historical Geography* **33**: 335–51.

Simonato Zasio, B. 1993. "Le Rive e Coste de' Monti". Proprietà collettive nella pedemontana feltrina (parte seconda)'. *Archivio storico di Belluno, Feltre e Cadore* **285**: 157–70.

Simonetto, M. 2001. *I lumi nelle campagne. Accademie e agricoltura nella Repubblica di Venezia 1768–1797*. Treviso: Fondazione Benettin Studi e Ricerche.

Simonetto, M. 2009a. 'Accademie agrarie italiane del XVIII secolo. Profili storici dimensione sociale (I)'. *Società e storia* **124**: 261–302.

Simonetto, M. 2009b. 'Accademie agrarie italiane del XVIII secolo. Profili storici dimensione sociale (II)'. *Società e storia* **125**: 445–63.

Sivaramakrishnan, K. 1999. *Modern Forests. Statemaking and Environmental Change in Colonial Eastern India*. Stanford: Stanford University Press.

Sofia, F. 1997. 'Manoscritti coperti e riscoperti: le statistiche dipartimentali di Melchiorre Gioia', in F. Cazzola (ed.), *Nei cantieri della ricerca. Incontri con Lucio Gambi*. Bologna: Clueb. pp. 163–77.

Soldani, S. (ed.). 2008. 'Le emozioni del Risorgimento'. *Passato e presente* **75**: 17–32.

Sombart, W. 1916–1927. *Der Moderne Kapitalismus*. Leipzig: Verlag von Duncker & Humblot.

Sperber, J. 2005. *The European Revolutions, 1848–1851*. New York: Cambridge University Press.

Stuber, M. 2008. *Wälder für Generationen: Konzeptionen der Nachhaltigkeit im Kanton Bern (1750–1880)*. Cologne: Böhlau Verlag.

Tello, E. 2009. 'Nuovi problemi, approcci e metodi per la storia economica ambientale delle società preindustriali e in via di industrializzazione'. *Studi storici* **3**: 607–31.

Thompson, E.P. 1975. *Whigs and Hunters. The Origin of the Black Act*. London: Allen Lane.

Thompson, E.P. 1978. 'Eighteenth-Century English Society: Class Struggle without Class?' *Social History* **3**/II: 133–65.

Thompson, E.P. 1993. *Customs in Common*. London: Penguin Books.

Tigrino, V. 2015. 'Risorse collettive e comunità locali: un approccio storico'. *Economia e società regionale* **33**/III: 23–44.

Tonetti, E. 1991. 'Amministrazione cittadina e rappresentanza di ceto nel Friuli della Restaurazione (1816–48)'. *Studi storici* **32**: 333–64.

Tonetti, E. 1992. 'Il Friuli nel Lombardo Veneto (1816–1848)', in *La provincia imperfetta. Il Friuli dal 1798 al 1848*. Udine: Accademia di Scienze Lettere e Arti di Udine. pp. 171–231.

Tonetti, E. 1997. *Governo austriaco e notabili sudditi. Congregazioni e municipi nel Veneto della Restaurazione (1816–1848)*. Venice: Istituto Veneto di Scienze, Lettere ed Arti.

Bibliography

Tonetti, E. 2003. 'I catasti per la storia delle proprietà, del regime agrario e delle mutazioni territoriali'. *Protagonisti* **84**: 113–35.

Toninelli, P.A. 2010. 'Energy and the Puzzle of Italy's Economic Growth'. *Journal of Modern Italian Studies* **15**/I: 107–27.

Torre, A. 2011. *Luoghi. La produzione di località in età moderna e contemporanea.* Rome: Donzelli.

Trivellato, F. 2000. *Fondamenta dei vetrai. Lavoro, tecnologia e mercato a Venezia tra Sei e Settecento.* Venice: Marsilio.

Vardi, L. 2012. *The Physiocrats and the World of the Enlightenment.* Cambridge: Cambridge University Press.

Vecchio, B. 1974. *Il bosco negli scrittori italiani del Settecento e dell'età napoleonica.* Turin: Einaudi.

Vecchio, B. 1994. 'Un documento in materia forestale nell'Italia del secondo Ottocento: i dibattiti parlamentari, 1869–1877'. *Storia urbana* **69**: 177–204.

Vecchio, B. 2010. 'Forest Visions in Early Modern Italy', in M. Armiero and M. Hall (eds), *Nature and History in Modern Italy.* Athens OH: Ohio University Press. pp. 108–25.

Vecchio, B., P. Piussi and M. Armiero. 2002. 'L'uso del bosco e degli incolti', in *Storia dell'agricoltura italiana,* III/1, *L'età contemporanea. Dalle 'Rivoluzioni agronomiche' alle trasformazioni del Novecento.* Florence: Edizioni Polistampa. pp. 129–216.

Vendramini, F. 1988. 'Boschi e legname nelle relazioni dei rettori veneti a Belluno', in D. Perco (ed.), *Zattere, zattieri e menadàs. La fluitazione del legname lungo il Piave.* Feltre: Castaldi. pp. 7–34.

Vendramini, F. 2000. 'Le alluvioni nel Bellunese al tramonto dell'Ottocento e il fallimento dell'impresa Tallachini'. *Archivio veneto* **190**: 103–25.

Vendramini, F. 2002. *Tutela e autotutela degli emigranti tra Otto e Novecento. Il segretariato dell'emigrazione di Belluno.* Belluno: Comunità Montana Bellunese-Associazione Bellunesi nel Mondo.

Vendramini, F. 2004. *Storia dell'amministrazione provinciale di Belluno,* I, *Dall'annessione alla Grande Guerra (1866–1918).* Belluno: Provincia di Belluno.

Vendramini, F. 2005. 'Aspetti della questione montana nella pubblicistica bellunese del secondo Ottocento', in A. Lazzarini and A. Amantia (eds), *La 'questione montagna' in Veneto e Friuli tra Otto e Novecento. Percezioni, Analisi e Interventi.* Belluno: Isbrec. pp. 51–90.

Vendramini, F. 2010. *Longarone 'ritrovato'. Dalla Repubblica di Venezia al Regno d'Italia.* Verona: Cierre.

Vergani, R. 1991. 'Le materie prime', in A. Tenenti and U. Tucci (eds), *Storia di Venezia,* XII, *Il mare.* Rome: Istituto della Enciclopedia Italiana. pp. 285–312.

Vergani, R. 2003. *Miniere e società nella montagna del passato. Alpi venete, secoli XIII–XIX.* Verona: Cierre.

Vergani, R. 2006. 'Legname per l'Arsenale: i boschi "banditi" nella repubblica di Venezia, secoli XV–XVII', in S. Cavaciocchi (ed.), *Ricchezza del Mare, Ricchezza dal Mare, secc. XIII–XVIII.* Florence: Le Monnier. pp. 401–04.

Vergani, R. 2010 'Venezia e la Terraferma: acque, boschi, ambiente'. *Ateneo veneto* **197**: 173–93.

Vianello, R. 1993. 'Famiglie di mercanti da legname a Venezia', in G. Caniato (ed.), *La via del fiume. Dalle Dolomiti a Venezia.* Verona: Cierre. pp. 299–312.

Viazzo, P.P. 1989. *Upland Communities. Environment, Population and Social Structure in the Alps Since the Sixteenth Century.* Cambridge-New York: Cambridge University Press.

Viazzo, P.P. 2000. 'Il modello alpino dieci anni dopo', in D. Albera and P. Corti (eds), *La montagna mediterranea: una fabbrica di uomini? Mobilità e migrazioni in una prospettiva comparata (secoli XV-XX)*. Cavalmaggiore: Gribaudo. pp. 31–46.

Viggiano, A. 2009. 'Il disegno dei confini. Comunità e ingegneri del censo nel Veneto napoleonico (1806–1813)'. *Ateneo veneto* **8**/I: 137–92.

Wall, D. 2014. *The Commons in History. Culture, Conflict, and Ecology.* Cambridge MA: The MIT Press.

Walter, J. 2001. 'Public Transcripts, Popular Agency and the Politics of Subsistence in Early Modern England', in Id. and M. Braddick (eds), *Negotiating Power in Early Modern Society. Order, Hierarchy and Subordination in Britain and Ireland.* Cambridge: Cambridge University Press. pp. 123–48.

Warde, P. 2002. 'Law, the "Commune", and the Distribution of Resources in Early Modern German State Formation'. *Continuity and Change* **17**: 183–211.

Warde, P. 2006a. *Ecology, Economy and State Formation in Early Modern Germany.* Cambridge: Cambridge University Press.

Warde, P. 2006b. 'Fear of Wood Shortage and the Reality of the Woodland in Europe, c.1450–1850'. *History Workshop Journal* **62**: 29–57.

Warde, P. 2015. 'Early Modern "Resource Crisis": the Wood Shortage Debates in Europe', in A.T. Brown, A. Burn and R. Doherty (eds), *Crisis in Economic and Social History.* Woodbridge: Boydell & Brewer. pp. 137–60.

Warde, P. 2018. *The Invention of Sustainability. Nature, Human Action, and Destiny, 1500–1870.* Cambridge: Cambridge University Press.

WCED (World Commission on Environment and Development). 1987. *Our Common Future.* Oxford: Oxford University Press.

Weber, E. 1976. *Peasants into Frenchmen. The Modernization of Rural France, 1870–1914.* Stanford: Stanford University Press.

Whited, T. 2000. *Forests and Peasant Politics in Modern France.* New Haven: Yale University Press.

Wing, J.T. 2015. *Roots of Empire. Forests and State Power in Early Modern Spain, c.1500–1750.* Leiden: Brill.

Wolf, E. 1957. 'Closed Corporate Peasant Communities in MesoAmerica and Central Java'. *Southwestern Journal of Anthropology* **13**/I: 1–18.

Worster, D. 1993. 'The Shaky Ground of Sustainable Development', in Id., *The Wealth of Nature. Environmental History and the Ecological Imagination.* New York: Oxford University Press. pp. 142–55.

Wrigley, E.A. 1988. *Continuity, Chance and Change. The Character of the Industrial Revolution in England.* Cambridge: Cambridge University Press.

Wrigley, E.A. 2016. *The Path to Sustained Growth. England's Transition from an Organic Economy to an Industrial Revolution.* Cambridge: Cambridge University Press.

Zanderigo Rosolo, G. 1982. *Appunti per la storia delle Regole del Cadore nei secoli XIII-XIV.* Belluno: Ibrsc.

Zanderigo Rosolo, G. 2013. *I laudi delle Regole di Candide, Lorenzago e San Vito in Cadore.* Belluno: Ibrsc.

Zangrando, F. 1991. 'La borghesia imprenditoriale: gli Zuliani e i Lazzaris', in S. De Vecchi

Bibliography

(ed.), *Opere nel tempo. Le tradizioni dell'industria e dell'artigianato tra i monti della provincia di Belluno*. Verona: Nuove Edizioni Dolomiti. pp. 110–12.

Zangrando, F. 1993. 'I cìdoli di Perarolo di Cadore, argani eccellenti e semplici ma giovevoli edifici', in G. Caniato (ed.), *La via del Fiume. Dalle Dolomiti a Venezia*. Verona: Cierre. pp. 165–70.

Zanier, C. (ed.). 1998. *Gherardo Freschi (1804–1893). Una figura di statura europea tra ricerca scientifica ed operare concreto*. Sesto al Reghena: Comune di Sesto al Reghena.

Zannini, A. 2005. 'La grande frattura. La demografia nel Bellunese nell'Ottocento rivisitata', in A. Lazzarini and A. Amantia (eds), *La 'questione montagna' in Veneto e Friuli tra Otto e Novecento. Percezioni, Analisi e Interventi*. Belluno: ISBREC. pp. 209–33.

Zannini, A. 2010. 'Sur la mer, près des montagnes. Venise et le circuit de production et vente du bois (XVIe–XIXe siècle)', in A. Cabantous, J.L. Chappey, R. Morieux, N. Richard and F. Walter (eds), *Mer et montagne dans la culture européenne (XVIe–XIXe siècle)*. Rennes: Press Universitaires de Rennes. pp. 43–55.

Zannini, A. 2011. 'I mercanti di legname delle Alpi orientali (secc. XV–XVIII). Note da alcuni studi recenti', in A. Csillaghy, A. Riem Natale, M. Romero Allué, R. De Giorgi, A. Del Ben and L. Gasparotto (eds), *Un tremore di foglie. Scritti e studi in onore di Anna Panicali*, II. Udine: Forum. pp. 471–78.

Zannini, A. 2012a. 'Bois, bétail et bras. L'économie des communautés alpines vénitiennes face aux changements des XVIIIe-XIXe siècles', in L. Brassart, J.P. Jessenne and N. Vivier (eds), *Clochemerle ou république villageoise? La conduite municipale des affaires villageoises en Europe du XVIII au XX siècle*. Lille: Presses Universitaires du Septentrion. pp. 175–88.

Zannini, A. 2012b. 'Ruined Landscape? Squilibri ambientali e costruzione dello Stato nelle Alpi orientali ad inizi Seicento', in G. Borghello (ed.), *Per Roberto Gusmani. Studi in ricordo*, I, *Linguaggi, culture, letterature*. Udine: Forum. pp. 493–511.

Zannini, A. 2012c. 'Un ecomito? Venezia (XV–XVIII sec.)', in G. Alfani, M. Di Tullio and L. Mocarelli (eds), *Storia economica e ambiente italiano (ca. 1400–1850)*. Milan: Franco Angeli. pp. 100–14.

Zannini, A. and D. Gazzi. 2003. *Contadini, emigranti, 'colonos'. Tra le Prealpi venete e il Brasile meridionale: storia e demografia, 1780–1910*, I-II. Treviso: Fondazione Benetton.

INDEX

Note: As this book is entirely about Cadore, this term will not be indexed.

Index

Index

Index